Politics, Leadership, and Justice

THE GREAT BOOKS FOUNDATION
50th Anniversary Series

PRESIDENT
Alice O. Letvin

EDITORIAL DIRECTOR
James L. Plecha

SENIOR EDITORS
Ann Speltz
Timothy Bagwell

SENIOR CONTRIBUTING EDITOR
Carolyn S. Saper

PRODUCTION EDITOR
Anne Gendler

COPY EDITORS
Mary Klein
Rebecca Johnson

EDITORIAL ASSISTANT
Heather Antti

ADULT PROGRAM DIRECTOR
Gary Schoepfel

Politics, Leadership, and Justice

The Great Books Foundation
A nonprofit educational organization

Published and distributed by

 The Great Books Foundation

A nonprofit educational organization

35 East Wacker Drive, Suite 2300
Chicago, IL 60601-2298

ISBN 1-880323-81-8

First Printing
9 8 7 6 5 4 3 2 1 0

Library of Congress Cataloging-in-Publication Data
Politics, leadership, and justice.
p. cm. — (50th anniversary series)
Contents: Second inaugural address / Abraham Lincoln — Letter from Birmingham jail / Martin Luther King Jr. — Sorrow-acre / Isak Dinesen — Kongi's harvest / Wole Soyinka — The Melian dialogue / Thucydides — Julius Caesar / William Shakespeare — Longing / Amos Oz — Poetry / Lao-tzu — Questions for Age of iron (J. M. Coetzee) — Questions for Paradise of the blind (Duong Thu Huong)
ISBN 1-880323-81-8
1. Literature — Collections. 2. Group reading. 3. Reader-response criticism. I. Great Books Foundation (U.S.) II. Series: Great Books Foundation 50th anniversary series.
PN6014.P59 1998
808.8—DC21 98-13670

CONTENTS

PREFACE

"So that's what Lao-tzu means when he says that people will act righteously and be happier if morality, justice, and wisdom are all thrown away!"
"Are women better equipped than men to deal with social upheaval?"
"Is there a correlation between being a successful politician and having a strong sexual drive?"

Anyone who has been in a book discussion group has experienced the joy of new insight. Sometimes an idea or question occurs to us during the group meeting. Often, it is afterward—sometimes much later—that an idea we had overlooked unexpectedly strikes us with new force. A good group becomes a community of minds. We share perspectives, questions, insights, and surprises. Our fellow readers challenge and broaden our thinking as we probe deeply into characters and ideas. They help us resolve questions, and raise new ones, in a creative process that connects literature with life.

It is this kind of experience that makes book discussion groups worthwhile, and that the Great Books Foundation fosters for thousands of readers around the world.

The Great Books Foundation is a pioneer of book discussion groups that bring together dedicated readers who wish to continue to learn throughout their lives. The literature anthologies published by the Foundation have been the focus of many enlightening discussions among people of all educational backgrounds and walks of life. And the *shared inquiry* method practiced by Great Books groups has proven to be a powerful approach to literature that solves many practical concerns of new discussion groups: How can we maintain a flow of ideas? What kinds of questions should we discuss? How can we keep the discussion focused on the reading so that we use our time together to really get at the heart of a work—to learn from it and each other?

With the publication of its 50th Anniversary Series, the Great Books Foundation continues and expands upon its tradition of helping all readers engage in a meaningful exchange of ideas about outstanding works of literature.

About *Politics, Leadership, and Justice*

The reading selections in *Politics, Leadership, and Justice* have been chosen to stimulate lively shared inquiry discussions. This collection brings together works from around the world that speak to each other on a theme of universal human significance. In this volume you will find classic works by the Chinese philosopher Lao-tzu and the ancient Greek historian Thucydides; drama by William Shakespeare and the Nobel Prize–winning Nigerian author Wole Soyinka; reflections on the American Civil War and the civil rights movement by Abraham Lincoln and Martin Luther King Jr.; and short fiction by Danish writer Isak Dinesen and the contemporary Israeli author Amos Oz.

These are carefully crafted works that readers will interpret in different ways. They portray characters whose lives and motivations are complex, embody concepts that go beyond simple analysis, and raise many questions to inspire extended reflection.

As an aid to reading and discussion, open-ended *interpretive questions* are included with each selection in the volume, and also for the recommended novels *Age of Iron* by the South African author J. M. Coetzee and *Paradise of the Blind* by the Vietnamese author Duong Thu Huong. A fundamental or *basic* interpretive question about the meaning of the selection is printed in boldface, followed by a list of related questions that will help you fully discuss the issue raised by the basic question. Passages for *textual analysis* that you may want to look at closely during discussion are suggested for each set of questions. Questions under the heading "For Further Reflection" can be used at the end of discussion to help your group consider the reading selection in a broader context.

About Shared Inquiry

The success of Great Books discussions depends not only on thought-provoking literature, but also on the shared inquiry method of discussion. A shared inquiry discussion begins with a basic interpretive question—a genuine question about the meaning of the selection that continues to be puzzling even after careful reading. As participants offer different possible answers to this question, the discussion leader or members of the group follow up on the ideas that are voiced, asking questions about how responses relate to the original question or to new ideas, and probing what specifically in the text prompted the response.

In shared inquiry discussion, readers think for themselves about the selection, and do not rely on critical or biographical sources outside the text for ideas about its meaning. Discussion remains focused on the text. Evidence for opinions is found in the selection. Because interpretive questions have no single "correct answer," participants are encouraged to entertain a range of ideas. The exchange of ideas is open and spontaneous, a common search for understanding that leads to closer, more illuminating reading.

Shared inquiry fosters a habit of critical questioning and thinking. It encourages patience in the face of complexity, and a respect for the opinions of others. As participants explore the work in depth, they try out ideas, reconsider simple answers, and synthesize interpretations. Over time, shared inquiry engenders a profound experience of intellectual intimacy as your group searches together for meaning in literature.

Improving Your Discussions

The selections in *Politics, Leadership, and Justice* will support seven meetings of your discussion group, with each selection being the focus of a single meeting. Discussions usually last about two hours, and are guided by a member of the group who acts as leader. Since the leader has no special knowledge or qualification beyond a genuine curiosity about the text, any member of the group may lead discussion. The leader carefully prepares the interpretive questions that he or she wants to explore with the group, and is primarily responsible for continuing the process of questioning that maintains the flow of ideas.

To ensure a successful discussion, we encourage you to make it a policy to read the selection twice. A first reading will familiarize you with the plot and ideas of a selection; on a second reading you will read more reflectively and discover many aspects of the work that deepen your thinking about it. Allowing a few days to pass between your readings will also help you approach a second reading with greater insight.

Read the selection actively. Make marginal comments that you might want to refer to in discussion. While our interpretive questions can help you think about different aspects of the work, jotting down your own questions as you read is the best way to engage with the selection and bring a wealth of ideas and meaningful questions to discussion.

During discussion, expect a variety of answers to the basic question. Follow up carefully on these different ideas. Refer to and read from the text often—by way of explaining your answer, and to see if the rest of the group understands the author's words the same way you do. (You will often be surprised!) As your group looks closely at the text, many new ideas will arise.

While leaders in shared inquiry discussion strive to keep comments focused on the text and on the basic interpretive question the group is discussing, the entire group can share responsibility for politely refocusing comments that wander from the text into personal anecdotes or issues that begin to sidetrack discussion.

Remember that during shared inquiry discussion you are investigating differing perspectives on the reading. Talk should focus foremost on characters in the story or play, not on participants' daily lives and concerns or current social topics. By maintaining this focus, each discussion will be new and interesting, with each participant bringing a different perspective to bear on the text. After the work has been explored thoroughly on its own terms, your thinking about important issues of the day or in your own life will be enhanced. We have found that it is best to formally set aside a time—perhaps the last half-hour of discussion or over coffee afterward—for members of the group to share personal experiences and opinions that go beyond a discussion of the selection.

Discussing the Poetry Selections

Many book groups shy away from the challenge of discussing poetry, but the shared inquiry method will enable you to make poetry a very satisfying part of your discussion group. Poetry, by its very nature, communicates ideas through suggestion, allusion, and resonance. Because meaning in poetry resides in the interaction between author and reader, and is brought to light through the pooling of different perspectives and readers' responses, poems are ideal for shared inquiry discussion.

It will be helpful to read aloud parts of the Tao Te Ching, our poetry selection for this volume, regularly during your discussion. Because poetry is usually more densely constructed than prose and highly selective in detail, it often lends itself to what we call *textual analysis*—looking closely at particular lines, words, and images as an entryway to discussing the whole work. Having readers share their different associations with a word or image can often help broaden interpretations.

Discussing the Novels

Many novels might come to mind that relate to the theme of politics, leadership, and justice. We have recommended *Age of Iron* and *Paradise of the Blind* as particularly enriching novels on this theme, and have provided interpretive questions that can be a significant aid to the reader. Even readers familiar with these novels will find a shared inquiry discussion of them a fresh and rewarding experience.

Most shared inquiry groups discuss a novel at a single discussion; some prefer to spread the discussion over more than one session, especially for longer novels. Since it is usually not realistic to expect participants to read a novel twice in full before discussion, we recommend that you at least reread parts of the novel that seemed especially important to you or that raised a number of questions in your mind. Our passages for textual analysis suggest parts of the novel where reading twice might be most valuable. You might even begin your discussion, after posing a basic question, by looking closely at one or two short passages to get people talking about central ideas and offering a variety of opinions that can be probed and expanded into a discussion of the whole work.

How the Great Books Foundation Can Help You

The Great Books Foundation can be a significant resource for you and your discussion group. Our staff conducts shared inquiry workshops throughout the country that will help you or your entire group conduct better discussions. Thousands of people—from elementary school teachers and college professors to those who just love books and ideas—have found our workshops to be an enjoyable experience that changes forever how they approach literature.

The Foundation publishes a variety of reading series that might interest you. We invite you to call us at 1-800-222-5870 or visit our Web site at http://www.greatbooks.org. We can help you start a book group, put you in touch with established Great Books groups in your area, or give you information about many special events—such as poetry weekends or week-long discussion institutes—sponsored by Great Books groups around the country.

Finally, we invite you to inquire about Junior Great Books for students in kindergarten through high school, to learn how you can help develop the next generation of book lovers and shared inquiry participants.

We hope you enjoy *Politics, Leadership, and Justice* and that it inaugurates many years of exciting discussions for your group. Great Books programs—for children as well as adults—are founded on the idea that readers discussing together can achieve insight and great pleasure from literature. We look forward, with you, to cultivating this idea through the next century.

Footnotes by the author are not bracketed; footnotes by the Great Books Foundation, an editor, or a translator are [bracketed].

Second Inaugural Address

~

Letter From Birmingham Jail

Abraham Lincoln

Martin Luther King Jr.

ABRAHAM LINCOLN (1809–1865) was the sixteenth president of the United States. Within six weeks of his inauguration to his first term of office in 1861, the army of the Southern secessionist states fired upon Fort Sumter in Charleston, South Carolina, igniting the American Civil War. In 1863, Lincoln issued the Emancipation Proclamation, which abolished slavery in the United States. On April 14, 1865—just five days after the surrender of the Confederate forces at Appomattox, Virginia—Abraham Lincoln was assassinated.

Second Inaugural Address

Abraham Lincoln

March 4, 1865

AT THIS SECOND APPEARING to take the oath of the presidential office, there is less occasion for an extended address than there was at the first. Then a statement, somewhat in detail, of a course to be pursued, seemed fitting and proper. Now, at the expiration of four years, during which public declarations have been constantly called forth on every point and phase of the great contest which still absorbs the attention, and engrosses the energies of the nation, little that is new could be presented. The progress of our arms, upon which all else chiefly depends, is as well known to the public as to myself; and it is, I trust, reasonably satisfactory and encouraging to all. With high hope for the future, no prediction in regard to it is ventured.

On the occasion corresponding to this four years ago, all thoughts were anxiously directed to an impending civil war. All dreaded it—all sought to avert it. While the inaugural address was being delivered from this place, devoted altogether to *saving* the Union without war, insurgent agents were in the city seeking to *destroy* it without war—seeking to dissolve the

Union, and divide effects, by negotiation. Both parties deprecated war; but one of them would *make* war rather than let the nation survive; and the other would *accept* war rather than let it perish. And the war came.

One eighth of the whole population were colored slaves, not distributed generally over the Union, but localized in the Southern part of it. These slaves constituted a peculiar and powerful interest. All knew that this interest was, somehow, the cause of the war. To strengthen, perpetuate, and extend this interest was the object for which the insurgents would rend the Union, even by war; while the government claimed no right to do more than to restrict the territorial enlargement of it. Neither party expected for the war, the magnitude, or the duration, which it has already attained. Neither anticipated that the *cause* of the conflict might cease with, or even before, the conflict itself should cease. Each looked for an easier triumph, and a result less fundamental and astounding. Both read the same Bible, and pray to the same God; and each invokes His aid against the other. It may seem strange that any men should dare to ask a just God's assistance in wringing their bread from the sweat of other men's faces; but let us judge not that we be not judged. The prayers of both could not be answered; that of neither has been answered fully. The Almighty has His own purposes. "Woe unto the world because of offenses! for it must needs be that offenses come; but woe to that man by whom the offense cometh!" If we shall suppose that American slavery is one of those offenses which, in the providence of God, must needs come, but which, having continued through His appointed time, He now wills to remove, and that He gives to both North and South, this terrible war, as the woe due to those by whom the offense came, shall we discern therein any departure from those divine attributes which the believers in a Living God always ascribe to Him? Fondly do we hope—fervently do we pray—that this mighty scourge of war may speedily pass away. Yet, if God wills that it continue, until all the wealth piled by the bondman's two hundred and fifty years of unrequited toil shall be sunk, and until every drop of blood drawn with the lash, shall be paid by another drawn with the sword, as was said three thousand years ago, so still it must be said "the judgments of the Lord, are true and righteous altogether."

With malice toward none; with charity for all; with firmness in the right, as God gives us to see the right, let us strive on to finish the work we are in; to bind up the nation's wounds; to care for him who shall have borne the battle, and for his widow, and his orphan—to do all which may achieve and cherish a just, and a lasting peace, among ourselves, and with all nations. ~

Martin Luther King Jr. (1929–1968) was born in Atlanta, Georgia, and attended Morehouse College and Crozer Theological Seminary before earning his Ph.D. at Boston University. In 1955 and 1956, Dr. King led African Americans in Montgomery, Alabama, in a boycott of the city's segregated bus lines. When Montgomery officials capitulated and desegregated their buses, Dr. King's name and his policy of nonviolent protest became nationally recognized. Dr. King formed and led the Southern Christian Leadership Conference, which organized civil rights activities in the South and later throughout the nation. In 1963, he led the famous civil rights march on Washington, D.C. Dr. King was awarded the Nobel Peace Prize in 1964. He was assassinated on April 4, 1968, in Memphis, Tennessee.

Letter from Birmingham Jail

Martin Luther King Jr.

April 16, 1963

MY DEAR FELLOW CLERGYMEN:

While confined here in the Birmingham city jail, I came across your recent statement calling my present activities "unwise and untimely." Seldom do I pause to answer criticism of my work and ideas. If I sought to answer all the criticisms that cross my desk, my secretaries would have little time for anything other than such correspondence in the course of the day, and I would have no time for constructive work. But since I feel that you are men of genuine good will and that your criticisms are sincerely set forth, I want to try to answer your statement in what I hope will be patient and reasonable terms.[1]

1. This response to a published statement by eight fellow clergymen from Alabama (Bishop C. C. J. Carpenter, Bishop Joseph A. Durick, Rabbi Hilton L. Grafman, Bishop Paul Hardin, Bishop Holan B. Harmon, the Reverend George M. Murray, the Reverend Edward V. Ramage, and the Reverend Earl Stallings) was composed under somewhat constricting circumstances. Begun on the margins of the newspaper in which the statement

I think I should indicate why I am here in Birmingham, since you have been influenced by the view which argues against "outsiders coming in." I have the honor of serving as president of the Southern Christian Leadership Conference, an organization operating in every southern state, with headquarters in Atlanta, Georgia. We have some eighty-five affiliated organizations across the South, and one of them is the Alabama Christian Movement for Human Rights. Frequently we share staff, educational, and financial resources with our affiliates. Several months ago the affiliate here in Birmingham asked us to be on call to engage in a nonviolent direct-action program if such were deemed necessary. We readily consented, and when the hour came we lived up to our promise. So I, along with several members of my staff, am here because I was invited here. I am here because I have organizational ties here.

But more basically, I am in Birmingham because injustice is here. Just as the prophets of the eighth century B.C. left their villages and carried their "thus saith the Lord" far beyond the boundaries of their hometowns, and, just as the Apostle Paul left his village of Tarsus and carried the gospel of Jesus Christ to the far corners of the Greco-Roman world, so am I compelled to carry the gospel of freedom beyond my own hometown. Like Paul, I must constantly respond to the Macedonian call for aid.

Moreover, I am cognizant of the interrelatedness of all communities and states. I cannot sit idly by in Atlanta and not be concerned about what happens in Birmingham. Injustice anywhere is a threat to justice everywhere. We are caught in an inescapable network of mutuality, tied in a single garment of destiny. Whatever affects one directly, affects all indirectly. Never again can we afford to live with the narrow, provincial "outside agitator" idea. Anyone who lives inside the United States can never be considered an outsider anywhere within its bounds.

---

appeared while I was in jail, the letter was continued on scraps of writing paper supplied by a friendly Negro trusty, and concluded on a pad my attorneys were eventually permitted to leave me. Although the text remains in substance unaltered, I have indulged in the author's prerogative of polishing it for publication.

You deplore the demonstrations taking place in Birmingham. But your statement, I am sorry to say, fails to express a similar concern for the conditions that brought about the demonstrations. I am sure that none of you would want to rest content with the superficial kind of social analysis that deals merely with effects and does not grapple with underlying causes. It is unfortunate that demonstrations are taking place in Birmingham, but it is even more unfortunate that the city's white power structure left the Negro community with no alternative.

In any nonviolent campaign there are four basic steps: collection of the facts to determine whether injustices exist; negotiation; self-purification; and direct action. We have gone through all these steps in Birmingham. There can be no gainsaying the fact that racial injustice engulfs this community. Birmingham is probably the most thoroughly segregated city in the United States. An ugly record of brutality is widely known. Negroes have experienced grossly unjust treatment in the courts. There have been more unsolved bombings of Negro homes and churches in Birmingham than in any other city in the nation. These are the hard brutal facts of the case. On the basis of these conditions, Negro leaders sought to negotiate with the city fathers. But the latter consistently refused to engage in good-faith negotiation.

Then, last September, came the opportunity to talk with leaders of Birmingham's economic community. In the course of the negotiations, certain promises were made by the merchants—for example, to remove the stores' humiliating racial signs. On the basis of these promises, the Reverend Fred Shuttlesworth and the leaders of the Alabama Christian Movement for Human Rights agreed to a moratorium on all demonstrations. As the weeks and months went by, we realized that we were the victims of a broken promise. A few signs, briefly removed, returned; the others remained.

As in so many past experiences, our hopes had been blasted, and the shadow of deep disappointment settled upon us. We had no alternative except to prepare for direct action, whereby we would present our very bodies as a means of laying our case before the conscience of the local and the national community. Mindful of the difficulties involved, we decided to undertake a process of self-purification. We began a series of workshops on nonviolence, and we repeatedly asked ourselves: "Are you able to accept blows without retaliating?" "Are you able to endure the ordeal of jail?" We decided to schedule our direct-action program for the Easter season, realizing that except for Christmas, this is the main shopping period of the year. Knowing that a strong economic-withdrawal program would be the by-product of direct action, we felt that this would be the best time to bring pressure to bear on the merchants for the needed change.

Then it occurred to us that Birmingham's mayoralty election was coming up in March, and we speedily decided to postpone action until after election day. When we discovered that the Commissioner of Public Safety, Eugene "Bull" Connor, had piled up enough votes to be in the run-off, we decided again to postpone action until the day after the run-off so that the demonstrations could not be used to cloud the issues. Like many others, we waited to see Mr. Connor defeated, and to this end we endured postponement after postponement. Having aided in this community need, we felt that our direct-action program could be delayed no longer.

You may well ask "Why direct action? Why sit-ins, marches, and so forth? Isn't negotiation a better path?" You are quite right in calling for negotiation. Indeed, this is the very purpose of direct action. Nonviolent direct action seeks to create such a crisis and foster such a tension that a community which has constantly refused to negotiate is forced to confront the issue. It seeks to so dramatize the issue that it can no longer be ignored. My citing the creation of tension as part of the work of the nonviolent resister may sound rather shocking. But I must confess that I am not afraid of the word "tension." I have earnestly opposed violent tension, but there is a type of constructive nonviolent tension which is necessary for growth. Just as Socrates felt that it was necessary to create a tension in the mind so that individuals could rise from the bondage of myths and half-truths to the unfettered realm of creative analysis and objective appraisal, so must we see the need for nonviolent gadflies to create the kind of tension in society that will help men rise from the dark depths of prejudice and racism to the majestic heights of understanding and brotherhood.

The purpose of our direct-action program is to create a situation so crisis-packed that it will inevitably open the door to negotiation. I therefore concur with you in your call for negotiation. Too long has our beloved Southland been bogged down in a tragic effort to live in monologue rather than dialogue.

One of the basic points in your statement is that the action that I and my associates have taken in Birmingham is untimely. Some have asked: "Why didn't you give the new city administration time to act?" The only answer that I can give to this query is that the new Birmingham administration must be prodded about as much as the outgoing one, before it will act. We are sadly mistaken if we feel that the election of Albert Boutwell as mayor will bring the millennium to Birmingham. While Mr. Boutwell is a much more gentle person than Mr. Connor, they are both segregationists, dedicated to maintenance of the status quo. I have hope that Mr. Boutwell will be reasonable enough to see the futility of massive resistance to desegregation. But he will not see this without pressure from devotees of civil rights. My friends, I must say to you that we have not made a single gain in civil rights without determined legal and nonviolent pressure. Lamentably, it is an historical fact that privileged groups seldom give up their privileges voluntarily. Individuals may see the moral light and voluntarily give up their unjust posture; but, as Reinhold Niebuhr has reminded us, groups tend to be more immoral than individuals.

We know through painful experience that freedom is never voluntarily given by the oppressor; it must be demanded by the oppressed. Frankly, I have yet to engage in a direct-action campaign that was "well-timed" in the view of those who have not suffered unduly from the disease of segregation. For years now I have heard the word "Wait!" It rings in the ear of every Negro with piercing familiarity. This "Wait" has almost always meant "Never." We must come to see, with one of our distinguished jurists, that "justice too long delayed is justice denied."

We have waited for more than 340 years for our constitutional and God-given rights. The nations of Asia and Africa are moving with jetlike speed toward gaining political independence, but we still creep at horse-and-buggy pace toward gaining a cup of coffee at a lunch counter. Perhaps it is easy for those who have never felt the stinging darts of segregation to say, "Wait." But when you have seen vicious mobs lynch your mothers and fathers at will and drown your sisters and brothers at whim; when you have seen hate-filled policemen curse, kick, and even kill your black brothers and sisters; when you see the vast majority of your twenty million Negro brothers smothering in an airtight cage of poverty in the midst of an affluent society; when you suddenly find your tongue twisted and your speech stammering as you seek to explain to your six-year-old daughter why she can't go to the public amusement park that has just been advertised on television, and see tears welling up in her eyes when she is told that Funtown is closed to colored children, and see ominous clouds of inferiority beginning to form in her little mental sky, and see her beginning to distort her personality by developing an unconscious bitterness toward white people; when you have to concoct an answer for a five-year-old son who is asking: "Daddy, why do white people treat colored people so mean?"; when you take a cross-country drive and find it necessary to sleep night after night in the uncomfortable corners of your automobile because no motel will accept you; when you are humiliated day in and day out by nagging signs reading "white" and "colored"; when your first name becomes "nigger," your middle name becomes "boy" (however old you are), and your last name becomes "John," and your wife and mother are never given the respected title "Mrs."; when you are harried by day and haunted by night by the fact that you are a Negro, living constantly at tiptoe stance, never quite knowing what to expect next, and are plagued with inner fears and outer resentments; when you are forever fighting a degenerating sense of "nobodiness"—then you will understand why we find it difficult to wait. There comes a time when the cup of endurance runs over, and men are no longer willing to be plunged into the abyss of despair. I hope, sirs, you can understand our legitimate and unavoidable impatience.

You express a great deal of anxiety over our willingness to break laws. This is certainly a legitimate concern. Since we so diligently urge people to obey the Supreme Court's decision of 1954 outlawing segregation in the public schools, at first glance it may seem rather paradoxical for us consciously to break laws. One may well ask: "How can you advocate breaking some laws and obeying others?" The answer lies in the fact that there are two types of laws: just and unjust. I would be the first to advocate obeying just laws. One has not only a legal but a moral responsibility to obey just laws. Conversely, one has a moral responsibility to disobey unjust laws. I would agree with St. Augustine that "an unjust law is no law at all."

Now, what is the difference between the two? How does one determine whether a law is just or unjust? A just law is a manmade code that squares with the moral law or the law of God. An unjust law is a code that is out of harmony with the moral law. To put it in the terms of St. Thomas Aquinas: An unjust law is a human law that is not rooted in eternal law and natural law. Any law that uplifts human personality is just. Any law that degrades human personality is unjust. All segregation statutes are unjust because segregation distorts the soul and damages the personality. It gives the segregator a false sense of superiority and the segregated a false sense of inferiority. Segregation, to use the terminology of the Jewish philosopher Martin Buber, substitutes an "I-it" relationship for an "I-thou" relationship and ends up relegating persons to the status of things. Hence segregation is not only politically, economically, and sociologically unsound, it is morally wrong and sinful. Paul Tillich has said that sin is separation. Is not segregation an existential expression of man's tragic separation, his awful estrangement, his terrible sinfulness? Thus it is that I can urge men to obey the 1954 decision of the Supreme Court, for it is morally right; and I can urge them to disobey segregation ordinances, for they are morally wrong.

Let us consider a more concrete example of just and unjust laws. An unjust law is a code that a numerical- or power-majority group compels a minority group to obey but does not make binding on itself. This is *difference* made legal. By the same token, a just law is a code that a majority compels a minority to follow and that it is willing to follow itself. This is *sameness* made legal.

Let me give another explanation. A law is unjust if it is inflicted on a minority that, as a result of being denied the right to vote, had no part in enacting or devising the law. Who can say that the legislature of Alabama which set up that state's segregation laws was democratically elected? Throughout Alabama all sorts of devious methods are used to prevent Negroes from becoming registered voters, and there are some counties in which even though Negroes constitute a majority of the population, not a single Negro is registered. Can any law enacted under such circumstances be considered democratically structured?

Sometimes a law is just on its face and unjust in its application. For instance, I have been arrested on a charge of parading without a permit. Now, there is nothing wrong in having an ordinance which requires a permit for a parade. But such an ordinance becomes unjust when it is used to maintain segregation and to deny citizens the First-Amendment privilege of peaceful assembly and protest.

I hope you are able to see the distinction I am trying to point out. In no sense do I advocate evading or defying the law, as would the rabid segregationist. That would lead to anarchy. One who breaks an unjust law must do so openly, lovingly, and with a willingness to accept the penalty. I submit that an individual who breaks a law that conscience tells him is unjust, and who willingly accepts the penalty of imprisonment in order to arouse the conscience of the community over its injustice, is in reality expressing the highest respect for law.

Of course, there is nothing new about this kind of civil disobedience. It was evidenced sublimely in the refusal of Shadrach, Meshach, and Abednego to obey the laws of Nebuchadnezzar, on the ground that a higher moral law was at stake. It was practiced superbly by the early Christians, who were willing to face hungry lions and the excruciating pain of chopping blocks rather than submit to certain unjust laws of the Roman Empire. To a degree, academic freedom is a reality today because Socrates practiced civil disobedience. In our own nation, the Boston Tea Party represented a massive act of civil disobedience.

We should never forget that everything Adolf Hitler did in Germany was "legal" and everything the Hungarian freedom fighters did in Hungary was "illegal." It was "illegal" to aid and comfort a Jew in Hitler's Germany. Even so, I am sure that, had I lived in Germany at the time, I would have aided and comforted my Jewish brothers. If today I lived in a Communist country where certain principles dear to the Christian faith are suppressed, I would openly advocate disobeying that country's antireligious laws.

I must make two honest confessions to you, my Christian and Jewish brothers. First, I must confess that over the past few years I have been gravely disappointed with the white moderate. I have almost reached the regrettable conclusion that the Negro's great stumbling block in his stride toward freedom is not the White Citizen's Counciler or the Ku Klux Klanner, but the white moderate, who is more devoted to "order" than to justice; who prefers a negative peace which is the absence of tension to a positive peace which is the presence of justice; who constantly says: "I agree with you in the goal you seek, but I cannot agree with your methods of direct action"; who paternalistically believes he can set the timetable for another man's freedom; who lives by a mythical concept of time and who constantly advises the Negro to wait for a "more convenient season." Shallow understanding from people of good will is more frustrating than absolute misunderstanding from people of ill will. Lukewarm acceptance is much more bewildering than outright rejection.

I had hoped that the white moderate would understand that law and order exist for the purpose of establishing justice and that when they fail in this purpose they become the dangerously structured dams that block the flow of social progress. I had hoped that the white moderate would understand that the present tension in the South is a necessary phase of the transition from an obnoxious negative peace, in which the Negro passively accepted his unjust plight, to a substantive and positive peace, in which all men will respect the dignity and worth of human personality. Actually, we who engage in nonviolent direct action are not the creators of tension. We merely bring to the surface the hidden tension that is already alive. We bring it out in the open, where it can be seen and dealt with. Like a boil that can never be cured so long as it is covered up but must be opened with all its ugliness to the natural medicines of air and light, injustice must be exposed, with all the tension its exposure creates, to the light of human conscience and the air of national opinion before it can be cured.

In your statement you assert that our actions, even though peaceful, must be condemned because they precipitate violence. But is this a logical assertion? Isn't this like condemning a robbed man because his possession of money precipitated the evil act of robbery? Isn't this like condemning Socrates because his unswerving commitment to truth and his philosophical inquiries precipitated the act by the misguided populace in which they made him drink hemlock? Isn't this like condemning Jesus because his unique God-consciousness and never-ceasing devotion to God's will precipitated the evil act of crucifixion? We must come to see that, as the federal courts have consistently affirmed, it is wrong to urge an individual to cease his efforts to gain his basic constitutional rights because the quest may precipitate violence. Society must protect the robbed and punish the robber.

I had also hoped that the white moderate would reject the myth concerning time in relation to the struggle for freedom. I have just received a letter from a white brother in Texas. He writes: "All Christians know that the colored people will receive equal rights eventually, but it is possible that you are in too great a religious hurry. It has taken Christianity almost two thousand years to accomplish what it has. The teachings of Christ take time to come to earth." Such an attitude stems from a tragic misconception of time, from the strangely irrational notion that there is something in the very flow of time that will inevitably cure all ills. Actually, time itself is neutral; it can be used either destructively or constructively. More and more I feel that the people of ill will have used time much more effectively than have the people of good will. We will have to repent in this generation not merely for the hateful words and actions of the bad people but for the appalling silence of the good people. Human progress never rolls in on wheels of inevitability; it comes through the tireless efforts of men willing to be coworkers with God, and without this hard work, time itself becomes an ally of the forces of social stagnation. We must use time creatively, in the knowledge that the time is always ripe to do right. Now is the time to make real the promise of democracy and transform our pending national elegy into a creative psalm of brotherhood. Now is the time to lift our national policy from the quicksand of racial injustice to the solid rock of human dignity.

You speak of our activity in Birmingham as extreme. At first I was rather disappointed that fellow clergymen would see my nonviolent efforts as those of an extremist. I began thinking about the fact that I stand in the middle of two opposing forces in the Negro community. One is a force of complacency, made up in part of Negroes who, as a result of long years of oppression, are so drained of self-respect and a sense of "somebodiness" that they have adjusted to segregation; and in part of a few middle-class Negroes who, because of a degree of academic and economic security and because in some ways they profit by segregation, have become insensitive to the problems of the masses. The other force is one of bitterness and hatred, and it comes perilously close to advocating violence. It is expressed in the various black nationalist groups that are springing up across the nation, the largest and best-known being Elijah Muhammad's Muslim movement. Nourished by the Negro's frustration over the continued existence of racial discrimination, this movement is made up of people who have lost faith in America, who have absolutely repudiated Christianity, and who have concluded that the white man is an incorrigible "devil."

I have tried to stand between these two forces, saying that we need emulate neither the "do-nothingism" of the complacent nor the hatred and despair of the black nationalist. For there is the more excellent way of love and nonviolent protest. I am grateful to God that, through the influence of the Negro church, the way of nonviolence became an integral part of our struggle.

If this philosophy had not emerged, by now many streets of the South would, I am convinced, be flowing with blood. And I am further convinced that if our white brothers dismiss as "rabble-rousers" and "outside agitators" those of us who employ nonviolent direct action, and if they refuse to support our nonviolent efforts, millions of Negroes will, out of frustration and despair, seek solace and security in black-nationalist ideologies—a development that would inevitably lead to a frightening racial nightmare.

Oppressed people cannot remain oppressed forever. The yearning for freedom eventually manifests itself, and that is what has happened to the American Negro. Something within has reminded him of his birthright of freedom, and something without has reminded him that it can be gained. Consciously or unconsciously, he has been caught up by the Zeitgeist, and with his black brothers of Africa and his brown and yellow brothers of Asia, South America, and the Caribbean, the United States Negro is moving with a sense of great urgency toward the promised land of racial justice. If one recognizes this vital urge that has engulfed the Negro community, one should readily understand why public demonstrations are taking place. The

Negro has many pent-up resentments and latent frustrations, and he must release them. So let him march; let him make prayer pilgrimages to the city hall; let him go on freedom rides—and try to understand why he must do so. If his repressed emotions are not released in nonviolent ways, they will seek expression through violence; this is not a threat but a fact of history. So I have not said to my people: "Get rid of your discontent." Rather, I have tried to say that this normal and healthy discontent can be channeled into the creative outlet of nonviolent direct action. And now this approach is being termed extremist.

But though I was initially disappointed at being categorized as an extremist, as I continued to think about the matter I gradually gained a measure of satisfaction from the label. Was not Jesus an extremist for love: "Love your enemies, bless them that curse you, do good to them that hate you, and pray for them which despitefully use you, and persecute you." Was not Amos an extremist for justice: "Let justice roll down like waters and righteousness like an ever-flowing stream." Was not Paul an extremist for the Christian gospel: "I bear in my body the marks of the Lord Jesus." Was not Martin Luther an extremist: "Here I stand; I cannot do otherwise, so help me God." And John Bunyan: "I will stay in jail to the end of my days before I make a butchery of my conscience." And Abraham Lincoln: "This nation cannot survive half slave and half free." And Thomas Jefferson: "We hold these truths to be self-evident, that all men are created equal. . . ." So the question is not whether we will be extremists, but what kind of extremists we will be. Will we be extremists for hate or for love? Will we be extremists for the preservation of injustice or for the extension of justice? In that dramatic scene on Calvary's hill three men were crucified. We must never forget that all three were crucified for the same crime—the crime of extremism. Two were extremists for immorality, and thus fell below their environment. The other, Jesus Christ, was an extremist for love, truth, and goodness, and thereby rose above his environment.

Perhaps the South, the nation, and the world are in dire need of creative extremists.

I had hoped that the white moderate would see this need. Perhaps I was too optimistic; perhaps I expected too much. I suppose I should have realized that few members of the oppressor race can understand the deep groans and passionate yearnings of the oppressed race, and still fewer have the vision to see that injustice must be rooted out by strong, persistent, and determined action. I am thankful, however, that some of our white brothers in the South have grasped the meaning of this social revolution and committed themselves to it. They are still all too few in quantity, but they are big in quality. Some—such as Ralph McGill, Lillian Smith, Harry Golden, James McBride Dabbs, Ann Braden, and Sarah Patton Boyle—have written about our struggle in eloquent and prophetic terms. Others have marched with us down nameless streets of the South. They have languished in filthy, roach-infested jails, suffering the abuse and brutality of policemen who view them as "dirty nigger-lovers." Unlike so many of their moderate brothers and sisters, they have recognized the urgency of the moment and sensed the need for powerful "action" antidotes to combat the disease of segregation.

Let me take note of my other major disappointment. I have been so greatly disappointed with the white church and its leadership. Of course, there are some notable exceptions. I am not unmindful of the fact that each of you has taken some significant stands on this issue. I commend you, Reverend Stallings, for your Christian stand on this past Sunday, in welcoming Negroes to your worship service on a nonsegregated basis. I commend the Catholic leaders of this state for integrating Spring Hill College several years ago.

But despite these notable exceptions, I must honestly reiterate that I have been disappointed with the church. I do not say this as one of those negative critics who can always find something wrong with the church. I say this as a minister of the gospel, who loves the church; who was nurtured in its bosom;

who has been sustained by its spiritual blessings and who will remain true to it as long as the cord of life shall lengthen.

When I was suddenly catapulted into the leadership of the bus protest in Montgomery, Alabama, a few years ago, I felt we would be supported by the white church. I felt that the white ministers, priests, and rabbis of the South would be among our strongest allies. Instead, some have been outright opponents, refusing to understand the freedom movement and misrepresenting its leaders; all too many others have been more cautious than courageous and have remained silent behind the anesthetizing security of stained-glass windows.

In spite of my shattered dreams, I came to Birmingham with the hope that the white religious leadership of this community would see the justice of our cause and, with deep moral concern, would serve as the channel through which our just grievances could reach the power structure. I had hoped that each of you would understand. But again I have been disappointed.

I have heard numerous southern religious leaders admonish their worshipers to comply with a desegregation decision because it is the law, but I have longed to hear white ministers declare: "Follow this decree because integration is morally right and because the Negro is your brother." In the midst of blatant injustices inflicted upon the Negro, I have watched white churchmen stand on the sideline and mouth pious irrelevancies and sanctimonious trivialities. In the midst of a mighty struggle to rid our nation of racial and economic injustice, I have heard many ministers say: "Those are social issues, with which the gospel has no real concern." And I have watched many churches commit themselves to a completely otherworldly religion which makes a strange, unbiblical distinction between body and soul, between the sacred and the secular.

I have traveled the length and breadth of Alabama, Mississippi, and all the other southern states. On sweltering summer days and crisp autumn mornings I have looked at the South's beautiful churches with their lofty spires pointing heavenward. I have beheld the impressive outlines of her massive religious-education buildings. Over and over I have found myself asking: "What kind of people worship here? Who is their God? Where were their voices when the lips of Governor Barnett dripped with words of interposition and nullification? Where were they when Governor Wallace gave a clarion call for defiance and hatred? Where were their voices of support when bruised and weary Negro men and women decided to rise from the dark dungeons of complacency to the bright hills of creative protest?"

Yes, these questions are still in my mind. In deep disappointment I have wept over the laxity of the church. But be assured that my tears have been tears of love. There can be no deep disappointment where there is not deep love. Yes, I love the church. How could I do otherwise? I am in the rather unique position of being the son, the grandson, and the great-grandson of preachers. Yes, I see the church as the body of Christ. But, oh! How we have blemished and scarred that body through social neglect and through fear of being nonconformists.

There was a time when the church was very powerful—in the time when the early Christians rejoiced at being deemed worthy to suffer for what they believed. In those days the church was not merely a thermometer that recorded the ideas and principles of popular opinion; it was a thermostat that transformed the mores of society. Whenever the early Christians entered a town, the people in power became disturbed and immediately sought to convict the Christians for being "disturbers of the peace" and "outside agitators." But the Christians pressed on, in the conviction that they were "a colony of heaven," called to obey God rather than man. Small in number, they were big in commitment. They were too God-intoxicated to be "astronomically intimidated." By their effort and example they brought an end to such ancient evils as infanticide and gladiatorial contests.

Things are different now. So often the contemporary church is a weak, ineffectual voice with an uncertain sound. So often it is an archdefender of the status quo. Far from being disturbed by the presence of the church, the power structure of the average community is consoled by the church's silent—and often even vocal—sanction of things as they are.

But the judgment of God is upon the church as never before. If today's church does not recapture the sacrificial spirit of the early church, it will lose its authenticity, forfeit the loyalty of millions, and be dismissed as an irrelevant social club with no meaning for the twentieth century. Every day I meet young people whose disappointment with the church has turned into outright disgust.

Perhaps I have once again been too optimistic. Is organized religion too inextricably bound to the status quo to save our nation and the world? Perhaps I must turn my faith to the inner spiritual church, the church within the church, as the true *ekklesia* and the hope of the world. But again I am thankful to God that some noble souls from the ranks of organized religion have broken loose from the paralyzing chains of conformity and joined us as active partners in the struggle for freedom. They have left their secure congregations and walked the streets of Albany, Georgia, with us. They have gone down the highways of the South on tortuous rides for freedom. Yes, they have gone to jail with us. Some have been dismissed from their churches, have lost the support of their bishops and fellow ministers. But they have acted in the faith that right defeated is stronger than evil triumphant. Their witness has been the spiritual salt that has preserved the true meaning of the gospel in these troubled times. They have carved a tunnel of hope through the dark mountain of disappointment.

I hope the church as a whole will meet the challenge of this decisive hour. But even if the church does not come to the aid of justice, I have no despair about the future. I have no fear about the outcome of our struggle in Birmingham, even if our motives are at present misunderstood. We will reach the goal of freedom in Birmingham and all over the nation, because the goal of America is freedom. Abused and scorned though we may be, our destiny is tied up with America's destiny. Before the pilgrims landed at Plymouth, we were here. Before the pen of Jefferson etched the majestic words of the Declaration of Independence across the pages of history, we were here. For more than two centuries our forebears labored in this country without wages; they made cotton king; they built the homes of their masters while suffering gross injustice and shameful humiliation—and yet out of a bottomless vitality they continued to thrive and develop. If the inexpressible cruelties of slavery could not stop us, the opposition we now face will surely fail. We will win our freedom because the sacred heritage of our nation and the eternal will of God are embodied in our echoing demands.

Before closing I feel impelled to mention one other point in your statement that has troubled me profoundly. You warmly commended the Birmingham police force for keeping "order" and "preventing violence." I doubt that you would have so warmly commended the police force if you had seen its dogs sinking their teeth into unarmed, nonviolent Negroes. I doubt that you would so quickly commend the policemen if you were to observe their ugly and inhumane treatment of Negroes here in the city jail; if you were to watch them push and curse old Negro women and young Negro girls; if you were to see them slap and kick old Negro men and young boys; if you were to observe them as they did on two occasions, refuse to give us food because we wanted to sing our grace together. I cannot join you in your praise of the Birmingham police department.

It is true that the police have exercised a degree of discipline in handling the demonstrators. In this sense they have conducted themselves rather "nonviolently" in public. But for what purpose? To preserve the evil system of segregation. Over the past few years I have consistently preached that nonviolence demands that the means we use must be as pure as the ends we seek. I have tried to make clear that it is wrong to use immoral means to attain moral ends. But now I must affirm that it is just as wrong, or perhaps even more so, to use moral means to preserve immoral ends. Perhaps Mr. Connor and his policemen have been rather nonviolent in public, as was Chief Pritchett in Albany, Georgia, but they have used the moral means of nonviolence to maintain the immoral end of racial injustice. As T. S. Eliot has said: "The last temptation is the greatest treason: To do the right deed for the wrong reason."

I wish you had commended the Negro sit-inners and demonstrators of Birmingham for their sublime courage, their willingness to suffer, and their amazing discipline in the midst of great provocation. One day the South will recognize its real heroes. They will be the James Merediths, with the noble sense of purpose that enables them to face jeering and hostile mobs, and with the agonizing loneliness that characterizes the life of the pioneer. They will be old, oppressed, battered Negro women, symbolized in a seventy-two-year-old woman in Montgomery, Alabama, who rose up with a sense of dignity and with her people decided not to ride segregated buses, and who responded with ungrammatical profundity to one who inquired about her weariness: "My feet is tired, but my soul is at rest." They will be the young high school and college students, the young ministers of the gospel and a host of their elders, courageously and nonviolently sitting in at lunch counters and willingly going to jail for conscience' sake. One day the South will know that when these disinherited children of God sat down at lunch counters, they were in reality standing up for what is best in the American dream and for the most sacred values in our Judaeo-Christian heritage, thereby bringing our nation back to those great wells of democracy which were dug deep by the founding fathers in their formulation of the Constitution and the Declaration of Independence.

Never before have I written so long a letter. I'm afraid it is much too long to take your precious time. I can assure you that it would have been much shorter if I had been writing from a comfortable desk, but what else can one do when he is alone in a narrow jail cell, other than write long letters, think long thoughts, and pray long prayers?

If I have said anything in this letter that overstates the truth and indicates an unreasonable impatience, I beg you to forgive me. If I have said anything that understates the truth and indicates my having a patience that allows me to settle for anything less than brotherhood, I beg God to forgive me.

I hope this letter finds you strong in the faith. I also hope that circumstances will soon make it possible for me to meet each of you, not as an integrationist or a civil-rights leader, but as a fellow clergyman and a Christian brother. Let us all hope that the dark clouds of racial prejudice will soon pass away and the deep fog of misunderstanding will be lifted from our fear-drenched communities, and in some not too distant tomorrow the radiant stars of love and brotherhood will shine over our great nation with all their scintillating beauty.

Yours for the cause of Peace and Brotherhood,
Martin Luther King Jr.

Interpretive Questions for Discussion

In his second inaugural address, why does Lincoln adopt the attitude of "judge not that we be not judged," even though he believes slavery to be an offense to God?

1. Why doesn't Lincoln feel triumphant regarding the successful course of the war? Why does he make no predictions about the war's outcome, but only express "high hope" for the future? (3)

2. According to Lincoln, did the North "accept" war because of its wish to preserve the Union, or because of its abhorrence of slavery? (3–4)

3. Does Lincoln blame the South for causing the war?

4. Why does Lincoln point out that "the government claimed no right to do more than to restrict the territorial enlargement" of slavery? (4) Is he suggesting that, in so compromising, the North was trying any means possible to avert bloodshed, or avoiding its moral responsibility?

5. According to Lincoln, why were people who had so much in common—even praying to the same God—unable to avoid such a terrible conflict? (4)

6. Why does Lincoln suggest that both North and South are being punished by God for the offense of American slavery? (4–5)

7. Why does Lincoln avoid calling for vengeance against the side who "would *make* war rather than let the nation survive"? (4)

8. Why does Lincoln think that, rather than a detailed speech outlining a course of action for the next four years, a brief statement about the sin of slavery and his wish that the nation bear "malice toward none" is the appropriate subject for his address? (3, 5)

Suggested textual analysis
Page 5: beginning, "With malice toward none;" to the end of the address.

According to Dr. King in "Letter from Birmingham Jail," why is most of the white community, including the clergy, blind to the justice of his protest?

1. What does Dr. King hope to accomplish by writing his letter to the Alabama clergymen?
2. Why do the Alabama clergymen consider Dr. King, who was well known as president of the Southern Christian Leadership Conference, to be an outsider in Birmingham? (8)
3. If Dr. King is sincere in saying that the Alabama clergymen are "men of genuine good will," how would he account for their failure to recognize that "injustice anywhere is a threat to justice everywhere"? (7–8)
4. Why does Dr. King call segregation a "disease"? (12)
5. Why does Dr. King find it especially difficult to explain racism to children? (12)
6. Why does Dr. King find "shallow understanding from people of good will" more frustrating than "absolute misunderstanding from people of ill will," and lukewarm acceptance "more bewildering than outright rejection"? (15–16)

7. Why is Dr. King confident that "national opinion" will reveal the injustices that African Americans face? (16)

8. Is Dr. King's letter intended to suggest that Christian segregationists, both moderate and extreme, are religious hypocrites who should be exposed?

Suggested textual analysis
Pages 14–18: beginning, "I hope you are able to see the distinction," and ending, "would inevitably lead to a frightening racial nightmare."

Do Abraham Lincoln and Martin Luther King Jr. share a philosophy of how to combat racial injustice?

1. Why does Lincoln say that everyone involved in the Civil War knew that slavery was "somehow" the cause of the conflict? Is he suggesting that racial injustice is a deeply complex issue or that most people find it a difficult problem to face? (4)

2. Why is Dr. King committed to *nonviolent* direct action, even in the face of rampant brutality against African Americans?

3. What does Lincoln mean when he says that both sides in the war "looked for an easier triumph, and a result less fundamental and astounding"? (4)

4. Would Dr. King call the Civil War a stage of "self-purification" for the nation? (9–10)

5. Why does Dr. King think that if one breaks an unjust law, he or she must do so openly and lovingly? (14–15)

6. Does the fact that Lincoln at first only tried to limit the expansion of slavery instead of abolishing the institution prove Dr. King's point that moderates pose the greatest threat to achieving social justice? (15–16)

7. Why does Dr. King think it difficult for his own people to see that it is "the more excellent way of love and nonviolent protest" that will achieve justice, and not "do-nothingism" or the hatred and despair of black nationalism? (17–18)

8. Do Lincoln and Dr. King share the same conception of a Living God who punishes the perpetrators of injustice?

Suggested textual analyses
Pages 4–5: from "One eighth of the whole population," and ending, "are true and righteous altogether."

Pages 22–24: beginning, "There was a time when the church was very powerful—" and ending, "the eternal will of God are embodied in our echoing demands."

For Further Reflection

1. Are Americans as deeply divided today as in the time of Lincoln? As in the time of Dr. King?

2. Would Americans today wage war on each other in order to preserve the Union from division?

3. Are moderates or extremists the greater impediment to establishing justice?

4. Has the "frightening racial nightmare" that Dr. King predicted would arise in America if racial equality were not attained already come about?

5. Are the nation and the world in "dire need of creative extremists"? For what causes?

6. Is it time for Americans to forgive each other for past injustices and "judge not that we be not judged"?

7. Do our leaders today lack a moral core? Do we romanticize past leaders, or do we really not have leaders today of the caliber of Lincoln and Dr. King?

8. Even though separation of church and state is a hallmark of American democracy, do our leaders need faith in God to see the nation through times of crisis?

9. Were the paths of righteous action clearer in the times of Lincoln and Dr. King than they are today?

Sorrow-Acre

Isak Dinesen

ISAK DINESEN (1885–1962) is the pen name of Danish author Karen Blixen, who wrote most of her works in English. Born Karen Christence Dinesen, she became Baroness Blixen-Finecke in 1914 when she married her cousin. The couple immigrated to British East Africa and bought a coffee plantation near Nairobi, where she began to write. Dinesen divorced her husband in 1921 but stayed in Africa and managed the plantation until 1931, when falling coffee prices forced her to return to Denmark, bankrupt. Suffering from ill health, Dinesen lived and wrote in her childhood home until her death. Her best-known works include *Out of Africa,* a memoir of her years in Kenya; *Seven Gothic Tales;* and *Winter's Tales,* in which "Sorrow-Acre" was first published in 1942.

THE LOW, undulating Danish landscape was silent and serene, mysteriously wide-awake in the hour before sunrise. There was not a cloud in the pale sky, not a shadow along the dim, pearly fields, hills, and woods. The mist was lifting from the valleys and hollows, the air was cool, the grass and the foliage dripping wet with morning dew. Unwatched by the eyes of man, and undisturbed by his activity, the country breathed a timeless life, to which language was inadequate.

All the same, a human race had lived on this land for a thousand years, had been formed by its soil and weather, and had marked it with its thoughts, so that now no one could tell where the existence of the one ceased and the other began. The thin gray line of a road, winding across the plain and up and down hills, was the fixed materialization of human longing, and of the human notion that it is better to be in one place than another.

A child of the country would read this open landscape like a book. The irregular mosaic of meadows and cornlands was a picture, in timid green and yellow, of the people's struggle for its daily bread; the centuries had taught it to plough and sow in this way. On a distant hill the immovable wings of a windmill, in a small blue cross against the sky, delineated a later stage in the career of bread. The blurred outline of thatched roofs—a low, brown growth of the earth—where the huts of the village thronged together, told the history, from his cradle to his grave, of the peasant, the creature nearest to the soil and dependent on it, prospering in a fertile year and dying in years of drought and pests.

A little higher up, with the faint horizontal line of the white cemetery wall round it, and the vertical contour of tall poplars by its side, the red-tiled church bore witness, as far as the eye reached, that this was a Christian country. The child of the land knew it as a strange house, inhabited only for a few hours every seventh day, but with a strong, clear voice in it to give out the joys and sorrows of the land: a plain, square embodiment of the nation's trust in the justice and mercy of heaven. But where, amongst cupular woods and groves, the lordly, pyramidal silhouette of the cut lime avenues rose in the air, there a big country house lay.

The child of the land would read much within these elegant, geometrical ciphers on the hazy blue. They spoke of power, the lime trees paraded round a stronghold. Up here was decided the destiny of the surrounding land and of the men and beasts upon it, and the peasant lifted his eyes to the green pyramids with awe. They spoke of dignity, decorum, and taste. Danish soil grew no finer flower than the mansion to which the long avenue led. In its lofty rooms life and death bore themselves with stately grace. The country house did not gaze upward, like the church, nor down to the ground like the huts; it had a wider earthly horizon than they, and was related to much noble architecture all over Europe. Foreign artisans had been called in to panel and stucco it, and its own inhabitants traveled and brought back ideas, fashions, and things of beauty. Paintings, tapestries, silver, and glass from distant countries had been made to feel at home here, and now formed part of Danish country life.

The big house stood as firmly rooted in the soil of Denmark as the peasants' huts, and was as faithfully allied to her four winds and her changing seasons, to her animal life, trees, and flowers. Only its interests lay in a higher plane. Within the domain of the lime trees it was no longer cows, goats, and pigs on which the minds and the talk ran, but horses and dogs. The wild fauna, the game of the land, that the peasant shook his fist at, when he saw it on his young green rye or in his ripening wheat field, to the residents of the country houses were the main pursuit and the joy of existence.

The writing in the sky solemnly proclaimed continuance, a worldly immortality. The great country houses had held their ground through many generations. The families who lived in them revered the past as they honored themselves, for the history of Denmark was their own history.

A Rosenkrantz had sat at Rosenholm, a Juel at Hverringe, a Skeel at Gammel-Estrup as long as people remembered. They had seen kings and schools of style succeed one another and, proudly and humbly, had made over their personal existence to that of their land, so that amongst their equals and with the peasants they passed by its name: Rosenholm, Hverringe, Gammel-Estrup. To the King and the country, to his family, and to the individual lord of the manor himself it was a matter of minor consequence which particular Rosenkrantz, Juel, or Skeel, out of a long row of fathers and sons, at the moment in his person incarnated the fields and woods, the peasants, cattle, and game of the estate. Many duties rested on the shoulders of the big landowners—towards God in heaven, towards the King, his neighbor, and himself—and they were all harmoniously consolidated into the idea of his duties towards his land. Highest amongst these ranked his obligation to uphold the sacred continuance, and to produce a new Rosenkrantz, Juel, or Skeel for the service of Rosenholm, Hverringe, and Gammel-Estrup.

Female grace was prized in the manors. Together with good hunting and fine wine it was the flower and emblem of the higher existence led there, and in many ways the families prided themselves more on their daughters than on their sons.

The ladies who promenaded in the lime avenues, or drove through them in heavy coaches with four horses, carried the future of the name in their laps and were, like dignified and debonair caryatides, holding up the houses. They were themselves conscious of their value, kept up their price, and moved in a sphere of pretty worship and self-worship. They might even be thought to add to it, on their own, a graceful, arch, paradoxical haughtiness. For how free were they, how powerful! Their lords might rule the country, and allow themselves many liberties, but when it came to that supreme matter of legitimacy which was the vital principle of their world, the center of gravity lay with them.

The lime trees were in bloom. But in the early morning only a faint fragrance drifted through the garden, an airy message, an aromatic echo of the dreams during the short summer night.

In a long avenue that led from the house all the way to the end of the garden, where, from a small white pavilion in the classic style, there was a great view over the fields, a young man walked. He was plainly dressed in brown, with pretty linen and lace, bare-headed, with his hair tied by a ribbon. He was dark, a strong and sturdy figure with fine eyes and hands; he limped a little on one leg.

The big house at the top of the avenue, the garden, and the fields had been his childhood's paradise. But he had traveled and lived out of Denmark, in Rome and Paris, and he was at present appointed to the Danish Legation to the Court of King George, the brother of the late, unfortunate young Danish Queen. He had not seen his ancestral home for nine years. It made him laugh to find, now, everything so much smaller than he remembered it, and at the same time he was strangely moved by meeting it again. Dead people came towards him and smiled at him; a small boy in a ruff ran past him with his hoop and kite, in passing gave him a clear glance and laughingly asked: "Do you mean to tell me that you are I?" He tried to catch him in the flight, and to answer him: "Yes, I assure you that I am you," but the light figure did not wait for a reply.

The young man, whose name was Adam, stood in a particular relation to the house and the land. For six months he had been heir to it all; nominally he was so even at this moment. It was this circumstance which had brought him from England, and on which his mind was dwelling, as he walked along slowly.

The old lord up at the manor, his father's brother, had had much misfortune in his domestic life. His wife had died young, and two of his children in infancy. The one son then left to him, his cousin's playmate, was a sickly and morose boy. For ten years the father traveled with him from one watering place to another, in Germany and Italy, hardly ever in other company than that of his silent, dying child, sheltering the faint flame of life with both hands, until such time as it could be passed over to a new bearer of the name. At the same time another misfortune had struck him: he fell into disfavor at Court, where till now he had held a fine position. He was about to rehabilitate his family's prestige through the marriage which he had arranged for his son, when before it could take place the bridegroom died, not yet twenty years old.

Adam learned of his cousin's death, and his own changed fortune, in England, through his ambitious and triumphant mother. He sat with her letter in his hand and did not know what to think about it.

If this, he reflected, had happened to him while he was still a boy, in Denmark, it would have meant all the world to him. It would be so now with his friends and schoolfellows, if they were in his place, and they would, at this moment, be congratulating or envying him. But he was neither covetous nor vain by nature; he had faith in his own talents and had been content to know that his success in life depended on his personal ability. His slight infirmity had always set him a little apart from other boys; it had, perhaps, given him a keener sensibility of many things in life, and he did not, now, deem it quite right that the head of the family should limp on one leg. He did not even see his prospects in the same light as his people at home. In England he had met with greater wealth and magnificence than they dreamed of; he had been in love with, and made happy by, an English lady of such rank and fortune that to her, he felt, the finest estate of Denmark would look but like a child's toy farm.

And in England, too, he had come in touch with the great new ideas of the age: of nature, of the right and freedom of man, of justice and beauty. The universe, through them, had become infinitely wider to him; he wanted to find out still more about it and was planning to travel to America, to the New World. For a moment he felt trapped and imprisoned, as if the dead people of his name, from the family vault at home, were stretching out their parched arms for him.

But at the same time he began to dream at night of the old house and garden. He had walked in these avenues in dream, and had smelled the scent of the flowering limes. When at Ranelagh an old gypsy woman looked at his hand and told him that a son of his was to sit in the seat of his fathers, he felt a sudden, deep satisfaction, queer in a young man who till now had never given his sons a thought.

Then, six months later, his mother again wrote to tell him that his uncle had himself married the girl intended for his dead son. The head of the family was still in his best age, not over sixty, and although Adam remembered him as a small, slight man, he was a vigorous person; it was likely that his young wife would bear him sons.

Adam's mother in her disappointment lay the blame on him. If he had returned to Denmark, she told him, his uncle might have come to look upon him as a son, and would not have married; nay, he might have handed the bride over to him. Adam knew better. The family estate, differing from the neighboring properties, had gone down from father to son ever since a man of their name first sat there. The tradition of direct succession was the pride of the clan and a sacred dogma to his uncle; he would surely call for a son of his own flesh and bone.

But at the news the young man was seized by a strange, deep, aching remorse towards his old home in Denmark. It was as if he had been making light of a friendly and generous gesture, and disloyal to someone unfailingly loyal to him. It would be but just, he thought, if from now the place should disown and forget him. Nostalgia, which before he had never known, caught hold of him; for the first time he walked in the streets and parks of London as a stranger.

He wrote to his uncle and asked if he might come and stay with him, begged leave from the Legation, and took ship for Denmark. He had come to the house to make his peace with it; he had slept little in the night, and was up so early and walking in the garden, to explain himself, and to be forgiven.

While he walked, the still garden slowly took up its day's work. A big snail, of the kind that his grandfather had brought back from France, and which he remembered eating in the house as a child, was already, with dignity, dragging a silver train down the avenue. The birds began to sing; in an old tree under which he stopped a number of them were worrying an owl; the rule of the night was over.

He stood at the end of the avenue and saw the sky lightening. An ecstatic clarity filled the world; in half an hour the sun would rise. A rye field here ran along the garden; two roe deer were moving in it and looked roseate in the dawn. He gazed out over the fields, where as a small boy he had ridden his pony, and towards the wood where he had killed his first stag. He remembered the old servants who had taught him; some of them were now in their graves.

The ties which bound him to this place, he reflected, were of a mystic nature. He might never again come back to it, and it would make no difference. As long as a man of his own blood and name should sit in the house, hunt in the fields, and be obeyed by the people in the huts, wherever he traveled on earth, in England or amongst the red Indians of America, he himself would still be safe, would still have a home, and would carry weight in the world.

His eyes rested on the church. In old days, before the time of Martin Luther, younger sons of great families, he knew, had entered the Church of Rome, and had given up individual wealth and happiness to serve the greater ideals. They, too, had bestowed honor upon their homes and were remembered in its registers. In the solitude of the morning half in jest he let his mind run as it listed; it seemed to him that he might speak to the land as to a person, as to the mother of his race. "Is it only my body that you want," he asked her, "while you reject my imagination, energy, and emotions? If the world might be brought to acknowledge that the virtue of our name does not belong to the past only, will it give you no satisfaction?" The landscape was so still that he could not tell whether it answered him yes or no.

After a while he walked on, and came to the new French rose garden laid out for the young mistress of the house. In England he had acquired a freer taste in gardening, and he wondered if he could liberate these blushing captives, and make them thrive outside their cut hedges. Perhaps, he meditated, the elegantly conventional garden would be a floral portrait of his young aunt from Court, whom he had not yet seen.

As once more he came to the pavilion at the end of the avenue his eyes were caught by a bouquet of delicate colors which could not possibly belong to the Danish summer morning. It was in fact his uncle himself, powdered and silk-stockinged, but still in a brocade dressing gown, and obviously sunk in deep thought. "And what business, or what meditations," Adam asked himself, "drags a connoisseur of the beautiful, but three months married to a wife of seventeen, from his bed into his garden before sunrise?" He walked up to the small, slim, straight figure.

His uncle on his side showed no surprise at seeing him, but then he rarely seemed surprised at anything. He greeted him, with a compliment on his matutinality, as kindly as he had done on his arrival last evening. After a moment he looked to the sky, and solemnly proclaimed: "It will be a hot day." Adam, as a child, had often been impressed by the grand, ceremonial manner in which the old lord would state the common happenings of existence; it looked as if nothing had changed here, but all was what it used to be.

The uncle offered the nephew a pinch of snuff. "No, thank you, Uncle," said Adam, "it would ruin my nose to the scent of your garden, which is as fresh as the Garden of Eden, newly created." "From every tree of which," said his uncle, smiling, "thou, my Adam, mayest freely eat." They slowly walked up the avenue together.

The hidden sun was now already gilding the top of the tallest trees. Adam talked of the beauties of nature, and of the greatness of Nordic scenery, less marked by the hand of man than that of Italy. His uncle took the praise of the landscape as a personal compliment, and congratulated him because he had not, in likeness to many young travelers in foreign countries, learned to despise his native land. No, said Adam, he had lately in England longed for the fields and woods of his Danish home. And he had there become acquainted with a new piece of Danish poetry which had enchanted him more than any English or French work. He named the author, Johannes Ewald, and quoted a few of the mighty, turbulent verses.

"And I have wondered, while I read," he went on after a pause, still moved by the lines he himself had declaimed, "that we have not till now understood how much our Nordic mythology in moral greatness surpasses that of Greece and Rome. If it had not been for the physical beauty of the ancient gods, which has come down to us in marble, no modern mind could hold them worthy of worship. They were mean, capricious, and treacherous. The gods of our Danish forefathers are as much more divine than they as the Druid is nobler than the Augur. For the fair gods of Asgaard did possess the sublime human virtues; they were righteous, trustworthy, benevolent, and even, within a barbaric age, chivalrous." His uncle here for the first time appeared to take any real interest in the conversation. He stopped, his majestic nose a little in the air. "Ah, it was easier to them," he said.

"What do you mean, Uncle?" Adam asked. "It was a great deal easier," said his uncle, "to the northern gods than to those of Greece to be, as you will have it, righteous and benevolent. To my mind it even reveals a weakness in the souls of our ancient Danes that they should consent to adore such divinities." "My dear uncle," said Adam, smiling. "I have always felt that you would be familiar with the modes of Olympus. Now please let me share your insight, and tell me why virtue should come easier to our Danish gods than to those of milder climates." "They were not as powerful," said his uncle.

"And does power," Adam again asked, "stand in the way of virtue?" "Nay," said his uncle gravely. "Nay, power is in itself the supreme virtue. But the gods of which you speak were never all-powerful. They had, at all times, by their side those darker powers which they named the Jotuns, and who worked the suffering, the disasters, the ruin of our world. They might safely give themselves up to temperance and kindness. The omnipotent gods," he went on, "have no such facilitation. With their omnipotence they take over the woe of the universe."

They had walked up the avenue till they were in view of the house. The old lord stopped and ran his eyes over it. The stately building was the same as ever; behind the two tall front windows, Adam knew, was now his young aunt's room. His uncle turned and walked back.

"Chivalry," he said, "chivalry, of which you were speaking, is not a virtue of the omnipotent. It must needs imply mighty rival powers for the knight to defy. With a dragon inferior to him in strength, what figure will St. George cut? The knight who finds no superior forces ready to hand must invent them, and combat windmills; his knighthood itself stipulates dangers, vileness, darkness on all sides of him. Nay, believe me, my nephew, in spite of his moral worth, your chivalrous Odin of Asgaard as a Regent must take rank below that of Jove, who avowed his sovereignty and accepted the world which he ruled. But you are young," he added, "and the experience of the aged to you will sound pedantic."

He stood immovable for a moment and then with deep gravity proclaimed: "The sun is up."

The sun did indeed rise above the horizon. The wide landscape was suddenly animated by its splendor, and the dewy grass shone in a thousand gleams.

"I have listened to you, Uncle," said Adam, "with great interest. But while we have talked you yourself have seemed to me preoccupied; your eyes have rested on the field outside the garden, as if something of great moment, a matter of life and death, was going on there. Now that the sun is up, I see the mowers in the rye and hear them whetting their sickles. It is, I remember you telling me, the first day of the harvest. That is a great day to a landowner and enough to take his mind away from the gods. It is very fine weather, and I wish you a full barn."

The elder man stood still, his hands on his walking stick. "There is indeed," he said at last, "something going on in that field, a matter of life and death. Come, let us sit down here, and I will tell you the whole story." They sat down on the seat that ran all along the pavilion, and while he spoke the old lord of the land did not take his eyes off the rye field.

"A week ago, on Thursday night," he said, "someone set fire to my barn at Rødmosegaard—you know the place, close to the moor—and burned it all down. For two or three days we could not lay hands on the offender. Then on Monday morning the keeper at Rødmose, with the wheelwright over there, came up to the house; they dragged with them a boy, Goske Piil, a widow's son, and they made their Bible oath that he had done it; they had themselves seen him sneaking round the barn by nightfall on Thursday. Goske had no good name on the farm; the keeper bore him a grudge upon an old matter of poaching, and the wheelwright did not like him either, for he did, I believe, suspect him with his young wife. The boy, when I talked to him, swore to his innocence, but he could not hold his own against the two old men. So I had him locked up, and meant to send him in to our judge of the district, with a letter.

"The judge is a fool, and would naturally do nothing but what he thought I wished him to do. He might have the boy sent to the convict prison for arson, or put amongst the soldiers as a bad character and a poacher. Or again, if he thought that that was what I wanted, he could let him off.

"I was out riding in the fields, looking at the corn that was soon ripe to be mowed, when a woman, the widow, Goske's mother, was brought up before me, and begged to speak to me. Anne-Marie is her name. You will remember her; she lives in the small house east of the village. She has not got a good name in the place either. They tell as a girl she had a child and did away with it.

"From five days' weeping her voice was so cracked that it was difficult for me to understand what she said. Her son, she told me at last, had indeed been over at Rødmose on Thursday, but for no ill purpose; he had gone to see someone. He was her only son, she called the Lord God to witness on his innocence, and she wrung her hands to me that I should save the boy for her.

"We were in the rye field that you and I are looking at now. That gave me an idea. I said to the widow: 'If in one day, between sunrise and sunset, with your own hands you can mow this field, and it be well done, I will let the case drop and you shall keep your son. But if you cannot do it, he must go, and it is not likely that you will then ever see him again.'

"She stood up then and gazed over the field. She kissed my riding boot in gratitude for the favor shown to her."

The old lord here made a pause, and Adam said: "Her son meant much to her?" "He is her only child," said his uncle. "He means to her her daily bread and support in old age. It may be said that she holds him as dear as her own life. As," he added, "within a higher order of life, a son to his father means the name and the race, and he holds him as dear as life everlasting. Yes, her son means much to her. For the mowing of that field is a day's work to three men, or three days' work to one man. Today, as the sun rose, she set to her task. And down there, by the end of the field, you will see her now, in a blue headcloth, with the man I have set to follow her and to ascertain that she does the work unassisted, and with two or three friends by her, who are comforting her."

Adam looked down, and did indeed see a woman in a blue headcloth, and a few other figures in the corn.

They sat for a while in silence. "Do you yourself," Adam then said, "believe the boy to be innocent?" "I cannot tell," said his uncle. "There is no proof. The word of the keeper and the wheelwright stand against the boy's word. If indeed I did believe the one thing or the other, it would be merely a matter of chance, or maybe of sympathy. The boy," he said after a moment, "was my son's playmate, the only other child that I ever knew him to like or to get on with." "Do you," Adam again asked, "hold it possible to her to fulfill your condition?" "Nay, I cannot tell," said the old lord. "To an ordinary person it would not be possible. No ordinary person would ever have taken it on at all. I chose it so. We are not quibbling with the law, Anne-Marie and I."

Adam for a few minutes followed the movement of the small group in the rye. "Will you walk back?" he asked. "No," said his uncle, "I think that I shall stay here till I have seen the end of the thing." "Until sunset?" Adam asked with surprise. "Yes," said the old lord. Adam said: "It will be a long day." "Yes," said his uncle, "a long day. But," he added, as Adam rose to walk away, "if, as you said, you have got that tragedy of which you spoke in your pocket, be as kind as to leave it here, to keep me company." Adam handed him the book.

In the avenue he met two footmen who carried the old lord's morning chocolate down to the pavilion on large silver trays.

As now the sun rose in the sky, and the day grew hot, the lime trees gave forth their exuberance of scent, and the garden was filled with unsurpassed, unbelievable sweetness. Towards the still hour of midday the long avenue reverberated like a sound-board with a low, incessant murmur: the humming of a million bees that clung to the pendulous, thronging clusters of blossoms and were drunk with bliss.

In all the short lifetime of Danish summer there is no richer or more luscious moment than that week wherein the lime trees flower. The heavenly scent goes to the head and to the heart; it seems to unite the fields of Denmark with those of Elysium; it contains both hay, honey, and holy incense, and is half fairyland and half apothecary's locker. The avenue was changed into a mystic edifice, a dryad's cathedral, outward from summit to base lavishly adorned, set with multitudinous ornaments, and golden in the sun. But behind the walls the vaults were benignly cool and somber, like ambrosial sanctuaries in a dazzling and burning world, and in here the ground was still moist.

Up in the house, behind the silk curtains of the two front windows, the young mistress of the estate from the wide bed stuck her feet into two little high-heeled slippers. Her lace-trimmed nightgown had slid up above her knee and down from the shoulder; her hair, done up in curling-pins for the night, was still frosty with the powder of yesterday, her round face flushed with sleep. She stepped out to the middle of the floor and stood there, looking extremely grave and thoughtful, yet she did not think at all. But through her head a long procession of pictures marched, and she was unconsciously endeavoring to put them in order, as the pictures of her existence had used to be.

She had grown up at Court; it was her world, and there was probably not in the whole country a small creature more exquisitely and innocently drilled to the stately measure of a palace. By favor of the old Dowager Queen she bore her name and that of the King's sister, the Queen of Sweden: Sophie Magdalena. It was with a view to these things that her husband, when he wished to restore his status in high places, had chosen her as a bride, first for his son and then for himself. But her own father, who held an office in the Royal Household and belonged to the new Court aristocracy, in his day had done the same thing the other way round, and had married a country lady, to get a foothold within the old nobility of Denmark. The little girl had her mother's blood in her veins. The country to her had been an immense surprise and delight.

To get into her castle-court she must drive through the farmyard, through the heavy stone gateway in the barn itself, wherein the rolling of her coach for a few seconds re-echoed like thunder. She must drive past the stables and the timber-mare, from which sometimes a miscreant would follow her with sad eyes, and might here startle a long string of squalling geese, or pass the heavy, scowling bull, led on by a ring in his nose and kneading the earth in dumb fury. At first this had been to her, every time, a slight shock and a jest. But after a while all these creatures and things, which belonged to her, seemed to become part of herself. Her mothers, the old Danish country ladies, were robust persons, undismayed by any kind of weather; now she herself had walked in the rain and had laughed and glowed in it like a green tree.

She had taken her great new home in possession at a time when all the world was unfolding, mating, and propagating. Flowers, which she had known only in bouquets and festoons, sprung from the earth round her; birds sang in all the trees. The newborn lambs seemed to her daintier than her dolls had been. From her husband's Hanoverian stud, foals were brought to her to give names; she stood and watched as they poked their soft noses into their mothers' bellies to drink. Of this strange process she had till now only vaguely heard. She had happened to witness, from a path in the park, the rearing and screeching stallion on the mare. All this luxuriance, lust, and fecundity was displayed before her eyes, as for her pleasure.

And for her own part, in the midst of it, she was given an old husband who treated her with punctilious respect because she was to bear him a son. Such was the compact; she had known of it from the beginning. Her husband, she found, was doing his best to fulfill his part of it, and she herself was loyal by nature and strictly brought up. She would not shirk her obligation. Only she was vaguely aware of a discord or an incompatibility within her majestic existence, which prevented her from being as happy as she had expected to be.

After a time her chagrin took a strange form: as the consciousness of an absence. Someone ought to have been with her who was not. She had no experience in analyzing her feelings; there had not been time for that at Court. Now, as she was more often left to herself, she vaguely probed her own mind. She tried to set her father in that void place, her sisters, her music master, an Italian singer whom she had admired; but none of them would fill it for her. At times she felt lighter at heart, and believed the misfortune to have left her. And then again it would happen, if she were alone, or in her husband's company, and even within his embrace, that everything round her would cry out: Where? Where? so that she let her wild eyes run about the room in search for the being who should have been there, and who had not come.

When, six months ago, she was informed that her first young bridegroom had died and that she was to marry his father in his place, she had not been sorry. Her youthful suitor, the one time she had seen him, had appeared to her infantile and insipid; the father would make a statelier consort. Now she had sometimes thought of the dead boy, and wondered whether with him life would have been more joyful. But she soon again dismissed the picture, and that was the sad youth's last recall to the stage of this world.

Upon one wall of her room there hung a long mirror. As she gazed into it new images came along. The day before, driving with her husband, she had seen, at a distance, a party of village girls bathing in the river, and the sun shining on them. All her life she had moved amongst naked marble deities, but it had till now never occurred to her that the people she knew should themselves be naked under their bodices and trains, waistcoats and satin breeches, that indeed she herself felt naked within her clothes. Now, in front of the looking glass, she tardily untied the ribbons of her nightgown, and let it drop to the floor.

The room was dim behind the drawn curtains. In the mirror her body was silvery like a white rose; only her cheeks and mouth, and the tips of her fingers and breasts had a faint carmine. Her slender torso was formed by the whalebones that had clasped it tightly from her childhood; above the slim, dimpled knee a gentle narrowness marked the place of the garter. Her limbs were rounded as if, at whatever place they might be cut through with a sharp knife, a perfectly circular transverse incision would be obtained. The side and belly were so smooth that her own gaze slipped and glided, and grasped for a hold. She was not altogether like a statue, she found, and lifted her arms above her head. She turned to get a view of her back, the curves below the waistline were still blushing from the pressure of the bed. She called to mind a few tales about nymphs and goddesses, but they all seemed a long way off, so her mind returned to the peasant girls in the river. They were, for a few minutes, idealized into playmates, or sisters even, since they belonged to her as did the meadow and the blue river itself. And within the next moment the sense of forlornness once more came upon her, a *horror vaccui* like a physical pain. Surely, surely someone should have been with her now, her other self, like the image in the glass, but nearer, stronger, alive. There was no one, the universe was empty round her.

A sudden, keen itching under her knee took her out of her reveries, and awoke in her the hunting instincts of her breed. She wetted a finger on her tongue, slowly brought it down and quickly slapped it to the spot. She felt the diminutive, sharp body of the insect against the silky skin, pressed the thumb to it, and triumphantly lifted up the small prisoner between her fingertips. She stood quite still, as if meditating upon the fact that a flea was the only creature risking its life for her smoothness and sweet blood.

Her maid opened the door and came in, loaded with the attire of the day—shift, stays, hoop, and petticoats. She remembered that she had a guest in the house, the new nephew arrived from England. Her husband had instructed her to be kind to their young kinsman, disinherited, so to say, by her presence in the house. They would ride out on the land together.

In the afternoon the sky was no longer blue as in the morning. Large clouds slowly towered up on it, and the great vault itself was colorless, as if diffused into vapors round the white-hot sun in zenith. A low thunder ran along the western horizon; once or twice the dust of the roads rose in tall spirals. But the fields, the hills, and the woods were as still as a painted landscape.

Adam walked down the avenue to the pavilion, and found his uncle there, fully dressed, his hands upon his walking stick and his eyes on the rye field. The book that Adam had given him lay by his side. The field now seemed alive with people. Small groups stood here and there in it, and a long row of men and women were slowly advancing towards the garden in the line of the swath.

The old lord nodded to his nephew, but did not speak or change his position. Adam stood by him as still as himself.

The day to him had been strangely disquieting. At the meeting again with old places the sweet melodies of the past had filled his senses and his mind, and had mingled with new, bewitching tunes of the present. He was back in Denmark, no longer a child but a youth, with a keener sense of the beautiful, with tales of other countries to tell, and still a true son of his own land and enchanted by its loveliness as he had never been before.

But through all these harmonies the tragic and cruel tale which the old lord had told him in the morning, and the sad contest which he knew to be going on so nearby, in the corn field, had re-echoed, like the recurrent, hollow throbbing of a muffled drum, a redoubtable sound. It came back time after time, so that he had felt himself to change colour and to answer absently. It brought with it a deeper sense of pity with all that lived than he had ever known. When he had been riding with his young aunt, and their road ran along the scene of the drama, he had taken care to ride between her and the field, so that she should not see what was going on there, or question him about it. He had chosen the way home through the deep, green wood for the same reason.

More dominantly even than the figure of the woman struggling with her sickle for her son's life, the old man's figure, as he had seen it at sunrise, kept him company through the day. He came to ponder on the part which that lonely, determinate form had played in his own life. From the time when his father died, it had impersonated to the boy law and order, wisdom of life and kind guardianship. What was he to do, he thought, if after eighteen years these filial feelings must change, and his second father's figure take on to him a horrible aspect, as a symbol of the tyranny and oppression of the world? What was he to do if ever the two should come to stand in opposition to each other as adversaries?

At the same time an unaccountable, a sinister alarm and dread on behalf of the old man himself took hold of him. For surely here the Goddess Nemesis could not be far away. This man had ruled the world round him for a longer period than Adam's own lifetime and had never been gainsaid by anyone. During the years when he had wandered through Europe with a sick boy of his own blood as his sole companion he had learned to set himself apart from his surroundings, and to close himself up to all outer life, and he had become insusceptible to the ideas and feelings of other human beings. Strange fancies might there have run in his mind, so that in the end he had seen himself as the only person really existing, and the world as a poor and vain shadow play, which had no substance to it.

Now, in senile wilfullness, he would take in his hand the life of those simpler and weaker than himself, of a woman, using it to his own ends, and he feared of no retributive justice. Did he not know, the young man thought, that there were powers in the world, different from and more formidable than the short-lived might of a despot?

With the sultry heat of the day this foreboding of impending disaster grew upon him, until he felt ruin threatening not the old lord only, but the house, the name, and himself with him. It seemed to him that he must cry out a warning to the man he had loved, before it was too late.

But as now he was once more in his uncle's company, the green calm of the garden was so deep that he did not find his voice to cry out. Instead a little French air which his aunt had sung to him up in the house kept running in his mind—"*C'est un trop doux effort . . .*" He had good knowledge of music; he had heard the air before, in Paris, but not so sweetly sung.

After a time he asked: "Will the woman fulfill her bargain?" His uncle unfolded his hands. "It is an extraordinary thing," he said animatedly, "that it looks as if she might fulfill it. If you count the hours from sunrise till now, and from now till sunset, you will find the time left her to be half of that already gone. And see! She has now mowed two-thirds of the field. But then we will naturally have to reckon with her strength declining as she works on. All in all, it is an idle pursuit in you or me to bet on the issue of the matter; we must wait and see. Sit down, and keep me company in my watch." In two minds Adam sat down.

"And here," said his uncle, and took up the book from the seat, "is your book, which has passed the time finely. It is great poetry, ambrosia to the ear and the heart. And it has, with our discourse on divinity this morning, given me stuff for thought. I have been reflecting upon the law of retributive justice." He took a pinch of snuff, and went on. "A new age," he said, "has made to itself a god in its own image, an emotional god. And now you are already writing a tragedy on your god."

Adam had no wish to begin a debate on poetry with his uncle, but he also somehow dreaded a silence, and said: "It may be, then, that we hold tragedy to be, in the scheme of life, a noble, a divine phenomenon."

"Aye," said his uncle solemnly, "a noble phenomenon, the noblest on earth. But of the earth only, and never divine. Tragedy is the privilege of man, his highest privilege. The God of the Christian Church Himself, when He wished to experience tragedy, had to assume human form. And even at that," he added thoughtfully, "the tragedy was not wholly valid, as it would have become had the hero of it been, in very truth, a man. The divinity of Christ conveyed to it a divine note, the moment of comedy. The real tragic part, by the nature of things, fell to the executors, not to the victim. Nay, my nephew, we should not adulterate the pure elements of the cosmos. Tragedy should remain the right of human beings, subject, in their conditions or in their own nature, to the dire law of necessity. To them it is salvation and beatification. But the gods, whom we must believe to be unacquainted with and incomprehensive of necessity, can have no knowledge of the tragic. When they are brought face to face with it they will, according to my experience, have the good taste and decorum to keep still, and not interfere.

"No," he said after a pause, "the true art of the gods is the comic. The comic is a condescension of the divine to the world of man; it is the sublime vision, which cannot be studied, but must ever be celestially granted. In the comic the gods see their own being reflected as in a mirror, and while the tragic poet is bound by strict laws, they will allow the comic artist a freedom as unlimited as their own. They do not even withhold their own existence from his sports. Jove may favor Lucianos of Samosata. As long as your mockery is in true godly taste you may mock at the gods and still remain a sound devotee. But in pitying, or condoling with your god, you deny and annihilate him, and such is the most horrible of atheisms.

"And here on earth, too," he went on, "we, who stand in lieu of the gods and have emancipated ourselves from the tyranny of necessity, should leave to our vassals their monopoly of tragedy, and for ourselves accept the comic with grace. Only a boorish and cruel master—a parvenu, in fact—will make a jest of his servants' necessity, or force the comic upon them. Only a timid and pedantic ruler, a *petit-maître,* will fear the ludicrous on his own behalf. Indeed," he finished his long speech, "the very same fatality, which, in striking the burgher or peasant, will become tragedy, with the aristocrat is exalted to the comic. By the grace and wit of our acceptance hereof our aristocracy is known."

Adam could not help smiling a little as he heard the apotheosis of the comic on the lips of the erect, ceremonious prophet. In this ironic smile he was, for the first time, estranging himself from the head of his house.

A shadow fell across the landscape. A cloud had crept over the sun; the country changed color beneath it, faded and bleached, and even all sounds for a minute seemed to die out of it.

"Ah, now," said the old lord, "if it is going to rain, and the rye gets wet, Anne-Marie will not be able to finish in time. And who comes there?" he added, and turned his head a little.

Preceded by a lackey, a man in riding boots and a striped waistcoat with silver buttons, and with his hat in his hand, came down the avenue. He bowed deeply, first to the old lord and then to Adam.

"My bailiff," said the old lord. "Good afternoon, Bailiff. What news have you to bring?" The bailiff made a sad gesture. "Poor news only, my lord," he said. "And how poor news?" asked his master. "There is," said the bailiff with weight, "not a soul at work on the land, and not a sickle going except that of Anne-Marie in this rye field. The mowing has stopped; they are all at her heels. It is a poor day for a first day of the harvest." "Yes, I see," said the old lord. The bailiff went on. "I have spoken kindly to them," he said, "and I have sworn at them; it is all one. They might as well all be deaf."

"Good bailiff," said the old lord, "leave them in peace; let them do as they like. This day may, all the same, do them more good than many others. Where is Goske, the boy, Anne-Marie's son?" "We have set him in the small room by the barn," said the bailiff. "Nay, let him be brought down," said the old lord; "let him see his mother at work. But what do you say—will she get the field mowed in time?" "If you ask me, my lord," said the bailiff, "I believe that she will. Who would have thought so? She is only a small woman. It is as hot a day today as, well, as I do ever remember. I myself, you yourself, my lord, could not have done what Anne-Marie has done today." "Nay, nay, we could not, Bailiff," said the old lord.

The bailiff pulled out a red handkerchief and wiped his brow, somewhat calmed by venting his wrath. "If," he remarked with bitterness, "they would all work as the widow works now, we would make a profit on the land." "Yes," said the old lord, and fell into thought, as if calculating the profit it might make. "Still," he said, "as to the question of profit and loss, that is more intricate than it looks. I will tell you something that you may not know: The most famous tissue ever woven was raveled out again every night. But come," he added, "she is close by now. We will go and have a look at her work ourselves." With these words he rose and set his hat on.

The cloud had drawn away again; the rays of the sun once more burned the wide landcape, and as the small party walked out from under the shade of the trees the dead-still heat was heavy as lead; the sweat sprang out on their faces and their eyelids smarted. On the narrow path they had to go one by one, the old lord stepping along first, all black, and the footman, in his bright livery, bringing up the rear.

The field was indeed filled with people like a marketplace; there were probably a hundred or more men and women in it. To Adam the scene recalled pictures from his Bible: the meeting between Esau and Jacob in Edom, or Boas' reapers in his barley field near Bethlehem. Some were standing by the side of the field, others pressed in small groups close to the mowing woman, and a few followed in her wake, binding up sheaves where she had cut the corn, as if thereby they thought to help her, or as if by all means they meant to have part in her work. A younger woman with a pail on her head kept close to her side, and with her a number of half-grown children. One of these first caught sight of the lord of the estate and his suite, and pointed to him. The binders let their sheaves drop, and as the old man stood still many of the onlookers drew close round him.

The woman on whom till now the eyes of the whole field had rested—a small figure on the large stage—was advancing slowly and unevenly, bent double as if she were walking on her knees, and stumbling as she walked. Her blue headcloth had slipped back from her head; the grey hair was plastered to the skull with sweat, dusty and stuck with straw. She was obviously totally unaware of the multitude round her; neither did she now once turn her head or her gaze towards the new arrivals.

Absorbed in her work she again and again stretched out her left hand to grasp a handful of corn, and her right hand with the sickle in it to cut it off close to the soil, in wavering, groping pulls, like a tired swimmer's strokes. Her course took her so close to the feet of the old lord that his shadow fell on her. Just then she staggered and swayed sideways, and the woman who followed her lifted the pail from her head and held it to her lips. Anne-Marie drank without leaving her hold on her sickle, and the water ran from the corners of her mouth. A boy, close to her, quickly bent one knee, seized her hands in his own and, steadying and guiding them, cut off a gripe of rye. "No, no," said the old lord, "you must not do that, boy. Leave Anne-Marie in peace to her work." At the sound of his voice the woman, falteringly, lifted her face in his direction.

The bony and tanned face was streaked with sweat and dust; the eyes were dimmed. But there was not in its expression the slightest trace of fear or pain. Indeed amongst all the grave and concerned faces of the field hers was the only one perfectly calm, peaceful, and mild. The mouth was drawn together in a thin line, a prim, keen, patient little smile, such as will be seen in the face of an old woman at her spinning wheel or her knitting, eager on her work, and happy in it. And as the younger woman lifted back the pail, she immediately again fell to her mowing, with an ardent, tender craving, like that of a mother who lays a baby to the nipple. Like an insect that bustles along in high grass, or like a small vessel in a heavy sea, she butted her way on, her quiet face once more bent upon her task.

The whole throng of onlookers, and with them the small group from the pavilion, advanced as she advanced, slowly and as if drawn by a string. The bailiff, who felt the intense silence of the field heavy on him, said to the old lord: "The rye will yield better this year than last," and got no reply. He repeated his remark to Adam, and at last to the footman, who felt himself above a discussion on agriculture, and only cleared his throat in answer. In a while the bailiff again broke the silence. "There is the boy," he said and pointed with his thumb. "They have brought him down." At that moment the woman fell forward on her face and was lifted up by those nearest to her.

Adam suddenly stopped on the path, and covered his eyes with his hand. The old lord without turning asked him if he felt incommoded by the heat. "No," said Adam, "but stay. Let me speak to you." His uncle stopped, with his hand on the stick and looking ahead, as if regretful of being held back.

"In the name of God," cried the young man in French, "force not this woman to continue." There was a short pause. "But I force her not, my friend," said his uncle in the same language. "She is free to finish at any moment." "At the cost of her child only," again cried Adam. "Do you not see that she is dying? You know not what you are doing, or what it may bring upon you."

The old lord, perplexed by this unexpected animadversion, after a second turned all round, and his pale, clear eyes sought his nephew's face with stately surprise. His long, waxen face, with two symmetrical curls at the sides, had something of the mien of an idealized and ennobled old sheep or ram. He made sign to the bailiff to go on. The footman also withdrew a little, and the uncle and nephew were, so to say, alone on the path. For a minute neither of them spoke.

"In this very place where we now stand," said the old lord, then, with hauteur, "I gave Anne-Marie my word."

"My uncle!" said Adam. "A life is a greater thing even than a word. Recall that word, I beseech you, which was given in caprice, as a whim. I am praying you more for your sake than for my own, yet I shall be grateful to you all my life if you will grant me my prayer."

"You will have learned in school," said his uncle, "that in the beginning was the word. It may have been pronounced in caprice, as a whim, the Scripture tells us nothing about it. It is still the principle of our world, its law of gravitation. My own humble word has been the principle of the land on which we stand, for an age of man. My father's word was the same, before my day."

"You are mistaken," cried Adam. "The word is creative—it is imagination, daring, and passion. By it the world was made. How much greater are these powers which bring into being than any restricting or controlling law! You wish the land on which we look to produce and propagate; you should not banish from it the forces which cause, and which keep up life, nor turn it into a desert by dominance of law. And when you look at the people, simpler than we and nearer to the heart of nature, who do not analyze their feelings, whose life is one with the life of the earth, do they not inspire in you tenderness, respect, reverence even? This woman is ready to die for her son; will it ever happen to you or me that a woman willingly gives up her life for us? And if it did indeed come to pass, should we make so light of it as not to give up a dogma in return?"

"You are young," said the old lord. "A new age will undoubtedly applaud you. I am old-fashioned, I have been quoting to you texts a thousand years old. We do not, perhaps, quite understand one another. But with my own people I am, I believe, in good understanding. Anne-Marie might well feel that I am making light of her exploit, if now, at the eleventh hour, I did nullify it by a second word. I myself should feel so in her place. Yes, my nephew, it is possible, did I grant you your prayer and pronounce such an amnesty, that I should find it void against her faithfulness, and that we would still see her at her work, unable to give it up, as a shuttle in the rye field, until she had it all mowed. But she would then be a shocking, a horrible sight, a figure of unseemly fun, like a small planet running wild in the sky, when the law of gravitation had been done away with."

"And if she dies at her task," Adam exclaimed, "her death, and its consequences, will come upon your head."

The old lord took off his hat and gently ran his hand over his powdered head. "Upon my head?" he said. "I have kept up my head in many weathers. Even," he added proudly, "against the cold wind from high places. In what shape will it come upon my head, my nephew?" "I cannot tell," cried Adam in despair. "I have spoken to warn you. God only knows." "Amen," said the old lord with a little delicate smile. "Come, we will walk on." Adam drew in his breath deeply.

"No," he said in Danish. "I cannot come with you. This field is yours; things will happen here as you decide. But I myself must go away. I beg you to let me have, this evening, a coach as far as town. For I could not sleep another night under your roof, which I have honored beyond any on earth." So many conflicting feelings at his own speech thronged in his breast that it would have been impossible for him to give them words.

The old lord, who had already begun to walk on, stood still, and with him the lackey. He did not speak for a minute, as if to give Adam time to collect his mind. But the young man's mind was in uproar and would not be collected.

"Must we," the old man asked, in Danish, "take leave here, in the rye field? I have held you dear, next to my own son. I have followed your career in life from year to year, and have been proud of you. I was happy when you wrote to say that you were coming back. If now you will go away, I wish you well." He shifted his walking stick from the right hand to the left and gravely looked his nephew in the face.

Adam did not meet his eyes. He was gazing out over the landscape. In the late mellow afternoon it was resuming its colors, like a painting brought into proper light; in the meadows the little black stacks of peat stood gravely distinct upon the green sward. On this same morning he had greeted it all, like a child running laughingly to its mother's bosom; now already he must tear himself from it, in discordance, and forever. And at the moment of parting it seemed infinitely dearer than any time before, so much beautified and solemnized by the coming separation that it looked like the place in a dream, a landscape out of paradise, and he wondered if it was really the same. But, yes—there before him was, once more, the hunting ground of long ago. And there was the road on which he had ridden today.

"But tell me where you mean to go from here," said the old lord slowly. "I myself have traveled a good deal in my days. I know the word of leaving, the wish to go away. But I have learned by experience that, in reality, the word has a meaning only to the place and the people which one leaves. When you have left my house—although it will see you go with sadness—as far as it is concerned the matter is finished and done with. But to the person who goes away it is a different thing, and not so simple. At the moment that he leaves one place he will be already, by the laws of life, on his way to another, upon this earth. Let me know, then, for the sake of our old acquaintance, to which place you are going when you leave here. To England?"

"No," said Adam. He felt in his heart that he could never again go back to England or to his easy and carefree life there. It was not far enough away; deeper waters than the North Sea must now be laid between him and Denmark. "No, not to England," he said. "I shall go to America, to the New World." For a moment he shut his eyes, trying to form to himself a picture of existence in America, with the gray Atlantic Ocean between him and these fields and woods.

"To America?" said his uncle and drew up his eyebrows. "Yes, I have heard of America. They have got freedom there, a big waterfall, savage red men. They shoot turkeys, I have read, as we shoot partridges. Well, if it be your wish, go to America, Adam, and be happy in the New World."

He stood for some time, sunk in thought, as if he had already sent off the young man to America, and had done with him. When at last he spoke, his words had the character of a monologue, enunciated by the person who watches things come and go, and himself stays on.

"Take service, there," he said, "with the power which will give you an easier bargain than this: That with your own life you may buy the life of your son."

Adam had not listened to his uncle's remarks about America, but the conclusive, solemn words caught his ear. He looked up. As if for the first time in his life, he saw the old man's figure as a whole, and conceived how small it was, so much smaller than himself, pale, a thin black anchorite upon his own land. A thought ran through his head: "How terrible to be old!" The abhorrence of the tyrant, and the sinister dread on his behalf, which had followed him all day, seemed to die out of him, and his pity with all creation to extend even to the somber form before him.

His whole being had cried out for harmony. Now, with the possibility of forgiving, of a reconciliation, a sense of relief went through him; confusedly he bethought himself of Anne-Marie drinking the water held to her lips. He took off his hat, as his uncle had done a moment ago, so that to a beholder at a distance it would seem that the two dark-clad gentlemen on the path were repeatedly and respectfully saluting one another, and brushed the hair from his forehead. Once more the tune of the garden room rang in his mind:

Mourir pour ce qu'on aime
C'est un trop doux effort . . .

He stood for a long time immobile and dumb. He broke off a few ears of rye, kept them in his hand, and looked at them.

He saw the ways of life, he thought, as a twined and tangled design, complicated and mazy; it was not given him or any mortal to command or control it. Life and death, happiness and woe, the past and the present, were interlaced within the pattern. Yet to the initiated it might be read as easily as our ciphers—which to the savage must seem confused and incomprehensible—will be read by the schoolboy. And out of the contrasting elements concord rose. All that lived must suffer; the old man, whom he had judged hardly, had suffered, as he had watched his son die, and had dreaded the obliteration of his being. He himself would come to know ache, tears, and remorse, and, even through these, the fullness of life. So might now, to the woman in the rye field, her ordeal be a triumphant procession. For to die for the one you loved was an effort too sweet for words.

As now he thought of it, he knew that all his life he had sought the unity of things, the secret which connects the phenomena of existence. It was this strife, this dim presage, which had sometimes made him stand still and inert in the midst of the games of his playfellows, or which had, at other moments—on moonlight nights, or in his little boat on the sea—lifted the boy to ecstatic happiness. Where other young people, in their pleasures or their amours, had searched for contrast and variety, he himself had yearned only to comprehend in full the oneness of the world. If things had come differently to him, if his young cousin had not died, and the events that followed his death had not brought him to Denmark, his search for understanding and harmony might have taken him to America, and he might have found them there, in the virgin forests of a new world. Now they have been disclosed to him today, in the place where he had played as a child. As the song is one with the voice that sings it, as the road is one with the goal, as lovers are made one in their embrace, so is man one with his destiny, and he shall love it as himself.

He looked up again, towards the horizon. If he wished to, he felt, he might find out what it was that had brought to him, here, the sudden conception of the unity of the universe. When this same morning he had philosophized, lightly and for his own sake, on his feeling of belonging to this land and soil, it had been the beginning of it. But since then it had grown; it had become a mightier thing, a revelation to his soul. Some time he would look into it, for the law of cause and effect was a wonderful and fascinating study. But not now. This hour was consecrated to greater emotions, to a surrender to fate and to the will of life.

"No," he said at last. "If you wish it I shall not go. I shall stay here."

At that moment a long, loud roll of thunder broke the stillness of the afternoon. It re-echoed for a while amongst the low hills, and it reverberated within the young man's breast as powerfully as if he had been seized and shaken by hands. The landscape had spoken. He remembered that twelve hours ago he had put a question to it, half in jest, and not knowing what he did. Here it gave him its answer.

What it contained he did not know; neither did he inquire. In his promise to his uncle he had given himself over to the mightier powers of the world. Now what must come must come.

"I thank you," said the old lord, and made a little stiff gesture with his hand. "I am happy to hear you say so. We should not let the difference in our ages, or of our views, separate us. In our family we have been wont to keep peace and faith with one another. You have made my heart lighter."

Something within his uncle's speech faintly recalled to Adam the misgivings of the afternoon. He rejected them; he would not let them trouble the new, sweet felicity which his resolution to stay had brought him.

"I shall go on now," said the old lord. "But there is no need for you to follow me. I will tell you tomorrow how the matter has ended." "No," said Adam, "I shall come back by sunset, to see the end of it myself."

All the same he did not come back. He kept the hour in his mind, and all through the evening the consciousness of the drama, and the profound concern and compassion with which, in his thoughts, he followed it, gave to his speech, glance, and movements a grave and pathetic substance. But he felt that he was, in the rooms of the manor, and even by the harpsichord on which he accompanied his aunt to her air from *Alceste,* as much in the center of things as if he had stood in the rye field itself, and as near to those human beings whose fate was now decided there. Anne-Marie and he were both in the hands of destiny, and destiny would, by different ways, bring each to the designated end.

Later on he remembered what he had thought that evening.

But the old lord stayed on. Late in the afternoon he even had an idea; he called down his valet to the pavilion and made him shift his clothes on him and dress him up in a brocaded suit that he had worn at Court. He let a lace-trimmed shirt be drawn over his head and stuck out his slim legs to have them put into thin silk stockings and buckled shoes. In this majestic attire he dined alone, of a frugal meal, but took a bottle of Rhenish wine with it, to keep up his strength. He sat on for a while, a little sunk in his seat; then, as the sun neared the earth, he straightened himself, and took the way down to the field.

The shadows were now lengthening, azure blue along all the eastern slopes. The lonely trees in the corn marked their site by narrow blue pools running out from their feet, and as the old man walked, a thin, immensely elongated reflection stirred behind him on the path. Once he stood still; he thought he heard a lark singing over his head, a springlike sound; his tired head held no clear perception of the season; he seemed to be walking, and standing, in a kind of eternity.

The people in the field were no longer silent, as they had been in the afternoon. Many of them talked loudly among themselves, and a little farther away a woman was weeping.

When the bailiff saw his master, he came up to him. He told him, in great agitation, that the widow would, in all likelihood, finish the mowing of the field within a quarter of an hour.

"Are the keeper and the wheelwright here?" the old lord asked him. "They have been here," said the bailiff, "and have gone away, five times. Each time they have said that they would not come back. But they have come back again, all the same, and they are here now." "And where is the boy?" the old lord asked again. "He is with her," said the bailiff. "I have given him leave to follow her. He has walked close to his mother all the afternoon, and you will see him now by her side, down there."

Anne-Marie was now working her way up towards them more evenly than before, but with extreme slowness, as if at any moment she might come to a standstill. This excessive tardiness, the old lord reflected, if it had been purposely performed, would have been an inimitable, dignified exhibition of skilled art; one might fancy the Emperor of China advancing in like manner on a divine procession or rite. He shaded his eyes with his hand, for the sun was now just beyond the horizon, and its last rays made light, wild, many-colored specks dance before his sight. With such splendor did the sunset emblazon the earth and the air that the landscape was turned into a melting pot of glorious metals.

The meadows and the grasslands became pure gold; the barley field nearby, with its long ears, was a live lake of shining silver.

There was only a small patch of straw standing in the rye field, when the woman, alarmed by the change in the light, turned her head a little to get a look at the sun. The while she did not stop her work, but grasped one handful of corn and cut it off, then another, and another. A great stir, and a sound like a manifold, deep sigh, ran through the crowd. The field was now mowed from one end to the other. Only the mower herself did not realize the fact; she stretched out her hand anew, and when she found nothing in it, she seemed puzzled or disappointed. Then she let her arms drop, and slowly sank to her knees.

Many of the women burst out weeping, and the swarm drew close round her, leaving only a small open space at the side where the old lord stood. Their sudden nearness frightened Anne-Marie; she made a slight, uneasy movement, as if terrified that they should put their hands on her.

The boy, who had kept by her all day, now fell on his knees beside her. Even he dared not touch her, but held one arm low behind her back and the other before her, level with her collar-bone, to catch hold of her if she should fall, and all the time he cried aloud. At that moment the sun went down.

The old lord stepped forward and solemnly took off his hat. The crowd became silent, waiting for him to speak. But for a minute or two he said nothing. Then he addressed her, very slowly.

"Your son is free, Anne-Marie," he said. He again waited a little, and added: "You have done a good day's work, which will long be remembered."

Anne-Marie raised her gaze only as high as his knees, and he understood that she had not heard what he said. He turned to the boy. "You tell your mother, Goske," he said, gently, "what I have told her."

The boy had been sobbing wildly, in raucous, broken moans. It took him some time to collect and control himself. But when at last he spoke, straight into his mother's face, his voice was low, a little impatient, as if he were conveying an everyday message to her. "I am free, Mother," he said. "You have done a good day's work that will long be remembered."

At the sound of his voice she lifted her face to him. A faint, bland shadow of surprise ran over it, but still she gave no sign of having heard what he said, so that the people round them began to wonder if the exhaustion had turned her deaf. But after a moment she slowly and waveringly raised her hand, fumbling in the air as she aimed at his face, and with her fingers touched his cheek. The cheek was wet with tears, so that at the contact her fingertips lightly stuck to it, and she seemed unable to overcome the infinitely slight resistance, or to withdraw her hand. For a minute the two looked each other in the face. Then, softly and lingeringly, like a sheaf of corn that falls to the ground, she sank forward onto the boy's shoulder, and he closed his arms round her.

He held her thus, pressed against him, his own face buried in her hair and headcloth, for such a long time that those nearest to them, frightened because her body looked so small in his embrace, drew closer, bent down, and loosened his grip. The boy let them do so without a word or a movement. But the woman who held Anne-Marie, in her arms to lift her up, turned her face to the old lord. "She is dead," she said.

The people who had followed Anne-Marie all through the day kept standing and stirring in the field for many hours, as long as the evening light lasted, and longer. Long after some of them had made a stretcher from branches of the trees and had carried away the dead woman, others wandered on, up and down the stubble, imitating and measuring her course from one end of the rye field to the other, and binding up the last sheaves, where she had finished her mowing.

The old lord stayed with them for a long time, stepping along a little, and again standing still.

In the place where the woman had died the old lord later on had a stone set up, with a sickle engraved in it. The peasants on the land then named the rye field "Sorrow-Acre." By this name it was known a long time after the story of the woman and her son had itself been forgotten.

Interpretive Questions for Discussion

Why does the old lord give Anne-Marie an almost impossible task to complete to save her son?

1. Why does the old lord set the task for Anne-Marie and not for her son, who is accused of the crime?
2. What does the old lord mean when he says that he and Anne-Marie are "not quibbling with the law"? (49)
3. Is the old lord being cruel or merciful toward Anne-Marie?
4. Why are we told that Anne-Marie, like her son, has a bad name in the village, and that rumor says she "did away with" a child she had when she was a girl? (48)
5. Why does it seem not to matter to the old lord whether Anne-Marie's son is guilty or innocent? (49)
6. Why are we told that Goske was the playmate of the old lord's deceased son, the only other child the lord's son had ever gotten along with or liked? (49)
7. Why is the old lord surprised by Adam's reactions to the suffering he has imposed on Anne-Marie? Why does he seem not to understand when Adam says that the consequences for Anne-Marie's death will come upon his head? (61–63)
8. Why does Anne-Marie seem calm, happy, and eager in her task? (60)

9. Why does the old lord stay all day to watch Anne-Marie mow the field? Why does he dress as he did at Court to meet Anne-Marie at the end of her ordeal?

10. Why does the old lord remain in the field along with the peasants many hours after Anne-Marie's body is borne away?

11. Why does the old lord say in acknowledgment of Anne-Marie's triumph, "You have done a good day's work, which will long be remembered"? (69) Why does he place in the field a stone with a sickle engraved on it to commemorate her accomplishment?

12. Why are we told that the story of Anne-Marie and her son was forgotten, but that the name the peasants had given to the field, "Sorrow-Acre," was not?

Suggested textual analyses
Pages 46–49: beginning, "What do you mean, Uncle?" and ending, "Adam handed him the book."

Pages 61–64: beginning, "In the name of God," and ending, "That with your own life you may buy the life of your son."

Why does Adam "surrender to fate and to the will of life" and change his mind about going to America?

1. Why does Adam delay returning to Denmark when his mother writes that he is heir to his uncle's estate? (41–42) Why is he "seized by a strange, deep, aching remorse" and "nostalgia" when he learns that his uncle has remarried? (43)

2. Why are we told that, in England, Adam had loved and been "made happy by" a noblewoman whose rank and fortune far surpassed that of his uncle? (42)

3. Why does Adam feel he will be safe as long as someone of his own lineage rules his uncle's estate? (43)

4. Why, at the beginning of his stay, is Adam moved to ask his ancestral lands, "Is it only my body that you want . . . while you reject my imagination, energy, and emotions"? (44)

5. After witnessing the suffering of Anne-Marie, why does Adam decide that England is "not far enough away"—that he must go to America? (64)

6. Why does pity for the old lord cause Adam to lose his abhorrence for what has been decreed for Anne-Marie? (64–65; cf. 56–57)

7. Why does Adam find peace in the idea that "all that lived must suffer"? Why does he find "harmony" and "unity" in his ancestral home? (65–66)

8. After deciding not to leave his uncle, why does Adam feel that his native landscape has spoken to him, but without his understanding what its answer contains? (66–67; cf. 44)

9. Why is the happiness that Adam feels at his decision to stay with his uncle threatened when the old lord thanks him? Why does Adam consciously reject his misgivings of the afternoon? (67)

10. Why doesn't Adam return to watch the end of Anne-Marie's ordeal as he told his uncle he would? Why does he feel, as he accompanies his aunt on the harpsicord, "as much in the center of things as if he had stood in the rye field itself"? (67)

Suggested textual analyses

Pages 40–43: beginning, "In a long avenue that led from the house," and ending, "to explain himself, and to be forgiven."

Pages 65–67: beginning, "His whole being had cried out for harmony," and ending, "which his resolution to stay had brought him."

Why is the righteous old lord the cause of so much misery—to his young wife, his nephew, Anne-Marie, and her son?

1. Why does the old lord proclaim that "power is in itself the supreme virtue"? (46)
2. Why does the old lord prefer the "mean, capricious, and treacherous" Greek gods to those of Scandinavia? Why does the old lord think that it belies a "weakness" in the soul to worship the "righteous and benevolent" Nordic gods? (45–46)
3. Why does the old lord believe that tragedy is the highest privilege of human beings? Why does he consider the members of his class, "who stand in lieu of the gods," to be immune from tragedy? (56–57)
4. Why, despite her great pleasure in country life, does the old lord's young wife feel that "the universe was empty round her" in her new home? (53)
5. Why is the old lord pleased to have the peasants witness Anne-Marie's ordeal? Why does he order Anne-Marie's son to watch his mother at work? (58)
6. Why does the old lord dismiss Adam's pleas to end Anne-Marie's ordeal by saying that to do so would be to make a mockery of her? (62)
7. Is Adam correct in thinking that his uncle is a despot who is using Anne-Marie for his own ends? (55)
8. Why does the old lord believe that his word is greater than a life? (61)
9. Why are we told that the keeper and the wheelwright—the men who accused Anne-Marie's son—came and left five times during her ordeal, and eventually stayed to the end? (68)

10. Is the powerful old lord neither a comic nor a tragic figure?

Suggested textual analysis
Pages 56–57: beginning, "After a time he asked:" and ending, "estranging himself from the head of his house."

For Further Reflection

1. Do Anne-Marie and her son receive justice at the hands of the old lord?
2. Is tragedy the essence of humanity? Does suffering give meaning to our lives?
3. Does the old lord deal wisely with a situation in which he must pass judgment without knowing the truth?
4. When it comes to maintaining and exacting justice, is the "word" greater than any single life?
5. Is "Sorrow-Acre" essentially a Christian story, or do its notions of justice and human suffering transcend any particular faith or culture?

KONGI'S HARVEST

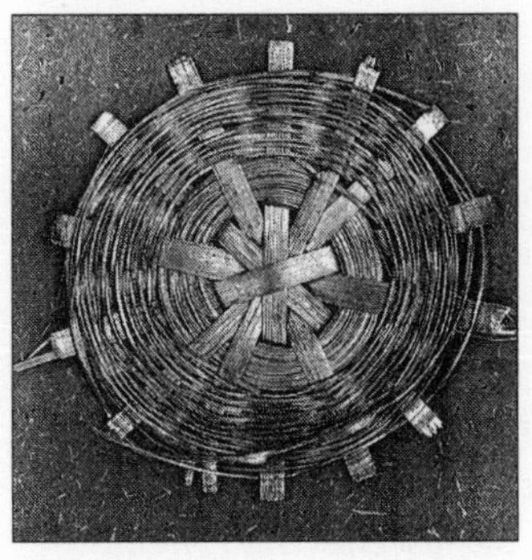

Wole Soyinka

WOLE SOYINKA (1934–) was born near Abeokuta, Nigeria. While his parents represented colonial influences—his father was headmaster of the British village school and his mother a devout Christian convert—Soyinka grew up learning Yoruba tribal traditions from his grandfather. He studied at universities in Nigeria and England and returned to Nigeria in 1960 to start his own theater company. During Nigeria's civil war, Soyinka spent more than two years as a political prisoner, mostly in solitary confinement. Upon his release in 1969, Soyinka left the country and did not return until after a change of power in 1975. In addition to dramatic works, Soyinka is known for his poetry, novels, essays, and memoirs, especially his autobiography *Aké: The Years of Childhood*. In 1986, he became the first African to win the Nobel Prize for literature.

Translations of the Yoruba songs in *Kongi's Harvest* are on pp. 183–185.

Characters

Oba Danlola	a traditional ruler
Sarumi	a junior Oba
Daodu	son to Sarumi and heir to Danlola's throne
Wuraola	Danlola's favourite wife
Ogbo Aweri	head of the Oba's defunct Conclave of Elders
Dende	servant to Danlola
Segi	a courtesan, Kongi's ex-mistress
Kongi	President of Isma
Organising Secretary	
First Aweri, Second Aweri, Third Aweri, Fourth Aweri, Fifth Aweri, Sixth Aweri	members of the Reformed Aweri Fraternity
Superintendent	
Captain of the Carpenters' Brigade	
Right and Left Ears of State	

Retinue, Drummers, Praise-singers, the Carpenters' Brigade, Photographer, Nightclub Habituées.

The action takes place on the eve and the day of the national celebrations of Isma.

HEMLOCK

A roll of drums such as accompanies a national anthem. Presumably the audience will rise. The curtain rises with them. Grouped solemnly behind it are OBA DANLOLA, WURAOLA *his favourite wife, his* OGBO AWERI, DENDE, *and* DANLOLA*'s retinue of drummers and buglers. They break into the following anthem:*

The pot that will eat fat
Its bottom must be scorched
The squirrel that will long crack nuts
Its footpad must be sore
The sweetest wine has flowed down
The tapper's shattered shins
And there is more, oh-oh
Who says there isn't more
Who says there isn't plenty a word
In a penny newspaper

Ism to ism for ism is ism
Of isms and isms on absolute-ism
To demonstrate the tree of life
Is sprung from broken peat
And we the rotted bark, spurned
When the tree swells its pot
The mucus that is snorted out
When Kongi's new race blows
And more, oh there's a harvest of words
In a penny newspaper

They say, oh how
They say it all on silent skulls
But who cares? Who but a lunatic
Will bandy words with boxes

With government rediffusion sets
Which talk and talk and never
Take a lone word in reply.

I cannot counter words, oh
I cannot counter words of
A rediffusion set
My ears are sore
But my mouth is *agbayun*
For I do not bandy words
No, I do not bandy words
With a government loudspeaker.

SUPERINTENDENT (*rushes in, agitated*): Kabiyesi, be your age. These antics may look well on a common agitator but really, an elder is an elder, and a king does not become a menial just because he puts down his crown to eat.

DANLOLA (*to the beat of* gbedu *drum, steps into slow, royal dance*): *E ma gun'yan Oba kere o*
E ma gun'yan Oba kere
Kaun elepini ko se e gbe mi
Eweyo noin ni i fi yo'nu
E ma gun'yan Oba kere

Don't pound the king's yam
In a small mortar
Don't pound the king's yam
In a small mortar
Small as the spice is
It cannot be swallowed whole
A shilling's vegetable must appease
A halfpenny spice.

SUPERINTENDENT: It won't work, Kabiyesi, it won't work. Every evening you gather your friends together and desecrate the National Anthem. It has to stop!

SARUMI: *Oba ni i f'epo inu ebo ra'ri*
Orisa l'oba
Oba ni i f'epo inu ebo r'awuje
Orisa l'oba.

None but the king
Takes the oil from the crossroads
And rubs it in his *awuje*
The king is a god.

SUPERINTENDENT: I say you desecrate our National Anthem. I have to do something about it. And stop that unholy noise.

(*Seizes the lead drummer by the wrist. Everything stops. Complete silence.*)

DANLOLA (*slowly*): You stopped the royal drums?

SUPERINTENDENT: I shall speak to the Secretary about this . . .

DANLOLA (*suddenly relaxed*): No, it is nothing new. Your betters
Stopped the drums a long time ago
And you the slave in khaki and brass buttons
Now lick your masters' spit and boast,
We chew the same tobacco.

SUPERINTENDENT (*turning to* SARUMI): Look, you better warn him . . .

SARUMI: We do not hear the jackal's call
When the Father speaks.

SUPERINTENDENT: This cannot continue. I shall insist that the Secretary put you all in different sections of the camp. This cannot go on.

DANLOLA: Good friend, you merely stopped
My drums. But they were silenced
On the day when Kongi cast aside
My props of wisdom, the day he
Drove the old Aweri from their seats.
What is a king without a clan
Of elders? What will Kongi be without . . .
Sarumi, what name was it again?

SARUMI: The Reformed Aweri Fraternity.

DANLOLA: A big name for little heads.
And now, he wants to eat
The first of the New Yam. The mashed
Weak yams on which the crow
Weaned our Leader his son still stick
Between his teeth and prove too tough
For his adult comfort, but he seeks
To eat the first of the New Yam.

(*The retainers burst into derisive laughter and the* SUPERINTENDENT *becomes incensed.*)

SUPERINTENDENT: You see if I don't do something about that subversive kind of talk. . . . E-eh!

(*He looks down and sees for the first time what* DANLOLA *has used for a wrapper under his* agbada. *Looks rapidly up at a flagpole in the middle of the yard and back again to* DANLOLA*'s legs.*)

SUPERINTENDENT: Kabiyesi, is that not our national flag?

DANLOLA: Did you not deprive me of my national trousers?

SUPERINTENDENT: Yes, to keep you from escaping.

DANLOLA: The nude shanks of a king
Is not a sight for children—
It will blind them.

When an Oba stops the procession
And squats on the wayside,
It's on an urgent matter
Which spares neither king nor god.
Wise heads turn away
Until he's wiped his bottom.

SUPERINTENDENT (*wildly*): We'll soon see about that. You want to cost me my job, do you?

(*He rushes at* DANLOLA *and whips off the flag.* DANLOLA *first rapidly gathers his* agbada *round his legs to protect his seminudity, then shrugs and tries to assume a dignified indifference.*)

DANLOLA: It was our fathers who said, not I—
A crown is a burden when
The king visits his favourite's
Chambers. When the king's wrapper
Falls off in audience, wise men know
He wants to be left alone. So—

(*Shoos him off with a contemptuous gesture.*)

SUPERINTENDENT (*going*): Too much indulgence, that's why. It's all the fault of the Organising Secretary permitting your wives and all these other creatures to visit you. And you are not even grateful.

DANLOLA (*bursts into laughter*): We curse a wretch denying cause
For gratitude deserved, but it is
A mindless clown who dispenses
Thanks as a fowl scatters meal
Not caring where it falls. Thanks?
In return for my long fingers of largesse
Your man knows I love to have my hairs
Ruffled well below the navel.
Denied that, are you or he the man
To stop me breaking out of camp?

And granting my retainers leave
To keep me weekend company—is that also
Reason for the grass to tickle (*slapping his belly*)
The royal wine gourd? Well?
What says the camp superintendent?
Shall I . . . ?

(*Makes a motion as if he means to prostrate himself.*)

RETAINERS (*step forward, shouting in alarm*): *Ewo!*[1]

DANLOLA: But he says I must. Let me
Prostrate myself to him.

(*Again the gesture. He and his retainers get involved in a mock struggle.*)

SUPERINTENDENT: I did not make any impious demands of you. All I asked was for more respect to constituted authority. I didn't ask for a curse on my head.

DANLOLA: Curse? Who spoke of curses?
To prostrate to a loyal servant
Of Kongi—is that a curse?

SUPERINTENDENT: Only a foolish child lets a father prostrate to him. I don't ask to become a leper or a lunatic. I have no wish to live on sour berries.

DANLOLA: All is well. The guard has waived
His rights and privileges. The father
Now prostrates himself in gratitude.

SUPERINTENDENT (*shouting*): I waived nothing. I had nothing to waive, nothing to excuse. I deny any rights and beg you not to cast subtle damnations on my head.

DANLOLA: Oh, but what a most suspicious mould
Olukori must have used for casting man.

1. Taboo.

Subtle damnations? If I was
Truly capable of that, would I
Now be here, thanking you for little
Acts of kindness flat on my face?

(*Again his act.*)

SUPERINTENDENT (*forestalls him by throwing himself down*): I call you all to witness. Kabiyesi, I am only the fowl droppings that stuck to your slippers when you strolled in the backyard. The child is nothing; it is only the glory of his forbears that the world sees and tolerates in him.

SARUMI: Ah, don't be angry with him
Oba Danlola, don't be angry
With your son. If the baobab shakes
Her head in anger, what chance
Has the rodent when
An earring falls
And hits the earth with thunder.

DANLOLA (*swelling, swelling . . .*): He paraded me to the world
L'ogolonto[2] I leave this abuse
To the judgement of the . . .

SUPERINTENDENT: Please—plead with him. Intercede for me.

SARUMI: Kabiyesi, a father employs only a small stick on his child, he doesn't call in the policeman to take him to gaol. Don't give voice to the awesome names on an Oba's tongue; when you feel kinder, they cannot easily be recalled. They must fulfill what task they were called to do.

(*The retainers intervene, pleading with* DANLOLA. *His drummers try to soothe him and* WURA *kneels to placate his anger. Gradually he calms down, slowly, as* SARUMI *sings.*)

2. Stark naked.

SARUMI: Ah, Danlola, my father,
Even so did I
Wish your frown of thunder away
When the Aweri were driven from
Their ancient conclave. Then you said . . .

DRUMMER: This is the last
That we shall dance together
They say we took too much silk
For the royal canopy
But the dead will witness
We never ate the silkworm.

SARUMI: They complained because
The first of the new yams
Melted first in an Oba's mouth
But the dead will witness
We drew the poison from the root.

(*As the king's men begin a dirge of* ege, DANLOLA *sits down slowly onto a chair, withdrawing more and more into himself.*)

DRUMMER: I saw a strange sight
In the market this day
The day of the feast of Agemo
The sun was high
And the king's umbrella
Beneath it. . . .

SARUMI: We lift the king's umbrella
Higher than men
But it never pushes
The sun in the face.

DRUMMER: I saw a strange sight
In the market this day

The sun was high
But I saw no shade
From the king's umbrella.

OGBO AWERI: This is the last
That we shall dance together
This is the last the hairs
Will lift on our skin
And draw together
When the *gbedu* rouses
The dead in *oshugbo*.[3] . . .

SARUMI: This is the last our feet
Shall speak to feet of the dead
And the unborn cling
To the hem of our robes
Oh yes, we know they say
We wore out looms
With weaving robes for kings
But I ask, is *popoki*[4]
The stuff to let down
To unformed fingers clutching up
At life?

OGBO AWERI: Did you not see us
Lead twins by the hand?
Did you not see us
Shade the albino's eyes
From the hard sun, with a fan
Of parrot feathers?
Even so did the god[5] enjoin
Whose hands of chalk
Have formed the cripple
And the human bat of day.

---

3. Shrine of Oro (cult of the dead).

4. Thick, coarse, woven cloth.

5. Obatala, a Yoruba deity.

SARUMI: Don't pound the king's yam
With a small pestle
Let the dandy's wardrobe
Be as lavish as the shop
Of the dealer in brocades
It cannot match an elder's rags.

DANLOLA (*almost to himself*): This dance is the last
Our feet shall dance together
The royal python may be good
At hissing, but it seems
The scorpion's tail is fire.

DRUMMER: The king's umbrella
Gives no more shade
But we summon no dirge master.
The tunnel passes through
The hill's belly
But we cry no defilement
A new-dug path may lead
To the secret heart of being.
Ogun is still a god
Even without his navel.

OGBO AWERI: Observe, when the monster child
Was born, Opele[6] taught us to
Abandon him beneath the buttress tree
But the mother said, oh no,
A child is still a child
The mother in us said, a child
Is still the handiwork of Olukori.

SARUMI: Soon the head swelled
Too big for pillow
And it swelled too big
For the mother's back

6. Vehicle for Ifa (divination).

And soon the mother's head
Was nowhere to be seen
And the child's slight belly
Was strangely distended.

DANLOLA (*comes forward, dancing softly*): This is the last
Our feet shall touch together
We thought the tune
Obeyed us to the soul
But the drums are newly shaped
And stiff arms strain
On stubborn crooks, so
Delve with the left foot
For ill luck; with the left
Again for ill luck; once more
With the left alone, for disaster
Is the only certainty we know.

(*The bugles join in royal cadences, the two kings dance slow, mournful steps, accompanied by their retinue. Coming down on the scene, a cage of prison bars separating* DANLOLA *from* SARUMI *and the other visitors, who go out backwards herded off by the* SUPERINTENDENT.)

FIRST PART

The action alternates between two scenes, both of which are present on different parts of the stage and are brought into play in turn, by lights. First, Kongi's retreat in the mountains, the Reformed Aweri Fraternity in session. KONGI *is seen dimly in his own cell, above the* AWERI. *Rising slowly, a chant in honour of Kongi.*

FOURTH AWERI: We need an image. Tomorrow being our first appearance in public, it is essential that we find an image.

FIFTH: Why?

THIRD: Why? Is that question necessary?

FIFTH: It is. Why do we need an image?

THIRD: Well, if you don't know that. . . .

FOURTH: He doesn't, so I'll answer the question. Especially as he seems to be staying awake at last.

FIFTH: Don't sneer. I've heard your snores twice at least this session.

FOURTH: Kindly return to the theme of this planning session. The problem of an image for ourselves.

SECOND: Isn't it enough just to go in as Kongi's disciples?

FOURTH: Magi is more dignified. We hold after all the position of the wise ones. From the recognition of us as the Magi, it is one step to his inevitable apotheosis.

FIRST: Which is to create a new oppositional force.

SECOND: Kongi is a great strategist. He will not take on too many opponents at once.

FIFTH: I still have not been told why we need an image.

THIRD: You are being very obstructive.

FIFTH: Why do we need an image?

FIRST: I suggest we pattern ourselves on our predecessors. Oh, I do admit they were a little old-fashioned, but they had er . . . a certain style. Yes, I think style is the word I want. Style. Yes, I think we could do worse than model ourselves on the old Aweri.

FIFTH: You mean, speak in proverbs and ponderous tone rhythms?

FOURTH: I'm afraid that is out anyway. Kongi would prefer a clean break from the traditional conclave of the so-called wise ones.

FIRST: They were remote, impersonal—we need these aspects. They breed fear in the common man.

SECOND: The paraphernalia helped too, don't forget that.

SIXTH: I have no intention of making myself look ridiculous in that outfit.

FOURTH: Welcome back to the discussion. I take it you know the subject.

SIXTH: No. Enlighten me.

FOURTH: The subject is an image for the Reformed Aweri Fraternity, of which you are a member in your waking moments.

FIFTH: And why do we need an image?

THIRD: Will you for Kongi's sake stop repeating that question?

FIFTH: When will you learn not to speak for Kongi?

FOURTH: Is this yet another effort to divert this discussion?

FIFTH: There is no discussion. Until Kongi makes up his mind just what image his is going to be this time, you can do nothing. I am going back to sleep.

FIRST: The emphasis of our generation is—youth. Our image therefore should be a kind of youthful elders of the state. A conclave of modern patriarchs.

THIRD: Yes, yes. Nice word patriarch, I'm glad you used it. Has a nice, reverent tone about it. Very nice indeed, very nice.

SECOND: I agree. Conjures up quite an idyllic scene.

THIRD: Yes, yes, children handing the patriarch his pipe at evening, crouching at his feet to sip raindrops of wisdom.

FIFTH: And dodging hot ashes as age shakes his rheumatic hand and the pipe overturns?

THIRD: You seem to turn a sour tongue on every progress we make in this discussion. Why don't you simply stay asleep?

FIFTH: When the patriarch overturns his pipe, make way. It is no time for piety.

THIRD: Well, now you've let off your crosswinds of advice, I hope your stomach pipes you sweeter to sleep.

FOURTH: We might consider a scientific image. This would be a positive stamp and one very much in tune with our contemporary situation. Our pronouncements should be dominated by a positive scientificism.

THIRD: A brilliant conception. I move we adopt it at once.

SIXTH: What image exactly is positive scientificism?

THIRD: Whatever it is, it is not long-winded proverbs and senile pronouncements. In fact we could say a step has already been taken in that direction. If you've read our Leader's last publication . . .

FIFTH: Ah yes. Nor proverbs nor verse, only ideograms in algebraic quantums. If the square of *XQY*(2*bc*) equals *QA* into the square root of *X*, then the progressive forces must prevail over the reactionary in the span of .32 of a single generation.

FOURTH: I trust you understood that as well as you remember it.

FIFTH: No. As well as *you* understand it.

FOURTH: I've had enough of your negative attitude . . . !

Coloured lights, and the sustained chord of a juju-band guitar gone typically mad brings on the nightclub scene, a few dancers on, the band itself offstage. DAODU *is dancing with* SEGI.

Enter SECRETARY *flanked by the* RIGHT AND LEFT EARS OF STATE. *Reactions are immediate to their entry. A few night-lifers pick up their drinks and go in, there are one or two aggressive departures, some stay on defiantly, others obsequiously try to attract attention and say a humble greeting.* DAODU *and* SEGI *dance on. The music continues in the background.*

SECRETARY (*approaches the pair*): Like a word with you. In private.

SEGI (*very sweetly*): You can see I'm occupied, Mr. Secretary.

SECRETARY: I don't mean you. Your boyfriend.

SEGI: He's busy too.

SECRETARY: Madam, I haven't come to make trouble.

SEGI (*very gently*): You couldn't, even if you wanted. Not here.

SECRETARY: I wouldn't be too sure of that.

SEGI: I would.

DAODU: What do you want with me?

SECRETARY: Not here. Let's find somewhere quiet.

(DAODU *leaves* SEGI *at a table and follows the* SECRETARY.)

SECRETARY (*with abrupt violence*): Your uncle is a pain in the neck.

DAODU: Who?

SECRETARY: Your uncle. You are Daodu, aren't you? Son of Sarumi by his wife number six. And Oba Danlola is your uncle and you the heir apparent to his throne. And I have come to tell you that your uncle is a damned stubborn goat, an obstructive, cantankerous creature, and a bloody pain in my neck.

DAODU: I'm sorry to hear that.

SECRETARY: Don't waste my time with apologies. You know who I am, of course.

DAODU: I don't believe so.

SECRETARY: Organising Secretary to the Leader. Those two, the Right and the Left Ears of State. The combination keeps the country nonaligned. Understand?

DAODU: I think so.

SECRETARY: And your guardian and uncle, Danlola, is a pain in my neck. Now tell me, what has he up his sleeves?

DAODU: Up his sleeves?

SECRETARY: Up those voluminous sleeves of his. What is he hiding in there for tomorrow?

DAODU: I thought he's been in detention for nearly a year.

SECRETARY: That doesn't stop him from messing me about. It only gives him an alibi.

DAODU: Hadn't you better turn him loose then?

SECRETARY: I might do that. Yes, I might do that. Hm. (*Looks slowly round.*) Does that woman have to keep looking at me like that?

DAODU: Does she bother you?

SECRETARY: Isn't there anywhere else we can go? I need to concentrate.

DAODU: I can ask her to go in if you like.

SECRETARY: Nonsense. Leave her where she is. I just wish she'd . . . what do they sing about her? What are they saying?

DAODU: The being of Segi
Swirls the night
In potions round my head

But my complaints
Will pass.

It is only
A madman ranting
When the lady
Turns her eyes,

Fathomless on those
I summoned as my go-between.

SECRETARY: Elegant. Very elegant. You know, I am very fond of music. Unfortunately I haven't much time for it. Moreover, one would hardly wish to be found in this sort of place.

DAODU: But you are here now.

SECRETARY: Yes, but only in the line of duty.

DAODU: You should take your duty more seriously and come more often.

SECRETARY: What? Oh . . . ha . . . ha, good idea, good idea.

DAODU: However, what brings you here to see me?

SECRETARY: Ah yes, we must get away from distractions and stick to business. (*Leans forward suddenly.*) But tell me, is she really as dangerous as they say? Some men I know have burns to show for their venture in that direction. The types too you'd think would know their way around.

DAODU: No. Listen to what they're singing now. *They* know Segi.

The wine-hour wind
That cools us
Leaves no prints behind

The spring
Has travelled long
To soothe our blistered feet

But last year's sands
Are still at the source
Unruffled.

SECRETARY: Just the same I wish she'd stop boring into my neck with her eyes.

DAODU: But she's gone.

SECRETARY (*spins round*): When? I didn't see her go.

DAODU: Her presence seemed to disturb you so I asked her to excuse us.

SECRETARY: You did? When?

DAODU: Just now.

SECRETARY (*narrowly*): I didn't see or hear you do anything. Are you trying to make a fool of me?

DAODU: No.

SECRETARY: Because I warn you, I'm a very dangerous man. I don't care what her reputation is, mine is also something to reckon with.

DAODU: Fame is a flippant lover
But Segi you made him a slave
And no poet now can rival
His devotedness.

The politician
Fights for place

With fat juices
On the tongue of generations

The judge
Is flushed down with wine
And pissed
Into the gutter

But Segi
You are the stubborn strand
Of meat, lodged
Between my teeth

I picked and picked
I found it was a silken thread
Wound deep down my throat
And makes me sing.

SECRETARY: And makes me thirsty, where is the waiter!

DAODU: Just behind you.

SECRETARY: Where? Oh, get us some beer.

DAODU: It's here.

SECRETARY: I don't remember ordering any.

DAODU: Segi did. She looks after her guests, especially important ones.

(SECRETARY *changes his mind about replying, digs instead into his pockets.*)

Naturally, it's on the house.

SECRETARY: No thank you. I prefer to pay for my drinks.

DAODU: The waiter won't take it.

SECRETARY: I hope at least I can buy drinks for my assistants. Where are they anyway?

DAODU: Inside, on duty.

SECRETARY: What is that supposed to mean?

DAODU: Keeping their ears open—isn't that what they're paid for? By the way, tell them not to stick their ears out too long or they might get slashed off. People are rather touchy here.

SECRETARY: No need to teach them their job.

DAODU: I thought I'd just mention it. Well, here's to duty.

(SECRETARY *grunts, drinks with the same pointlessly angry gestures. Lights fade. Kongi's chant. Change of lights into next scene.*)

(SECRETARY *speaks as he enters.*)

SECRETARY: How goes the planning session?

FIFTH: I am starving.

SECRETARY: That is a normal sensation with people who indulge in fasting.

FIFTH: I do not indulge in fasting. I am fasting under duress.

SECRETARY: I know nothing of that.

FIFTH: Nor do I. But you ask my stomach about it.

THIRD: Damn your greedy stomach.

(*Enter* KONGI. *They rise quickly.*)

KONGI: Do they have all the facts?

SECRETARY: I was just beginning . . .

KONGI: Do it now. There is little time left.

SECRETARY: The Leader's image for the next Five-Year Development Plan will be that of a benevolent father of the nation.

This will be strongly projected at tomorrow's Harvest festival, which has been chosen as the official start to the Five-Year Plan. The keyword is Harmony. Total Harmony.

KONGI: I want an immediate disputation on the subject. Then a planning session. (*Goes off.*)

FIFTH: And what, may I ask, does that mean in practical terms? What is the obstructive lump?

SECRETARY: Oba Danlola.

SECOND: What! That man again?

SECRETARY: He still refuses to give up the New Yam?

FIRST: Why is it necessary for him to give it up? He's in detention, isn't he?

FIFTH: I could do with a bit of yam right now.

SIXTH: Me too. New or old, I couldn't care less.

THIRD: Can't you two shut up your greedy mouths for a change?

FOURTH: If you can, just for a few moments, I would like to set the subject up in neat patterns for a formal disputation. The central problem, I take it, is this reactionary relic of the kingship institution.

SECRETARY: If by that you mean Danlola, yes.

FIRST: The man is in P.D. The state has taken over his functions. What exactly is the problem?

FOURTH: An act of public submission, obviously. Kongi must have his submission in full view of the people. The wayward child admits his errors and begs his father's forgiveness.

FIRST: You'll never do it. I know that stubborn old man, you'll never do it.

FOURTH: Kongi achieves all.

FIRST: Don't read me that catechism of the Carpenters' Brigade, man. Be practical.

FOURTH: I am being practical. Now let us see the problem as part of a normal historic pattern. This means in effect that—Kongi must prevail.

FIFTH: Page two, section 3b of the Carpenters' Credo.

FOURTH: Look here . . .

FIFTH: If you must catechize, at least sing it like the Carpenters. I take it they are the ones wailing from below.

SECOND: It's a horrible noise. I'd like to push a rock down on their heads.

SIXTH: Couldn't you find another choir to serenade the Leader?

SECRETARY: Gentlemen, please. All we want is some way of persuading King Danlola to bring the New Yam to Kongi with his own hands. I have organized the rest—the agricultural show to select the prizewinning yam, the feast, the bazaar, the music, the dance. Only one thing is missing—Oba Danlola. And gentlemen, that problem is yours. Kongi desires that the king perform all his customary spiritual functions, only this time, that he perform them to him, our Leader. Kongi must preside as the Spirit of Harvest, in pursuance of the Five-Year Development Plan.

FOURTH: An inevitable stage in the process of power reversionism.

SECRETARY: Call it what you like. Kongi wants a solution, and fast.

FOURTH: All right. We will hold a formal disputation.

SECRETARY: And the keyword, Kongi insists, must be—Harmony. We need that to counter the effect of the recent bomb throwing. Which is one of the reasons why the culprits of that outrage will be hanged tomorrow.

(*A nervous silence. They look at one another, stare at their feet.*)

FOURTH: An exercise in scientific exorcism—I approve.

(*Followed by murmurs and head nodding of agreement by the majority.*)

(*Loud chord on guitar and into the next scene.*)

(*Segi's Club*)

SECRETARY: And what about you, sir? What do *you* have in mind?

DAODU: Me?

SECRETARY: Yes, you. Tomorrow is State Festival.

DAODU: The Harvest?

SECRETARY: Naturally.

DAODU: I am looking forward to it. We are bound to take the first prize for the New Yam.

SECRETARY: Who are we?

DAODU: We? My farm, of course. You know I own a farm.

SECRETARY: Of course I know you own a farm. There is very little I don't know, let me tell you. What I don't understand is . . . no, wait a minute, I like to be sure of my facts before I jump. Now, did you say you are going to take the first prize tomorrow?

DAODU: Yes.

SECRETARY: You will compete in the agricultural show?

DAODU: Obviously.

SECRETARY: There is something not quite right somewhere. Or could it be that you are not yet aware that this time it is not your uncle who will eat the New Yam, but our Leader.

DAODU: I know all about that. What is it they say . . . the old order changeth—right?

SECRETARY: Cheers. Wish we had more democratic princes like you. (*He cheers up considerably.*) When you think of it, I shouldn't be surprised at all. There's a lot about you which marks you out to be quite exceptional. Mind you, I won't deny that once or twice you actually had us worried. Ye-e-es, we really thought at one stage we would have to do something about you.

DAODU: Why?

SECRETARY: Well . . . (*looks round him*), I'll be quite honest with you. We felt you were not quite . . . how should I put it . . . quite with us, that you were not pulling along with us. I mean we already had farm cooperatives but you had to start a farmers' community of your own!

DAODU: But it worked.

SECRETARY: Of course it worked! Damn it, man, were you trying to show us up? (*A waiter refills his glass; he downs it.*) It was bad for our morale, man, really bad.

DAODU: I am sorry to hear that.

SECRETARY (*waves him aside*): No you're not. I don't know how you did it but you got results. And your workers—contented sows the whole bloody lot of them. Oh our people sing too, but not in tune if you get my meaning. See what I mean? Very bad for the morale. Listen, I don't mind telling you . . . we sent in a few spies just to see what you were up to, but you know what happened?

DAODU (*mock ignorance*): No. Tell me.

SECRETARY: They never came back.

DAODU: Really! I am sorry about that.

SECRETARY: Will you stop saying you're sorry! (*Downs the rest of his beer and calls for more.*) Anyway, we couldn't do much about you. As long as you were contributing to the national economy . . . you see, my personal motto is Every Ismite must do his Mite . . . hey, did you hear that?

DAODU (*looking round*): What?

SECRETARY: No, me. Didn't you hear what I said. Came out just now, just like that, spontaneous. Every Ismite must do his Mite. How is that for a rallying slogan for tomorrow, eh? Find me a pen quickly before it goes. My memory is like a basket when I've had a few beers.

DAODU: Let me write it for you.

(*Scribbles it on a beer pad and gives it to him.*)

SECRETARY: Let me read it. Every-Ismite-Must-Do-His-Mite! Hey, you've added something to it.

DAODU: Don't you like it? I've just thought of it too.

SECRETARY: Ismite-Is-Might! Did you think that up?

DAODU: A moment ago.

SECRETARY: What! You are . . . a prince of slogans. A prince of slogans. Waiter! Waiter! Bring more beer. You know, this is the most profitable night I've had in a long time. You wait until I get this to the Leader. (*He rises, flushed and excited.*) End of the celebrations. Kongi raises his right fist—his favourite gesture have you noticed?—raises his right fist and says just the one word—Ismite . . .

LAYABOUTS: Is Might!

SECRETARY: Ismite . . .

LAYABOUTS: Is Might.

(*More people come in from the club and gather round.*)

SECRETARY: Ismite . . .

CROWD (*thunderously*): Is Might!

(SECRETARY *stops suddenly, then turns to examine his supporters and sinks back into his chair, his face wrinkled in disgust.*)

SECRETARY: Does no one come here except prostitutes and cutthroats?

(*In twos and threes the habituées melt slowly away.*)

(*Kongi's Retreat*)

FOURTH: Now, a systematic examination of the data. What have we got on our plates?

FIFTH: A few crumbs of mouldy bread, isn't it?

THIRD: What did you say?

FIFTH: I said a few crumbs of bread. What else do we ever get on our plates?

FOURTH: Can't you keep your mind on the subject? I used a common figure of speech and you leap straight onto the subject of food.

FIFTH: If your mind wasn't licking round the subject all the time how come you always pick that kind of expression?

SIXTH: He's right. It was a most unfortunate choice of words—what have we got on our plates? After several days of slow starvation what other answer do you expect?

THIRD: Can we return to the subject? We need a way to persuade that old reactionary to . . .

FIFTH: Starve him. Try starving him to death!

FOURTH: That would hardly solve the problem. It needs a live person to make even a symbolic act of capitulation.

THIRD: Especially when harmony is the ultimate goal. The ultimate goal.

FOURTH: I think I see something of the Leader's vision of this harmony. To replace the old superstitious festival by a state ceremony governed by the principle of Enlightened Ritualism. It is therefore essential that Oba Danlola, his bitterest opponent, appear in full antiquated splendour surrounded by his Aweri Conclave of Elders who, beyond the outward trappings of pomp and ceremony and a regular supply of snuff, have no other interest in the running of the state.

SIXTH: Who says?

FOURTH: Kongi says. The period of isolated saws and wisdoms is over, superseded by a more systematic formulation of comprehensive philosophies—*our* function, for the benefit of those who still do not know it.

THIRD: Hear hear.

FOURTH: And Danlola, the retrogressive autocrat, will with his own hands present the Leader with the New Yam, thereby acknowledging the supremacy of the State over his former areas of authority, spiritual or secular. From then on, the State will adopt towards him and to all similar institutions the policy of glamourized fossilism.

THIRD: Hear hear, very precisely put.

SECOND: You still haven't said how you are going to do it?

FOURTH: I beg your pardon.

SECOND: How will you make the king take part in this—public act of submission?

FOURTH: Just what is the difficulty? I have outlined the main considerations, haven't I?

SECOND: Outlining the considerations is not exactly a solution.

FOURTH: You all expect me to do all the thinking, don't you?

FIFTH: Don't look at me. I've told you I can't think on an empty stomach.

THIRD: Can't you lay off your filthy stomach?

FIFTH: I can't. Why the hell couldn't Kongi do his fasting alone? I'll tell you why. He loves companions in misery.

FIRST: Look, man, enough of you. You didn't have to come.

FIFTH: Yah? I'd like to see any of us refusing that order. And anyway, he said nothing of fasting at the time. Just disputations and planning.

SIXTH: Very true. I knew nothing of the fasting part of it until we were cut off from all contact.

THIRD: Don't you arrogate yourselves to being his companions in misery. You get something to eat. Kongi doesn't eat at all.

FIFTH: All part of his diabolical cleverness. A little bit of dry bread every day just to activate the stomach devils. Much better if we'd gone all out like him.

FIRST: Hey, go easy, man. You're asking for P.D. if you go on in that tone.

FIFTH: At least you get fed. And if you have money you can live like a king—ask our dear Organising Secretary if you don't believe me.

SECRETARY: You are suggesting something nasty, Sir?

FIFTH: Don't act innocent with me. If a detainee pays your price you'll see to his comforts. I bet our royal prisoner has put on weight since he came under your charge.

SECRETARY: This is slander.

FIFTH: Sue me.

SECRETARY: I refuse to listen to any more of this.

FIFTH: And a full sex life too I bet. Are you going to tell me you don't issue weekend permits to his wives?

SECRETARY: You are taking advantage of your privileged position.

FIFTH: I waive it, you shameless bribe collector. Say whatever is on your mind, or take me to court. I waive my philosophic immunity.

SECRETARY: All right. So I take bribes. It only puts me on the same level with you.

THIRD: What!

SECOND: I smell corruption.

SIXTH: Let's hear it. Come on, out with it.

SECRETARY: You've been bought. You've all been bought.

FOURTH (*on his feet*): Withdraw that statement!

THIRD: Immediately.

FIRST: This has me curious. Has anyone been accepting money on my behalf? All I ask is my cut.

FOURTH: It is an unforgivable insult.

FIFTH: Let the man speak. Which of us has been taking money?

SECRETARY: Oh, not money, I know the sight of cash is printed over with INSULT for upright men like you and intellectual minds. Oh no, not cash. But position, yes, position! And the power of being so close to power, "Well, it's difficult but I'll see what I can do." "You understand, my private feelings cannot come into this but that's the position. Oh yes, if you think that will help, do mention the fact that I sent you." And the dark impersonal protocol suits, and the all-purpose face, the give-nothing-away face in conference corridors, star-struck with the power of saying, "Yes, I think I could arrange for you to meet the President." Of course you've been bought. Bribed with the bribe of an all-powerful signature across a timeless detention order.

(*A brief pause.*)

FIFTH: Hm. What do you think of that, gentlemen?

THIRD: A rotten exposition.

SECRETARY: Well, I never did claim to be a theoretician.

SIXTH: I confess I found it very absorbing.

FIFTH: Me too. I quite forgot my hunger for a while.

THIRD: Will you leave your stomach out of it!

SIXTH: Why does that always set you raving?

THIRD: I suffer from ulcers.

SIXTH: Don't we all? Mine are crying out for a decent meal.

THIRD: I tell you it's my ulcers.

SIXTH: I know, I know. You wait until we all break the fast on that New Yam.

FIRST: Which we have not yet secured. Isn't it time we returned to that subject?

FIFTH: You carry on with it. I think I'll have a word with our Organising Secretary first. We may both find a common ground of understanding. Come this way, my friend.

SECRETARY: Kindly resume the disputations. Kongi expects an answer soon.

(*They move to one side.*)

FIFTH: Danlola was in your charge. Kongi rightly expects that you should have broken all his resistance by now. But you haven't, have you?

SECRETARY: He is a stubborn ass.

FIFTH: Well, maybe. Your problem could be quite simple, only it will have to depend on your powers of persuasion.

SECRETARY: What else do you think I've been doing all these months?

FIFTH: Working on that wrong person. Now, before I tell you what to do, we must settle on a fee.

SECRETARY: You . . . want me to pay you?

FIFTH: Naturally. I am a professional theoretician. I must be paid for my services.

SECRETARY: Nothing doing.

FIFTH (*turning away*): In that case I shall contribute my solution to the general pool and let my colleagues take the credit for it.

SECRETARY: Wait.

FIFTH: That's better. You can't pretend that you wouldn't be glad to succeed where he failed.

SECRETARY: But suppose it doesn't work, this mysterious solution of yours.

FIFTH: I can't see why it shouldn't.

SECRETARY: All right, let's hear it.

FIFTH: First, the fee.

SECRETARY: I thought you lot were supposed to be above this sort of thing.

FIFTH: You'll be surprised. Let's get back to business. I know you're making quite a bit out of the Harvest.

SECRETARY: All right, you name your terms.

FIFTH: No, that's not the way it's usually done. You make me an offer. And don't think I'm a novice at this game.

SECRETARY: All right. What about . . . ?

(*Casually holds out a closed fist.* FIFTH AWERI *shakes his head.*)

No? I've known contracts for a ten-mile road settled for less than . . .

(*Two closed fists.*)

You are a hard man. Of course I must admit that the cost of living rises all the time. My contacts in the Ministry of Housing tell me that a modest office block was won by a round figure close to . . .

(*Cups his two hands together, slowly.*)

A juicy, streamlined shape I think . . .

(FIFTH AWERI *turns his back.* SECRETARY *speaks hastily.*)

But by no means final. An artist must experiment with shapes. I would add, by way of attraction, a pair of ears. . . .

(*He sticks out the two thumbs. Obtaining only a wooden response, he throws up his hands angrily.*)

Well in that case take your solution where you please. Just how much do you think I will make for myself from organising the Harvest anyway. I may as well hand you my entire profits.

FIFTH (*chuckling*): Oh, I've always longed to see that done by a professional.

SECRETARY: You would appear to be something of one yourself.

FIFTH: No, to tell you the truth, my interest has been purely clinical.

SECRETARY: Do you mean you don't want a fee after all?

FIFTH: You bet I do. (*Gives a quick look round, desperately.*) Food, man, food. A bit of the Harvest before the banquet. I've had enough of this starvation act. Smuggle in some food tonight.

SECRETARY: Is that all?

FIFTH: But do it carefully. Their noses are so pinched from hunger, they will smell out any food within a two-mile radius.

SECRETARY: Well, well. Any particular preference?

FIFTH: Yes, food. Just food.

SECRETARY: It's a deal. Now . . .

FIFTH: My solution? Simple. Kongi is the man you have to tackle.

SECRETARY: Please, don't try to make a fool of me.

FIFTH: I am deadly serious. Persuade him to grant some form of amnesty. Then go to Danlola and tell him that in exchange for the New Yam, a few of the detainees will be set free.

SECRETARY: And you think that will have the slightest effect on the old man? He'll say they will be chucked right back again at the first excuse.

FIFTH: Good. In that case, you will need something more substantial, won't you?

SECRETARY: Like what, for heaven's sake?

FIFTH: Think. If Kongi were persuaded to grant a reprieve to the men condemned to death . . .

SECRETARY: You are out of your mind.

FIFTH: If you are able to assure Danlola that they will be reprieved . . .

SECRETARY: You are raving. Kongi does not want the New Yam that badly.

FIFTH: You are good at these things. Rack your brain for some way of getting him in the right mood.

SECRETARY: You don't know how he hates those men. He wants them dead—you've no idea how desperately.

FIFTH: I do. But tell him he can kill them later in detention. Have them shot trying to escape or something. But first, demonstrate his power over life and death by granting them a last-minute reprieve. That's it, work on that aspect of it, the drama of a last-minute reprieve. If I know my Kongi that should appeal to his flair for gestures.

SECRETARY: It might work.

FIFTH: It will. (*Going.*) And don't come back without my fee. I can't last much longer.

(*Segi's Club*)

DAODU: Those are Segi's friends you insulted.

SECRETARY: They are not her type.

DAODU: I assure you they are.

SECRETARY: She belongs in a different class.

DAODU: She won't agree with you.

SECRETARY: What do you come to do here anyway? Are you Segi's lover?

DAODU: Yes.

SECRETARY: I should have said, current lover.

DAODU: I *am* her current lover.

SECRETARY: There is something I don't understand. This is not the Segi we hear of. This one seemed to look at you as a woman should. The Segi we know never does.

DAODU: You keep postponing what you want to say about the Harvest.

SECRETARY: This place bothers me. I have a sixth sense about things, that is how I survive in this job. Something is missing. There should be a pungent odour of fornication about places like this. Is business slack tonight or something?

DAODU: I'll ask Segi if you like.

SECRETARY: No, no, leave her out of it. She'll confuse me. It was bad enough when I wasn't even drunk.

DAODU: Then what did you come to see me about?

SECRETARY: We closed down these quarters once, didn't we?

DAODU: I don't know.

SECRETARY: Yes, we did. All the prostitutes were sent off to a rehabilitation camp, and on graduation they became the Women's Auxiliary Corps, a sort of female leg of the Carpenters' Brigade.

DAODU: You must have missed out some.

SECRETARY: Oh no, we were very thorough. Make no mistake about that, we picked the kind of men for the job who would be thorough.

DAODU: Then these came after the er . . . the purge.

SECRETARY: Impossible. It couldn't have flourished so quickly.

DAODU: Why not? Some of the credit is, in fact, yours. Do you mean you don't recognise any of them?

SECRETARY: What do you mean? I am not in the habit of consorting with . . .

DAODU: Sit down. Take a look at that one over there . . . don't you know who she is?

SECRETARY (*looks intently, gives up*): She doesn't mean a thing to me.

DAODU: Go inside then. Look in the bar and in the dark corners. See if there is someone you remember.

(*As the* SECRETARY *rises,* SEGI *comes out. He pulls himself right against a wall as if he does not want her to touch him.* SEGI *goes past him without a glance, sits at her former table.* SECRETARY *stops suddenly, turns round, and stares.* SEGI *keeps her eyes on* DAODU, *who in turn continues to look at the* SECRETARY, *in half-mockery. From inside, the music rises.*)

DAODU: Don't you like the music anymore? They're saying—

Your eyes were bathed
In tender waters
Milk of all mothers
Flowed through your fingers
At your hour of birth

And they say of her skin, it is a flash of *agbadu*[7] through the sun and into cool shadows. Of her nipples, palm nuts, red flesh and black shadows, and violent as thorns.

7. Black, glistening snake.

SECRETARY: I can remember her. If I tried hard. But my brain is all addled.

DAODU: A coiled snake
Is beautiful asleep
A velvet bolster
Laid on flowers

If the snake would
Welcome me, I do not wish
A softer pillow than
This lady's breasts

But do not fool with one
Whose bosom ripples
As a python coiled
In wait for rabbits.

SECRETARY (*shuts his eyes tightly and holds his head*): I know I can remember. Isn't she the same one of whom they warn

Do not stay by the sea
At night
Mammy Watta frolics by the sea
At night
Do not play
With the Daughter of the sea. . . .

It's picking at my mind but it just will not surface.

DAODU: She is still, but only as
The still heart of a storm.
Segi, turn on me eyes
That were bathed in tender seas
And tender springs

(*The* SECRETARY*'s face becomes clear suddenly, he opens his eyes, stares hard at* SEGI.)

DAODU: Your eyes are
Cowrie shells, their cups
Have held much brine

It rained
Beads of grace
That hour of your birth

But it fell
From baleful skies.

SECRETARY: I am never wrong. I know now who she is. And the rest of them. Why are they here? Is this another vigil?

DAODU: For the condemned, yes. Not for Kongi.

SECRETARY: I am not really frightened. Yours is a strangely cheerful vigil.

DAODU: We are a cheerful lot. Moreover (*looks at his watch*), we are expecting news.

SECRETARY: I came here with a proposal.

DAODU: Which you haven't made.

SECRETARY: If she is who I'm sure now she is, this should interest her.

DAODU: Shall I call her over?

SECRETARY: No. You can tell her afterwards—if you wish.

DAODU: Well? The proposal.

SECRETARY: Five men are awaiting execution.

DAODU: We know that.

SECRETARY: They will be reprieved—if your uncle cooperates. Think about it—I'll be back.

(*Flees, looking nervously back.*)

(*Kongi's Retreat*)

(*The* AWERI *are dozing.* KONGI *descends from his cell.*)

KONGI: I can't hear voices.

SECRETARY: I think they are meditating.

KONGI: Meditating is my province. They are here to hold disputations.

(*He looks over the partition.*)

That is no meditation. They are fast asleep!

SECRETARY (*joins him at the screen*): You're right. They are sleeping.

KONGI: They are always sleeping. What is the matter with them?

SECRETARY: I heard one or two of them mention hunger.

KONGI: Hunger? They are fed daily, aren't they? I see to their food myself.

SECRETARY: I think they haven't got used to the diet.

KONGI: Damn their greedy guts. I eat nothing at all.

SECRETARY: Not everyone can be a Kongi.

KONGI: Strike the gong and wake them up.

(SECRETARY *strikes the gong; there is no response.*)

SECRETARY: They are practically dead.

KONGI: Dead? How dead? I don't remember condemning any of them to death. Or maybe I should?

SECRETARY: You still need them, Leader.

KONGI: But they are sleeping.

SECRETARY: Let me try again.

(*Strikes the gong.*)

I think they are really out. They've been overworking their brains, I think.

KONGI: Overwork? Nonsense. They do nothing but quarrel among themselves. Every time I set them a subject for disputation they quarrel like women and then fall asleep. What do they find to quarrel about?

SECRETARY: Philosophy can be a violent subject.

KONGI: You think so? I wonder sometimes. You should have seen them during the writing of my last book. I couldn't think for the squabbles.

SECRETARY: Oh, that must have been plain jealousy.

KONGI: Jealousy? Of whom are they jealous?

SECRETARY: Of one another, my Leader. You shouldn't give your books to only one person to write.

KONGI: Really? But he's the best disputant of the lot. I like his style. You shall hear the Harvest speech he's prepared for me. Four and a half hours—no joke, eh?

SECRETARY: Well, it causes dissension. At least let one of the others select the title or write the footnotes.

KONGI (*pleased no end*): Dear, dear, I had no idea they were so jealous. Very disturbing. I like harmony, you realise. But I never seem to find it. And among my philosophers especially, there must be perfect harmony.

SECRETARY: Then write more books. Write enough to go round all of them.

KONGI: Oh, would that be wise? It wouldn't do to become too prolific, you know. I wouldn't want to be mistaken for a full-time author.

SECRETARY: Your duty to the country, and to the world, demands far more works from you than you produce at present. Moreover, it will make your theoreticians happy.

KONGI: Hm. I think I'll trust your judgement. Tell them they can begin work on my next book as soon as the new one is released.

SECRETARY: Who is to write it, my Leader?

KONGI: Let them toss for it.

(*Kongi's chant swells louder.*)

SECRETARY: Can you hear them, my Leader?

KONGI: What?

SECRETARY: Your Carpenters' Brigade. They have been keeping vigil with you at the foot of the mountain.

KONGI: An inspired creation of mine, don't you think?

SECRETARY: They would lay down their lives for you.

KONGI: I trust no one. They will be in attendance tomorrow?

SECRETARY: Need you ask that?

KONGI: They complement my sleepy Aweris here. These ones look after my intellectual needs, the Brigade take care of the occasional physical requirements.

SECRETARY: They will not be needed tomorrow.

KONGI: Just the same, let them stand by. Nothing must disturb the harmony of the occasion . . . ah, I like that song.

SECRETARY: It is an invocation to the Spirit of Harvest to lend you strength.

KONGI (*violently*): I *am* the Spirit of Harvest.

(*The* AWERI *stir.*)

SECRETARY: S-sh. They are waking up.

KONGI (*alarmed, looks round wildly*): Who? The people?

(*Recovers slowly, angrily begins to climb the steps leading to his cell.* SECRETARY *follows him, appeasing.*)

KONGI: I *am* the Spirit of Harvest.

SECRETARY: Of course, my Leader, the matter is not in dispute.

KONGI: I am the SPIRIT of Harvest.

SECRETARY: Of course, my Leader.

KONGI: I am the Spirit of HAAR-VEST!

SECRETARY: Of course, my Leader. And a benevolent Spirit of Harvest. This year shall be known as the year of Kongi's Harvest. Everything shall date from it.

KONGI (*stops suddenly*): Who thought that up?

SECRETARY: It is among the surprise gifts we have planned for our beloved Leader. I shouldn't have let it slip out. . . .

KONGI (*rapt in the idea*): You mean, things like 200 K.H.

SECRETARY: A.H., my Leader. After the Harvest. In a thousand years, one thousand A.H. And last year shall be referred to as 1 B.H. There will only be the one Harvest worth remembering.

KONGI: No, K.H. is less ambiguous. The year of Kongi's Harvest. Then for the purpose of backdating, B.K.H. Before Kongi's Harvest. No reason why we should conform to the habit of two initials only. You lack imagination.

SECRETARY: It shall be as you please, my Leader.

KONGI: Now you see why it is all the more important that everything goes forward tomorrow as I wish it? I want the entire nation to subscribe to it. Wake up those hogs!

SECRETARY: It isn't necessary, my Leader. I think the little problem of Danlola is nearly solved.

KONGI: Another of your ideas?

SECRETARY: Leave it all to me. I er . . . oh yes, I ought to mention one other matter. I . . . have reason to believe that a press photographer might find his way into your retreat in spite of all our precautions for your privacy.

(*Enter photographer.*)

KONGI: Oh dear, you know I wouldn't like that at all.

(*He strikes a pose of anguish, camera clicks.*)

SECRETARY: In fact we think we know who it is. A foreign journalist, one of the best. He plans to leak it to a chain of foreign newspapers under the caption—Last Day of Meditation; A Leader's Anguish! I have seen some of his work, the work of a genius. He has photographed at least nine heads of state.

KONGI: I wouldn't like it at all.

SECRETARY: If we catch him we shall expel him at once.

KONGI: No, after the Harvest.

SECRETARY: Of course after the Harvest. The Leader's place of meditation should be sacrosanct.

(KONGI *moves to an opening, and poses his best profile.*)

KONGI: Twilight gives the best effect—of course I speak as an amateur.

(*Click.*)

SECRETARY: But you are right. I have noticed its mystical aura in the mountains. I think our man is bound to come at twilight.

KONGI: I don't like being photographed.

SECRETARY: I'll ensure it never happens again.

KONGI: Take care of it and let me hear no more on the subject. Some of these journalists are remarkably enterprising. Nothing you do can stop them.

(*Returns to his table and goes through a series of "Last Supper" poses*—iyan *(pounded yam) serving variation—while the photographer takes picture after picture.*)

SECRETARY: Yes, my Leader.

KONGI: Then go and look after everything. . . . What's the matter? Is there anything else?

SECRETARY: Only the question of amnesty, my Leader.

KONGI: Oh, I leave that to you. Release all those who have served their court sentences.

SECRETARY: Too trivial a gesture, my Leader. Too trivial for one who holds the power of life and death.

KONGI (*suddenly wary*): What do you have in mind exactly?

SECRETARY: The men awaiting execution.

KONGI: I thought so. Who put you up to it?

SECRETARY: Another of my ideas.

KONGI: I like the ones that went before. But not this one.

SECRETARY: It's all part of one and the same harmonious idea, my Leader. A Leader's Temptation . . . Agony on the Mountains . . . The Loneliness of the Pure . . . The Uneasy Head . . . A Saint at Twilight . . . The Spirit of the Harvest . . . The Face of Benevolence . . . The Giver of Life . . . who knows how many other titles will accompany such pictures round the world. And then, my Leader, this is the Year of Kongi's Harvest! The Presiding Spirit as a life-giving spirit—we could project that image into every heart and head, no matter how stubborn.

(*As the* SECRETARY *calls each shot,* KONGI *poses it and the photographer shoots, bows, and departs.*)

KONGI: But those men . . .

SECRETARY: A life-giving Spirit of Harvest, by restoring life, increasing the manpower for the Five-Year Development Plan . . . I could do anything with that image.

KONGI: Hm.

SECRETARY: Such a gesture would even break the back of the opposition. A contemptuous gift of life would prove that their menace is not worth your punishment.

KONGI: Tell you what. You get all the leaders of the dissident groups to appear on the dais with me tomorrow—all of them, and at their head, that wretched king himself and his entire court, bearing the New Yam in his hands. Right? You get him to do that. Him at the head of all the opposing factions. Well? Is there anything else?

SECRETARY: But my Leader, you haven't completed the message.

KONGI: What more do you want? I say I want a total, absolute submission—in full view of the people.

SECRETARY: And of the world press—haven't I promised it, my Leader?

KONGI: Then get on with it. There isn't much time left, you know.

SECRETARY: But the reprieve. You said nothing of that.

KONGI: Didn't I? Oh, all right. Tell your Danlola I'll reprieve those men if he cooperates fully. Now go.

SECRETARY: Leader, my magnanimous Leader!

KONGI: But look here, we must make it a last-minute reprieve. It will look better that way, don't you think? Kongi's act of clemency remains a confidential decision until a quarter of an hour before the hanging—no, five minutes. That's enough of a safety margin, isn't it? It had better be!

SECRETARY: It will do, my Leader.

KONGI: So keep it under until then. Now go.

(SECRETARY *runs off.* KONGI *stands for a moment, sunk in a new pose, thoughtful. Seizes the iron bar suddenly and strikes the gong. Strides among the startled* AWERI.)

KONGI: Dispute me whether it is politic to grant reprieves to the five men awaiting execution. And DISPUTE you hear! I shall go and meditate upon it.

(*Segi's Club*)

SECRETARY: Well?

DAODU: This is a certainty?

SECRETARY: I have Kongi's word. Now I want your uncle's word that he will cooperate with us.

DAODU: I shall obtain it. On those conditions, he cannot refuse me.

SECRETARY: And no one need lose face over it.

(*He is once more expansive, calls for beer.*)

Who really cares for the Festival of New Yam anyway? It is all a matter of face. The struggle began, involved others, and no one dared give ground for the very stink of face. But I have devised a clean solution.

DAODU: The New Yam for the lives of five men. It's a generous bargain.

SECRETARY: Four men. One is dead, hanged himself by the belt. Heard about it on my way here. Publicly, we shall give it out that, as part of the Harvest amnesty, the government has been pleased to release Oba Danlola and a few others, then, as a gesture of reciprocity—the exact words of my official release—as a gesture of reciprocity—the Oba will voluntarily surrender the first yam.

DAODU: The enactment of it alone should appeal to him. Kabiyesi loves to act roles. Like kingship. For him, kingship is a role.

SECRETARY: Now where did I hear that before? Seems I heard it . . . that's right. Now that's funny, isn't it? One of the Aweri said exactly the same thing of Kongi. "A flair for gestures," he said.

DAODU: Maybe that's why they hate each other's guts.

SECRETARY: Professional jealousy, eh? Ha, ha, couldn't agree with you more. Well then, I'll take Kongi, and you deal with your uncle. I can count on you?

DAODU: As an ally. I shall see him tonight—you will make the arrangements?

SECRETARY: Go and see him now; you'll be admitted. Let him know that the lives of four men hang on his decision.

DAODU: He won't refuse me.

SECRETARY: I must go now. I have to tell Kongi all is well.

DAODU: I thought he was meditating in the mountains.

SECRETARY: I am allowed to go up and see him—on urgent state matters, of course.

DAODU: Of course.

(SECRETARY *goes, looks round, looks off into the club.*)

SECRETARY: Where are those fools gone? (*To a waiter.*) You. Call me those two creatures I came in with.

(*The waiter and a couple of layabouts move as if to cut off his retreat, quietly menacing.*)

DAODU: I think they are gone.

SECRETARY: Gone? Where? I didn't see them leave.

DAODU: They shouldn't have come here.

SECRETARY: As servants of the State they can go anywhere. Anywhere!

DAODU: Too many people remember them. They shouldn't have come here.

SECRETARY (*looks round fearfully*): What are you trying to say? I thought we were allies.

DAODU: So we are. I have promised you my uncle's public submission.

SECRETARY: What happened to my Ears of State?

DAODU: You forget. I'm only a farmer. I don't run this place.

SECRETARY: Well, who does?

DAODU (*points*): Over there. Ask her.

(SECRETARY *stares at her, experiencing fear.* SEGI *rises, comes forward slowly.*)

SECRETARY: You witch! What have you done to them?

DAODU: This is Segi. Once she said to herself, this man's lust, I'll smother it with my beauty.

SECRETARY: Lust?

DAODU: For power.

SEGI: Surely you must know me.

SECRETARY: Kongi's mystery woman. You couldn't be anybody else.

SEGI: Why did you come here?

SECRETARY: A mistake. Just call me the Ears of State and I'll leave.

SEGI: They have already left.

SECRETARY: When? Why?

DAODU: They left with Segi's friends.

SECRETARY (*sits down, dog-tired*): Oh! yes, it's all clear now. Your father . . . one of the condemned men.

SEGI: You understand.

SECRETARY: I suppose this means I am also your prisoner?

DAODU: No, ally.

SECRETARY: In that case . . . I don't wish to remain here.

DAODU: I'll see you out.

(*The layabouts look questioningly at* SEGI, *who engages in a silent duel with* DAODU. DAODU *firmly takes the* SECRETARY *by the arm and moves forward. The men make way.* SEGI *is obviously angry, and turns away.*)

SECRETARY: Don't forget my mission.

DAODU: I won't. You understand, your men had to go with others—for safety. Naturally we were suspicious.

SECRETARY: No, no. I've been trying to get those men reprieved.

DAODU: I'll take your message to Oba Danlola.

SECRETARY: My . . . bargaining position is somewhat weaker. . . . When I left Kongi I had five lives. Then they told me one had hanged himself. And now . . . I suppose by now her father has escaped?

DAODU: An hour ago.

SECRETARY: That leaves me only three.

DAODU: It's enough to bargain with, for a New Yam.

SECRETARY: I'm glad you think so. I'll see you at the feast.

(*He slouches off, a heavy, pathetic figure.* DAODU *turns to meet* SEGI, *smiles to break her anger.*)

DAODU: My eyes of rain, Queen of the Harvest night.

SEGI (*slowly relenting, half-ashamed*): I was so afraid.

DAODU: There is nothing more to fear.

SEGI: I will never be afraid again.

DAODU: Two less for Kongi's grim collection. I am glad the live one is your father.

SEGI: I feel like dancing naked. If I could again believe I would say it was a sign from heaven.

DAODU: Yes, if I were awaiting a sign, this would be it. It may turn me superstitious yet.

SEGI: I want to dance on *gbegbe* leaves; I know now I have not been forgotten.

DAODU: I'll rub your skin in camwood, you'll be flames at the hide of night.

SEGI: Come with me, Daodu.

DAODU: Now? There is still much to do before you meet us at the gates.

SEGI: Come through the gates tonight. Now. I want you in me, my Spirit of Harvest.

DAODU: Don't tempt me so hard. I am swollen like prize yam under earth, but all harvest must await its season.

SEGI: There is no season for seeds bursting.

DAODU: My eyes of kernels, I have much preparation to make.

SEGI: I shall help you.

DAODU: Segi, between now and tomorrow's eve, I must somehow obtain some rest.

SEGI: Let me tire you a little more.

DAODU: You cannot know how weary I am. . . . A child could sneeze me off my legs with a little pepper.

SEGI: I must rejoice, and you with me. I am opened tonight. I am soil from the final rains.

DAODU: Promise you won't keep me long. I still have to meet my troublesome king.

SEGI: Only a bite, of your Ismite.

DAODU: Only a bite?

SEGI: Only a mite.

DAODU: Oh, Segi! I had thought tonight, at least, I would keep my head.

(*Enter two women, bearing an unfinished robe.*)

SEGI: Ah, you must try this on before we go. It isn't finished yet but it will be ready for you tomorrow.

DAODU: This!

SEGI: They'll work on it all night if necessary.

DAODU: I didn't mean that, but . . . must I really wear this?

SEGI: Stand still!

(*They drape the robe round him.*)

DAODU: In the name of everything, what am I supposed to be?

SEGI: The Spirit of Harvest.

DAODU: I feel like the prince of orgies, I feel like some decadent deity.

SEGI: Well, that's the idea.

DAODU: Can't something simpler do?

SEGI: No. Now stand still. Be solemn for a moment.

(*She comes round, surveys him. Suddenly she kneels and clings to the hem of his robes. The other women kneel too.*)

My prince . . . my prince . . .

DAODU: Let me preach hatred, Segi. If I preached hatred I could match his barren marathon, hour for hour, torrent for torrent . . .

SEGI: Preach life, Daodu, only life . . .

DAODU: Imprecations then, curses on all inventors of agonies, on all Messiahs of pain and false burdens . . .

SEGI: Only life is worth preaching, my prince.

DAODU (*with mounting passion*): On all who fashion chains, on farmers of terror, on builders of walls, on all who guard against the night but breed darkness by day, on all whose feet are heavy and yet stand upon the world . . .

SEGI: Life . . . life . . .

DAODU: On all who see, not with the eyes of the dead, but with eyes of Death. . . .

SEGI: Life then. It needs a sermon on life . . . love . . .

DAODU (*with violent anger*): Love? Love? You who gave love, how were you requited?

SEGI (*rises*): My eyes were open to what I did. Kongi *was* a great man, and I loved him.

DAODU: What will I say then? What can one say on life against the batteries and the microphones and the insistence of one indefatigable madman? What is there strong enough about just living and loving? What!

SEGI: It will be enough that you erect a pulpit against him, even for one moment.

DAODU (*resignedly*): I hate to be a mere antithesis to your Messiah of Pain.

(SEGI *begins to disrobe him. The women go off with the garment.*)

(*The song in the background comes up more clearly—a dirge.*)

DAODU: Do they all know where they may be tomorrow, by this time?

SEGI: You shouldn't worry about my women. They accepted it long ago.

DAODU: My men also. They have waited a long time for this.

SEGI: This, the last night, is mine by right. Ours.

DAODU: Ours. Suddenly I have lost my tiredness. First let me go and speak with my awkward king, then I'll come back to you. (*Going.*)

SEGI: Shall I stop the wake—since there is to be a reprieve?

DAODU: No, let it continue. I find grief sharpens my appetite for living.

SEGI: And loving? Come back quickly, Daodu, I'll be waiting.

(DAODU *goes off; the dirge rises. All lights come on for the next scene. There is no break.*)

(*Kongi's Retreat*)

(KONGI, *shaking with anger, the* SECRETARY *cowering before him.*)

KONGI: Escaped?

SECRETARY: Not from my camp, my Leader. It wasn't from my camp.

KONGI: Escaped? Escaped?

SECRETARY: Only one, sir. The other hanged himself.

KONGI: I want him back. I want him back, you hear?

SECRETARY: He shall be caught, my Leader.

KONGI: I want him back—alive if possible. If not, ANY OTHER WAY! But I want him back!

SECRETARY: It shall be done at once, my Leader.

KONGI: Get out! GO AND BRING HIM BACK!

(SECRETARY *turns to escape.*)

And hear this! The amnesty is OFF! The reprieve is OFF! The others hang tomorrow.

SECRETARY: My Leader, your promise!

KONGI: No Amnesty! No Reprieve! Hang every one of them! Hang them!

SECRETARY: Your promise, my Leader. The word of Kongi!

KONGI: And find me the other one for hanging—GET OUT! GET OUT! GET . . . AH . . . AH . . . AH . . .

(*His mouth hanging open, from gasps into spasms and violent convulsions,* KONGI *goes into an epileptic fit. Over his struggle for breath rises Kongi's chant.*)

SECOND PART

Oba Danlola's palace. Plenty of bustle and activity as if a great preparation were in progress. DANLOLA *is trying out one thing, rejecting it, and trying on another.*

DANLOLA: Oh, what a homecoming this is!
I obtained much better service
In the detention camp.

DENDE: But you did order a sceptre, Kabiyesi.

DANLOLA: Do you dare call this a sceptre?
This dung-stained goat prod, this
Makeshift sign at crossroads, this
Thighbone of the crow that died
Of rickets? Or did you merely
Steal the warped backscratcher
Of your hunchback uncle?

DENDE: I got no cooperation at all
From the blacksmith. It was the best
I found in the blacksmith's foundry.

DANLOLA: Some soup-pot foundry. Find me
Such another ladle and I'll
Shove it up your mother's fundaments.

DAODU (*storms in; stops short as he sees signs of activity*): I was told you would not take part in today's procession.

DANLOLA: The ostrich also sports plumes but
I've yet to see that wise bird
Leave the ground.

DAODU: But all this preparation . . .

DANLOLA: When the dog hides a bone does he not
Throw up sand? A little dust in the eye
Of His Immortality will not deceive
His clever Organising Secretary. We need to
Bury him in shovelfuls.

(*Re-enter* DENDE.)

You horse manure! Is this a trip
To gather mangoes for the hawker's tray?
Tell me, did I ask for a basket fit
To support your father's goitre? I thought
I specially designed a copper salver.

DENDE: The smith had done nothing at all
About it.

DANLOLA: The smith! The smith! All I hear
Is of some furnace blower called
The smith!

DAODU (*sharply, to* DENDE): Send for the smith.

DANLOLA: I have more important preparations
Than to break wind with the smith.
Take that thing right back to where
It was aborted from, and tell him
I want my copper salver.

DENDE: Copper, Kabiyesi?

DANLOLA: Copper, yes. Copper the colour of earth
In harvest. Do you think I'll serve the first
Of our New Yam in anything but copper?

DAODU: Since you don't intend to be present anyway, why all this energy?

DANLOLA: The Big Ear of the Man Himself
Has knocked twice on my palace gates—
Twice in one morning—and his spies
Have sneaked in through the broken wall
Of my backyard, where women throw their piss
As many times today.

DAODU: And why does he suspect you?

DANLOLA: I have, dear son, a reputation for
Falling ill on these state occasions.
And, to tell the truth, they make me
Ill. So my friends the Eyes and Ears
Of State set prying fingers to sieve
My chamber pot, diagnose my health,
And analyse every gesture.

DAODU: Isn't it much simpler to go? After all, you did promise . . .

DANLOLA: I promised nothing that I will not
Fulfill.

DAODU: You gave your word.

DANLOLA: Indeed I gave my word and if you like
I swear again to exhaust your eyes and ears
With that word undergoing fulfillment.

DAODU: You should go. It's a small thing to sacrifice—I thought we agreed on that and you gave your word.

DANLOLA: You should, my son, when you deal in politics
Pay sharp attention to the word. I agreed
Only that I would prepare myself
For the grand ceremony, not
That I would go. Hence this bee hum fit
For the world's ruling heads jammed
In annual congress. When my servants
Are later questioned, they'll bear witness
How I set the royal craftsmen slaving
At such short notice to make me ready
To present the New Yam to my Leader.

DAODU: How do you expect him—them—to take your absence?

DANLOLA: As an act of God. Perhaps I'll be
Smitten with a heart attack from
My loyal efforts. Or it could be
The Oracle forbade me budging from
My chamber walls today. As the Man
Himself has often screamed, we are
A backward superstitious lot, immune
To Kongi's adult education schemes.

DAODU: I should have believed it. I was warned you might go back on your word.

DANLOLA: Now where could you have picked that up?
In those dives of *tombo* where you pass
The hours of sleep?

DAODU: I see it's not Kongi's men alone who have an efficient spy system.

DANLOLA: For us, even the dead lend their eyes
And ears, as do also the unborn.

DAODU: But you find something wrong with the eyes of the living?

DANLOLA: They are the eyes of fear. But tell me,
How is the woman?

DAODU: Who?

DANLOLA: Who? Are you playing lawyer to
Oba Danlola, the Ears of wind on dry
Maize leaves? I asked, how fares
The woman whose eyes unblinking as
The eyes of the dead have made you drunk?

DAODU: I don't know what woman you mean.

DANLOLA (*bursts suddenly into laughter*): They say you can always tell the top
By the way it dances. If anyone had doubts
Whose son you are, you've proved you are
No bastard. A-ah, you have picked yourself
A right cannibal of the female species.

DAODU: I think I'll go on to watch the procession. . . .

DANLOLA: Stay where you are! Tell me, do you
Know that woman's history? I have myself
Wandered round some dens of Esu, once,
And clambered over sweet hillocks
In the dark, and not missed my way. But
Daodu, that woman of yours, she scares
The pepper right up the nostrils
Of your old man here. She has left victims
On her path like sugar cane pulp
Squeezed dry.

DAODU: Men know nothing of Segi. They only sing songs about her.

DANLOLA: Much better not to know, believe your father.
Oh, you have chosen to be swallowed whole
Down the oyster throat of the witch

Of nightclubs. Segi! Son, she'll shave
Your skull and lubricate it in oil.

(*Enter* DENDE.)

DENDE: Kabiyesi . . . about the er—your royal canopy.

DANLOLA: Well—is it ready at last?

DENDE: No sir. Er—it seems
The snakeskins have all been used up.

DANLOLA: Then use the one you moulted
Yesterday, you single-gut
Hunter of toads!

(*Enter* SECRETARY.)

Ah, you were surely
Summoned by my head. You see yourself
How the courtesan is one hour escalating
Her brocade head-tie, and the devil wind
Whisks it out of sight just when the sun
Has joined to make it dazzle men.

SECRETARY: Kabiyesi, what is the matter?

DANLOLA: The matter? The things they bring me
Anyone would think I was headed
For a pauper's funeral.

SECRETARY: But you will be late. The things you have on you will do just as well.

DANLOLA: What! These trimmings may serve
A wayward lunatic, but my friend,
We must meet the Leader as
A conquering hero, not welcome him
Like some corner-corner son-in-law.

DENDE (*enters*): Perhaps you would prefer this, Kabiyesi.
It belonged to my great
Grandfather on my mother's side. . . .

DANLOLA: Oh, what a joy you must have been
To your great progenitors until
They died of overjoy! The Leader
Visits us today—is that not enough?
Must I ask him also to make a sword
Of state, fit to grace his presence?

SECRETARY: All this is quite unnecessary, Kabiyesi. We appreciate your zeal and I assure you it will not go unmentioned. But it is your presence our Leader requires. . . .

DANLOLA: You wish to make me a laughingstock?

SECRETARY: You know how we deal with those who dare make fun of the Leader's favoured men.

DANLOLA: Then, my dear son-in-politics, this being
The only way in which our dignity
May be retained without the risk
Of conflict with the new authority,
Let us be seen in public only as
Befits our state. Not to add the fact
That this is Harvest. An Oba must emerge
In sun colours as a laden altar.

SECRETARY: Kabiyesi, I don't suggest for a moment that . . .

DANLOLA: I know we are the masquerade without
Flesh or spirit substance, but we can
Afford the best silk on our government
Pension. Now you! Tell the smith he must
Produce the sword I ordered specially.

DENDE: He says that would require at least . . .

DANLOLA: Enough, enough, I'll use this as it is.
Get a new cover on it, some titbit
Of leather—and don't tell me you have
No leftover scraps enough to hide
A rusty scabbard. I know your pumice
Stomach can digest it. Move!
A-ah, my good Organising Secretary of
His Immortality our Kongi, you see
What agonies these simple ceremonies
Demand of us?

SECRETARY: You really haven't that much time you know. It would be simpler . . .

DANLOLA: You haven't met my heir, have you?
Lately returned from everywhere and still
Trying to find his feet. Not surprisingly.
It must be hard to find one's feet in such
Thin arrowheads. Daodu, before you
Flaps the Big Ear of His Immortality.
Make friends with him. Your decaying
Father is most deeply in his debt.
In these trying times, it is good to know
The Big Ear of his government.

SECRETARY: Your uncle is a most difficult man.

DANLOLA: Difficult? Me difficult? Why should
A father be difficult and obstruct
His children's progress? No, I have told you
Listen less to those who carry tales
From sheer envy.

SECRETARY (*to* DAODU): What is he up to?

(DANLOLA *pricks up his ears.*)

DAODU: I'm not sure. I am still feeling the ground.

DANLOLA: You'll feel the ground until
It gives way under you. What,
I ask you, is there to feel?
Oh, never mind, I suppose it gives
You children pleasure to pretend
There are new cunnings left for
The world to discover . . . Dende!

DENDE (*runs in*): Kabiyesi.

DANLOLA: Dende, do you realize you keep
A whole nation waiting?

DENDE: Kabiyesi, you asked me to stuff
The crown with cotton.

DANLOLA: Ah, so I did. Age has shrunk
The tortoise and the shell is full
Of air pockets. My head
Now dances in my crown like a cola nut
In the pouch of an *ikori* cap.
Well, why do you stand there? Waiting
Still for the cotton fall of the next
Harmattan?

(DENDE *runs off.*)

SECRETARY: Couldn't you manage it at all? We are really short of time.

DANLOLA: Manage it? Will there not be six times
At the least when we must up and bow
To Kongi? These are no bones
To rush an old man after a crown
That falls off his head and rolls
Into a gutter.

(*Royal drums heard in distance.*)

SECRETARY: I will have to leave you. The other Obas are already arriving. Someone has to be there to group each entourage in their place.

DANLOLA: You must hurry or the confusion
Will be worse than shoes before the
Praying ground at Greater Beiram.

SECRETARY: Kabiyesi, please follow quickly. It will make my task easier if I can get all the Obas settled before our Leader arrives.

(*Enter* DENDE.)

DANLOLA: No, not that one! Is that a crown
To wear on such a day?

DENDE: But I took it from . . .

DANLOLA: The same dunghill you use for a pillow!

DENDE: But Kabiyesi, this is your favourite
Crown. It belonged to Kadiri, the great
Ancestor warrior of your lineage.

DANLOLA: Who rests in peace we pray. And now
My pious wish is—burn it! Burn it
With firewood from the desiccated trunk
Of your family tree.

SECRETARY (*stares, speechless, and turns in desperation to* DAODU): Are you coming to the square?

DAODU: Oh, I don't really know.

DANLOLA: He never really knows, that thoughtful
Son of mine. Go with the man. If anyone
Can conjure you a seat close to the Great
Visitor himself, he can.

SECRETARY: Yes, I was going to suggest that. Why don't you come now? I'm sure I can squeeze you in somewhere.

DAODU: In a minute.

SECRETARY: Good. Kabiyesi, we shall expect you.

(*He goes.*)

DANLOLA: And I, you. But here, within
My audience chambers. I have done enough
Of this play-acting.

(*Begins leisurely to remove his trappings. Drums, bugles, etc. announce the approach of* OBA SARUMI *and retinue.* DENDE *rushes in.*)

DENDE: Kabiyesi, Oba Sarumi is at the palace gates.

DANLOLA: Let him enter. I suppose he wants
Our four feet to dance together
To the meeting place.

PRAISE-SINGER (*leads in, singing*): *E ma gun'yan Oba kere o*
E ma gun'yan Oba kere

(*Enter* SARUMI, *prostrates himself.*)

DANLOLA: Get up, get up man. An Oba Grade I
By the grace of Chieftaincy Succession
Legislation Section II, nineteen-twenty-one
Demands of you, not this lizard posture,
But a mere governmental bow—from
The waist, if you still have one.

SARUMI (*joining the singer*): *E ma gun'yan Oba kere o*
E ma gun'yan Oba kere
Kaun elepini o se e gbe mi
Eweyo noin ni i fi yo'nu
E ma gun'yan Oba kere

DANLOLA: Go and tell that to the Leader's men.
Their yam is pounded, not with the pestle
But with stamp and a pad of violet ink
And their arms make omelet of
Stubborn heads, via police truncheons.

SARUMI: *Oba ni f'itan ebo ha'yin*
Orisa l'oba

DANLOLA: At least get up from that position
Sit down and go easy on my eyes.
I can't look down without my glasses.

SARUMI (*rises, still singing*): *Oba ni f'epo inu ebo r'awuje*
Orisa l'oba.

DANLOLA: *Orisa l'oba?* Hadn't you better see
The new *orisa* in the market square
Before you earn yourself a lock-up
For reactionary statements.

SARUMI: Kabiyesi, your voice was the dawn pigeon
Which summoned us from drowsy mats
We do not know the jackal's call
We do not hear the bonded overseer
When the father speaks.

DANLOLA: Wise birdlings learn to separate
The pigeon's cooing from the shrill alarm
When Ogun stalks the forests.

SARUMI: The boldest hunter knows when
The gun must be unspiked. When a squirrel
Seeks sanctuary up the *iroko* tree
The hunter's chase is ended. . . .
In Oba Danlola's palace his sons
Speak out their minds.

(*Dances.*)

PRAISE-SINGER: *Ogun o l'oun o j'oba*
Ogun o l'oun o j'oba
Jeje l'Ogun se jeje
T'ijoye gb'ade Ire wa ba baba ode o
Ogun o l'oun o j'oba

DANLOLA: You'll be more at home performing
At the Festival of Traditional Arts.

SARUMI: *Ma binu si mi Oba. . . .*

DANLOLA: Look, if you want to please me, dip
In your regal pouch and find me
Some cola nut. Playing a clown's part
For the Eye and Ear of His Immortality
Has turned my blood to water. I need
The stain of cola to revive
Its royal stain.

SARUMI (*gives him cola*): *Orogbo ebo, awuje Oba. . . .*

DANLOLA: Don't tell me this is cola nut
From a wayside bowl! Dende!

DENDE (*rushes in*): Kabiyesi.

DANLOLA: Bring the schnapps. Esu alone knows
Where this cola nut was picked. Not that
It matters. The schnapps should take
Good care of sacrificial germs. I suppose
After all your exercise, some schnapps
Would come in handy too.

(SARUMI'*s dance grows positively ecstatic,* DAODU *remains intensely frustrated but undecided.*)

SARUMI: *Ma ma binu si mi Oba*
B'esumare se binu si'takun
To ta kete, to ta kete
To ran'ri s'agbede meji orun

Ma binu si mi Oba
Bi Sango se binu s'araiye.
To di pe manamana ni fi i
Mba omo enia soro

Ma binu si mi Oba
B'iwin ope se binu s'elemu
To re alangba lu'le
Bi eni ha kuruna l'ori

(DANLOLA *begins slowly to glow, to expand, to be visibly affected by the praise-singing.*)

Oba o se e te
Bi eni te r'awe
B'ajanaku o rora rin
A t'egun mole
A d'atiro tiro tiro
Oba o se e gbon
Bi eni gbon t'akun
Igbon oba, awon eru
Ogbon oba, iwon eru
Esin to r'ebo ti o sare
Tin nta felefele
Enu alantakun ni o bo.

DANLOLA, *totally swelled, steps down from his throne and falls in step with* SARUMI. *The two Obas cavort round the chamber in sedate, regal steps and the bugles blast a steady refrain. Danlola's wives emerge and join in; the atmosphere is full of the ecstasy of the dance. At its height* DAODU *moves with sudden decision, pulls out the ceremonial whisk of Danlola, and hits the lead drum with the heavy handle. It bursts. There is a dead silence.* DANLOLA *and* DAODU *face each other in a long, terrible silence.*

SARUMI (*in a horrified whisper*): *Efun!*

DANLOLA (*shakes his head slowly*): No. Your son has his senses Intact. He must know what he is doing.

SARUMI: *Efun! Efun!* Someone has done this to him. Some enemy has put a curse on my first-born.

DANLOLA (*climbing back to his throne, wearily*): Life gets
more final every day. That prison
Superintendent merely lay his hands
On my lead drummer, and stopped
The singing, but you, our son and heir,
You've seen to the song itself.

DAODU: Kabiyesi . . .

DANLOLA: It is a long long time my limbs
Rejoiced that way. I swear a snake
Ran wildly through my veins and left
Its moulting in my train. . . . A-ah
Matters will go hard upon
A royal favourite tonight. I feel
Life resurrected within me and I
Shall resurrect my dance on softer springing
Than this dung-baked floor. In fact
To confess the truth, I doubt
If matters can await the dark.
Call me that Dende.

DAODU: I only want a few words. . . .

DANLOLA: I know the drums were silenced long
Before you, but you have split
The gut of our make-believe. Suddenly
The world has run amok and left you
Alone and sane behind.

DAODU: In that case, you know I have a reason.

DANLOLA: And I do not choose to hear it.

When the next-in-line claps his hand
Over a monarch's mouth, it is time
For him to take to the final sleep
Or take to drink and women.

DAODU: It is vital that you hand the Leader what he wants. I cannot explain it now. Time is short and we have much to do. But I must have your word that you will play your part.

DANLOLA: Make my excuses to him—my son-in-politics
Will help you. Tell His Immortality
I sprained my back rehearsing dances
In honour of his visit. He loves to see
His Obas prancing to amuse him after all
And excess zeal should be a credit.

DAODU: I have no thoughts of Kongi. This matter concerns us, your children. Don't ask me to say more—I cannot now. I dare not. Kabiyesi, this is no time for trivialities. We shall all have our dance tonight, when it matters, and I promise you the event will make its own amends.

DANLOLA: I wish you luck. Dende!
Where on earth is that fool!
I am not young like you, and these
Sudden surges must be canalized.
Who knows? There may be another son
From this, if so, rest assured
I'll name him after you—to mark
This morning's work.

DAODU: You swore to me. Early this morning you swore to me.

DANLOLA (*with sudden unexpected anger*): And so, you child, did Kongi.
Did he not promise a reprieve
For the condemned men, in return
For the final act of my humiliation?
Well, did he not?

DAODU: Yes, and I know our man will remind him of it.

DANLOLA: Then perhaps you have not heard
What the wooden box announced
As I returned to palace. Such a welcoming
I've never known. Did not one
Of the dying enemies of Kongi
Seize suddenly on life by jumping
Through the prison walls?

DAODU: I heard about it.

DANLOLA: And the radio has put out a price
Upon his head. A life pension
For his body, dead or alive. That,
Dear child, is a new way to grant
Reprieves. Alive, the radio blared,
If possible; and if not—DEAD!
I didn't say it, the radio did.
In my primitive youth, that would be called
A plain incitement to murder.

DAODU: It means nothing. Nothing can alter what today will bring. And your compliance is a vital part of it.

DANLOLA: My vital part shall exhaust itself
In my favourite's bed. Call me Wuraola.
Go hand Kongi the New Yam yourself
But count me out.

SARUMI: Kabiyesi, age is nectar
May the royal household ever
Savour its blessings.

DANLOLA: Take your son with you,
Prepare him for my crown and beads
This king is done.

SARUMI: Kabiyesi, live long, reign long and peaceful. Our line does not seek this kind of succession which bears a silent curse. I know my son has something for old ears like ours. You have to listen.

DANLOLA: Out of my way.

DAODU (*desperately*): The woman you warned me about, Segi, the witch of nightclubs as you labelled her, is the daughter of this man who has escaped. And she wants the Harvest to go on as we all planned, as much as I.

(DANLOLA *turns slowly round.*)

DANLOLA: Is this the truth about that woman?

DAODU: The truth.

DANLOLA (*hesitates and a farseeing look comes into his eyes*):
There was always something more, I knew,
To that strange woman beyond
Her power to turn grown men to infants.

(*He looks long and kindly at* DAODU, *then incredulous.*)

And this woman, you say
Her father is already free, and yet
She wants the Harvest to be held
As . . . planned?

DAODU: She does.

DANLOLA: And what harvest do you children
Mean to give the world?

DAODU: Kabiyesi, is it not you elders who say . . . ?

DANLOLA: The eyes of divination never close
But whoever boasts Ifa greeted him
With open lips . . . well, so be it. Sarumi,
It seems our son will make us mere

Spectators at our own feast. But
Who are we to complain? Dada knows
He cannot wrestle, will he then preach restraint
To his eager brother?

SARUMI: Kabiyesi!

DANLOLA: Well, I will not bear the offering
Past the entrance to the mosque
Only a phoney drapes himself in deeper indigo
Than the son of the deceased.

SARUMI (*with gratitude*): Kabiyesi!

DANLOLA: Dende!

(*He sweeps out, the others hurrying after him.*)

Immediately the big parade drum is heard with its One-Two, One-Two-Three, penny whistles blow to the tune of the Carpenters' Song and the Carpenters' Brigade march in, uniformed, heavy mallets swinging from their waists. They clear the stage and reset it for the harvest scene—decorated dais, buntings, flags, etc. On a huge cyclorama which completely dominates the stage, pictures are projected of various buildings, factories, dams, etc., all clearly titled Kongi Terminus, Kongi University, Kongi Dam, Kongi Refineries, Kongi Airport, etc. Finally, of course, a monster photo of the great man himself. They sing their anthem as they work, and form and execute a couple of parade movements to the last verse or two.

We are the nation's carpenters
We build for Isma land
From the forests of Kuramba
They bring the timber wild
And we saw and plane and tame the wood
To bring the grains to light
Converting raw material
To "Made in Ismaland."

Men of peace and honour
Are the Carpenters' Brigade
But primed for fight or action
To defend our motherland
We spread the creed of Kongism
To every son and daughter
And heads too slow to learn it
Will feel our mallets' weight.

Though rough and ready workers
Our hearts are solid gold
To beat last year's production
Is our target every year
We're total teetotallers
Except on local brew
For it's guts of toughened leather
That survive on Isma gin.

Our hands are like sandpaper
Our fingernails are chipped
Our lungs are filled with sawdust
But our anthem still we sing
We sweat in honest labour
From sunrise unto dawn
For the dignity of labour
And the progress of our land.

For Kongi is our father
And Kongi is our man
Kongi is our mother
Kongi is our man
And Kongi is our Saviour
Redeemer, prince of power
For Ismà and for Kongi
We're proud to live or die!

(*The carpenters end with a march downstage with stiff mallet-wielding arms pistoning up in the Nazi salute.*

DENDE, *also in uniform, is seen among them trying gamely to keep in step. Enter the* SECRETARY, *declaiming as he enters.*)

SECRETARY: Kongi comes! And with his carpenters
Spitting fire on his enemies.
Comrades, our not-so-comrade comrades
Have their bottoms ready greased
For singeing, and do not know it. . . .
Hey . . . that is one new face, a very
Mouse among wildcats. Come here.
You seem at once familiar and yet
Completely out of place.

CAPTAIN: A new recruit. Newly defected
From the reactionary camp. You there!
Fall out!

SECRETARY: We must beware of spies.

CAPTAIN: I've put him through the standard tests.
He's no fifth columnist.

SECRETARY: Your name?

DENDE: Dende.

SECRETARY: The name is even more familiar.
Who was your last employer?

CAPTAIN: The king himself. Our mortal enemy.

SECRETARY: What!

CAPTAIN: A triumph for the cause, sir.
It should be good for seven weeks
Of propaganda.

SECRETARY: Hm. That, I'll admit, is one way
Of viewing the matter. But look here
A joke is a joke; is he combat worthy?

CAPTAIN: Not as a fighter, sir. But, as we are
Somewhat short on the muscle side—
The celebrations started a little early
For some carpenters, and that vigil
Beneath Kongi's hill of meditation proved
A disaster, a most debilitating
Orgy. Even these must nibble cola nuts
To keep awake. So I thought, maybe
We could use him for odd jobs
And errands. I admit he is
A sorry looking crow, but at least
He swells the ranks.

SECRETARY: Well, I shall be on hand to assume
Full command, if it proves necessary.
I warn you, this is Kongi's day.
I've organised towards it for the past
Twelve months. If anything goes wrong
He'll have my head, but first I'll scrape
Your heads clean with your chisels
Without using lather.

CAPTAIN: I will die for Kongi!

SECRETARY: Let us hope that will not
Prove necessary. I'd better take this runt
With me. If any need arises, he will rush
My orders back and forth. Now once again
Bear it in mind—this is my last
Organising job before retirement
And I wish to retire to my village
Not to a detention camp. Is that clear?

CAPTAIN: We will die for Kongi!

SECRETARY: After my retirement. Now listen
All of you. Far be it from me to sun
My emblems in the square, but merit . . .

DENDE: Is like pregnancy, never seen
But makes its proclamation.

SECRETARY: Well, well, well, the wonder actually
Boasts a voice. Tell me, why did you
Desert the palace? Were you bored
With swapping saws with that disgusting
Lecher?

CAPTAIN: We went parading past the palace—
Just to show the flag you know—
Suddenly there he was doggedly
Marching behind the ranks.
I shooed him off but he swore
He was resolved to be a carpenter.

(*They all burst out laughing.*)

CAPTAIN: Silence! 'Tention! As you were!

DENDE: I like the uniform. I asked Kabiyesi
To make me a uniform but he refused.

(*Again they fall to laughing.*)

CAPTAIN: Silence! 'Tention! The representative
Of our commander-in-chief, the Organising
Secretary, the Right Hand of Kongi
Our beloved Leader, will now address
The Carpenters' Brigade.

SECRETARY: Comrades, as I began to say, far be it
From me to sun my emblems but I am not
Without experience in the planning
Of moves and strategies on occasions
Such as this. And while it is true
That certain rules of strategy exist
In the manual of the Carpenters' Brigade
Yet is it the mark of genius when

A Field Marshal makes his own. The simplest
Part, you'll be surprised, is
The strategic disposition of your men
As laid down in your book of fundamentals
A man is either born to such basic
Know-how, or he should change his trade.
Even this warrior's progeny here
Can juggle men—what say you, sir?

DENDE: Politicians, Kabiyesi used to say,
Are as the seeds in a game of *ayo*
When it comes to juggling.

SECRETARY: The boy approaches genius.

DENDE: Wise partymen must learn the cunning
To crab and feint, to regroup and then
Disband like hornets.

SECRETARY: I should have come to the same
Training school as you. Now tell me,
What are the realities of conflict
As propounded by your royal sage?

DENDE: First, always outnumber the enemy.

SECRETARY: The man is a profound realist.

DENDE: And when outnumbered, run!

CAPTAIN: A fifth columnist, I knew it!
He's here to demoralize the carpenters.

SECRETARY: Nonsense. Athletics is a noble
Exercise. No need to be ashamed
Or coy about it.

CAPTAIN: This is disgraceful.

SECRETARY: Nothing of the sort. You are privileged
To learn today the ultimate realities

Of war. As your Strategist and Field Marshal
For this occasion, it shall be my duty
To instruct you when events demand
Its application. Come, you lion of Isma.

(*They cross to the other side. He speaks to a group offstage.*)

It's safe to enter now. The stalwarts
Have taken up position.

(*Enter the* AWERI. *They take their places on the dais.* SECRETARY *goes off.*)

THIRD: Your speech is too short.

FOURTH: What are you talking about? It runs to four hours and a half.

THIRD: Then you didn't listen to the news. The President over the border has just spoken for seven. And you know he fancies himself something of a rival to Kongi.

FOURTH: Disaster!

THIRD: Kongi won't like it at all. Can't you scribble something?

FOURTH: Impossible.

THIRD: He won't like it at all.

FOURTH: All right, all right. Don't keep on about it.

THIRD: But what are you going to do?

FOURTH: I'm dry. My brain is shrunk from hunger. I can't think.

THIRD: Add a diatribe on the condemned men.

FOURTH: It's down already. And I've run out of names to call them.

THIRD: Include an exposition on Kongi's reasons for withdrawing the reprieve.

FOURTH: It's all down in the President's prerogatives.

THIRD: Then you've really had it.

FOURTH: Unless . . . you say you listened to the news . . . anything about the one who escaped?

THIRD: He is still at large.

FOURTH: Then there is nothing I can add.

THIRD: I'm afraid not. (*With quiet malice.*) I'm afraid you've really had it.

(*Re-enter* SECRETARY *with* DENDE.)

SECRETARY: Something is not quite right.
My Number Seven sense refuses
To be silenced. Look here, batman,
Runner, aide-de-camp, or whatever
You call yourself, go and find me
A vantage point for observation
And remember friend, I have to keep
The entire square under observation
So, select some point quite distant
And reasonably protected. I hope
Your legs are in good training,
My instructions may likely be
Fast and furious. Well, get going man
And remember, not too near. My hearing
And eyesight are in top condition
And anyway, there are enough loudspeakers
To deafen the dead . . . damn! another one
Of these brigades and organisations.
Where on earth do I fit them?

(*Approaching, a male group singing to the rhythm of cutlasses scraping on hoes.*)

Which reminds me, where are the
Women's Auxiliary Corps? The job
Of cooking the New Yam is theirs.
Lateness means trouble. Captain! Captain!
Where is your women's wing? Have I
Gone blind or are there really no signs
Of cooking preparations?

CAPTAIN: They should have been here to cheer in
My men. We intend to lodge a vigorous
Complaint.

SECRETARY: To hell with that part of it.
I've warned you, if anything goes wrong . . .

CAPTAIN: I had no time to check on them.
I was busy reviving what remained
Of the carpenters.

SECRETARY (*his fingers desperately stuck in his ears*): And who are those metallic lunatics?

DENDE: It sounds like men from Prince Daodu's
Farming settlement.

CAPTAIN: Show-offs, that's all they are
Bloody show-offs.

SECRETARY: That noise, just because they won
The New Yam competition. God, and that
Is one more black mark against
My performance today. I did my best
To rig the results in favour of
The state cooperatives, but that man
Anticipated every move. And then his yam!
Like a giant wrestler with legs
And forearms missing. If only I had
Thought of it in time, I would have

Disqualified him on the grounds
Of it being a most abnormal specimen.

CAPTAIN: Perhaps our women's wing have stayed away
In protest.

SECRETARY: Make one more suggestion like that
And I'll dress you and your carpenters
In women's clothes, and make you do
The cooking.

CAPTAIN: No, no, please . . . they are sure to come.
I could send someone to hurry them
If you . . .

SECRETARY: Don't get nervous. I'd have a harder time
Explaining why your carpenters
Were not on hand. You stick to your job.
Remember, your job is to guard the yam
Every bit of the way. We don't want
Some fatal spice slipped into it, do we?

CAPTAIN: We will die for Kongi.

SECRETARY: Good. You have just volunteered
To act as taster. I shall come personally
And supervise the tasting—after the yam
Is cooked, and after it is pounded.

(*The* CAPTAIN*'s jaw drops.*)

Cheer up. Nothing is likely
To be tried. But it is just the idea
Of revenge which might occur
To our good friends the old Aweri.
So, keep good watch. You, run and stop
Daodu's yokels at the gate. I cannot
Let them in here—security reasons.
Only state-approved institutions

May enter Kongi Square. Mind you
They may appoint a delegate, someone
To bring in the winning yam—only one!

(DENDE *runs off.*)

I hope Daodu comes himself, at least
He can act civilised.

(*Royal drums and bugles. Enter* DANLOLA, SARUMI, *the old Aweri, and retinue.* SECRETARY *rushes to group them.*)

Kabiyesi! I had begun to rack my brain
For some excuse I hadn't used before
To explain your absence.

DANLOLA: I have only come to see our son dance.

SECRETARY: Dance? Daodu? Does that one dance?
I know he shuffles about in that club
Of Segi's, but don't tell me he will
Actually perform in honour of Kongi.

DANLOLA: I do not know in whose honour
Daodu intends to dance or make others dance
But he bade us to the feast saying
Come see a new Harvest jig, so,
Here we are.

SARUMI: Our sons tell us we've grown too old
To dance to Kongi's tunes. We've come
To see them do better.

SECRETARY: I know his farm won the competition,
But as for dancing. . . . I mean, his men
Are not even permitted here. So how . . . ?

DANLOLA: The bridegroom does not strain his neck
To see a bride bound anyway for his

Bedchamber. So let you and I wait
Like the patient bridegroom.

SECRETARY: Well, well, wonders will never end.
Winning that prize has really turned
Your prince's head . . . oh, I trust . . . I mean
About the other matter, our agreement
Still stands? You will present the yam?

DANLOLA: If the young sapling bends, the old twig
If it resists the wind, can only break.

SECRETARY: You are not angry that the amnesty
Has been revoked? My ancestors will
Bear witness—I did my best.

DANLOLA: It's a foolish elder who becomes
A creditor, since he must wait until
The other world, or outlive his debtors.

SECRETARY: Live long, Kabiyesi, we only await
Our women, and then the ceremony
Can begin at last.

(*Enter the women, singing, led by* SEGI, *who carries Daodu's cloak. They dance onto the stage, bearing mortar and pestle, cooking utensils, a cloth-beating unit, etc. They throw up their arms in derision and mock appeal to the world in general, singing—*)

Won ma tun gb'omiran de o
Kongi ni o je'yan oba.

(*They curtsey to the seated Obas, perform a brief insulting gesture as they dance past the Reformed* AWERI. *The* SECRETARY *has stood speechless at the sight of* SEGI, *now recovers himself sufficiently to approach her.* SEGI *signals to the women to stop.*)

SECRETARY: What do you want here? You should not even
Dream of coming here.

SEGI: But I belong to the Women's Corps.

SECRETARY (*frantic*): Since when? I do not remember you
Being remotely rehabilitated.

SEGI (*waving at the women*): Are all these approved people?

SECRETARY: Yes. They are all in the Women's Corps.

SEGI: They appointed me their leader. By a normal
Democratic process.

SECRETARY: Captain! Get your men to veto
The appointment.

SEGI: They also voted to ally with Daodu's Farm Settlement.
We have deserted the carpenters.

SECRETARY: Aha. There you have overreached
Yourself. You cannot do that unless
By express dispensation of Kongi.

SEGI: Yes, but nothing can be done about that until after the Harvest, is there? We can seek approval—later—if it is still necessary.

SECRETARY (*goes near, near-pleading*): Woman, what are you planning to do?

SEGI: Nothing. We heard Daodu and his men would dance for Kongi and we came to second his steps.

SECRETARY: Will you all stop saying that!
What of a sudden is all this concern
With Daodu's jitterbug. For one thing
It is not on the official programme.

SEGI: His New Yam won . . .

SECRETARY: The competition—yes! yes! We all know it.
But so what? Is that enough excuse
To turn my pageant into a Farmers' Cabaret?

SEGI: Have the farmers come?

SECRETARY: Yes, but I stopped them at the gate
Which is exactly where they will
Be left until the very end.

SEGI: I know. At the gate where we promised
We would welcome them.
(*To the women.*) Let's go.
Daodu may come in of course? He won . . .

SECRETARY: Yes, he won, he won! Segi, I beg of you
Don't ruin twelve months of preparation. . . .

(*The women resume their song, dance out, leaving behind a handful of them to attend to cooking preparations. Two women begin a steady rhythm with the cloth-beaters, giving Daodu's cloak a final sheen for the big occasion.*)

What can I do? He is entitled
To make a speech, and if like the Obas
He chooses to dance for Kongi
What is wrong in that? I only hope
It doesn't get out of hand, what with Segi's
Wild women abetting him.

CAPTAIN: Let him make a fool of himself.

SECRETARY (*slumping down wearily*): Oh, I don't know, I don't know at all.
Daodu is a cultured man. I had half-hoped
For some illiterate farm clod who would
Mumble the usual slogans and take
His farm stench off as fast as I chose

To cry "Shoo." But these new educated
Rascals! He's bound to show off and annoy
Somebody, or else make some ideological
Blunder, and then I get the blame.

Re-enter the women singing the same song and bearing DAODU *aloft. Others carry the farming implements which they have taken from Daodu's men and use them to supply a noisy rhythm.* DAODU *carries the winning yam above the triumphal entry. They set him down,* SEGI *takes the cloak from the women and fits it around his shoulders.*

SEGI: It is my turn to ask—you are not afraid?

DAODU: No. After all, only a little speech. Nothing need come of it.

SEGI: It seems suddenly futile, putting one's head into the lion's jaws.

DAODU: Nothing may come of it.

SEGI: Nothing may come of it and then you will do something else, and that will be more final.

DAODU: Then pray that something does come of it.

SEGI: It is wrong to feel so selfish, but now that my father has escaped, I wish this plan was never made.

DAODU: I did not work for this merely for your father, Segi. At least, so I tell myself.

SEGI: I know. Forgive me.

DAODU: All I fear is that I won't be allowed to finish what I have to say.

SEGI: You will have enough time. They all have husbands, sons, and brothers rotting in forgotten places. When they form a tight ring about you, only death will break it.

SECRETARY (*coming forward*): I might have known it. I never saw
A man make christmas over such a trifle
As the prize for a monster yam.

DAODU: It is a monster yam, it grew from Kongi's soil.

SECRETARY: Make your speech snappy, that's all
I ask of you. Five minutes at the most.
Just be happy and honoured and all that
Stuff, and remember to feel proud to be
A son of Isma. If you exceed five minutes
It will be my duty to cut you off.
Captain, stand by, here comes our Leader!

SECRETARY: Now! Ismite . . .

BRIGADE: Is Might!

SECRETARY: Ismite . . .

BRIGADE: Is Might!

SECRETARY: Ismite . . .

BRIGADE: Is Might . . .

SECRETARY: Now—One—Two—Three.

(*An orchestra strikes up the national anthem. They all rise. Enter* KONGI; *he stands under the flag until the end of the tune and is then fussily led to his seat by the* SECRETARY. KONGI *selects his pose and remains fixed in it throughout.*)

(*The* SECRETARY *signals frantically to* DAODU *to begin his presentation speech and to make it snappy.* DAODU *fastidiously adjusts his robe, takes out a small piece of paper.*)

SECRETARY: Well, it looks like a short speech anyway, so that's not the danger. (*Looks round nervously, sweating profusely.*) So where is it? Something is bound to go wrong. Something always goes wrong.

(*The women form a ring around* DAODU *with their pestles.* SECRETARY *stares in disbelief, especially at their hard, determined faces.*)

I don't think I'll bother to find out. Dende, take me to that observation post. Something tells me this is the moment to start supervising from a distance.

(*Half-runs off, dragging* DENDE *along.*)

DAODU (*looking straight at* KONGI): An impotent man will swear he feels the pangs of labour; when the maniac finally looks over the wall, he finds that there, agony is the raw commodity which he has spent lives to invent.

(*Stretches out his arms suddenly, full length.*)

Where I have chosen to return in joy, only fools still insist that my fate must be to suffer.

(*The tightness with which he has spoken thus far breaks into laughter; his arms come down.*)

This trip, I have elected to sample the joys of life, not its sorrows, to feast on the pounded yam, not on the rind of yam, to drink the wine myself, not leave it to my ministers for frugal sacraments, to love the women, not merely wash their feet at the well. In pursuit of which, let this yam, upon which I spent a fortune in fertilizers and in experiments with a multitude of strains, let it be taken out, peeled, cooked, and pounded, let bitter-leaf soup simmer in the women's pots and smoked fish release the goodness of the seas; that the Reformed Aweri Fraternity may belch soundly instead of merely salivating, that we may hereby repudiate all Prophets of Agony, unless it be recognized that pain may be endured only in the pursuit of ending pain and fighting terror.

(*Handing over the yam to* DANLOLA.)

DAODU: So let him, the Jesus of Isma, let him, who has assumed the mantle of a Messiah, accept from my farming settlement this gift of soil and remember that a human life once buried cannot, like this yam, sprout anew. Let him take from the palm only its wine and not crucify lives upon it.

(KONGI *has remained rapt in his pose.*)

DANLOLA: I don't think he heard a thing.

DAODU: Don't let that worry you. In a few more moments he will be woken up. And then it will be too late.

DANLOLA (*looks up sharply, apprehensive, turns slowly round to look at* KONGI, *shrugs*): As you wish.

Followed by the old Aweri, DANLOLA *bears the New Yam to* KONGI. KONGI *places his hands over it in benediction and in that moment there is a burst of gunfire which paralyses everyone.* KONGI *looks wildly round for some means of protection. The* SECRETARY *rushes in a moment later, obviously shaken. Hesitates, looking at* SEGI *especially but drawn dutifully to* KONGI. *He goes up to him and whispers in his ear.* KONGI *relaxes gradually, swells with triumph. He begins to chuckle, from a low key his laughter mounts, louder and more maniacal. His eye fixed on* SEGI *as a confident spider at a fly, he breaks off suddenly, snaps an urgent instruction to the* SECRETARY. *The man hesitates but* KONGI *insists, never taking his eye off* SEGI. *The* SECRETARY *slowly approaches her.*

SECRETARY: I wish you'd kept out of sight. Why did you have to let Kongi see you?

SEGI: I wanted him to. Anyway, what is it?

SECRETARY: I would have waited but he says I'm to tell you at once. Your father . . . oh, Segi, what were you people planning, for God's sake. What was he doing here?

SEGI: Go on. Have they caught him?

SECRETARY: Didn't you hear the shots?

DAODU: Oh God!

SEGI: He's dead?

SECRETARY (*nods*): What was he trying? Why was he here? Doesn't anyone know it's never any use.

SEGI: Go away.

SECRETARY: But why did he have to come back? Why didn't he just keep running, why?

DAODU: He's watching. He's watching.

SEGI: Let him watch. He shan't see me break.

DAODU: You mean to continue?

SEGI: Yes, let it all end tonight. I am tired of being the mouse in his cat-and-mouse game.

SECRETARY: I'm done for, I know it. I'm heading for the border while there is time. Oh, there is going to be such a clamp-down after this. . . .

SEGI: Where have they taken him?

SECRETARY: In a schoolroom just across the square.

SEGI: I'll be back directly, Daodu. Let everything go on as planned.

DAODU: Such as what? After what has happened, what?

SEGI: So he came back? Why didn't you tell me?

DAODU: I could do nothing to stop him. When he heard that the reprieve had been withdrawn . . . there was simply nothing I could do. He said he had to do it and no one else.

SEGI: It doesn't matter.

DAODU: We've failed again, Segi.

SEGI: No, not altogether.

DAODU: What else can one do now?

SEGI: The season is Harvest, so let there be plenty of everything. The best and the richest. Let us see only what earth has fattened, not what has withered within it.

DAODU: What are you talking about? What do I do now?

SEGI: Sing, damn him, sing! Let none of our people know what has happened. Is it not time for Kongi's speech?

SECRETARY: Yes, he'll begin any moment. He's very much awake now.

DAODU: There should have been no speech. We failed again.

SEGI: Then forget he is there. Let the yam be pounded. I shall return soon with a season's gift for the Leader.

(*The women relieve* OBA DANLOLA *of the yam, take it away as* KONGI *rises slowly, triumphant.*)

KONGI: The Spirit of Harvest has smitten the enemies of Kongi. The justice of earth has prevailed over traitors and conspirators. There is divine blessing on the second Five-Year Development Plan. The spirit of resurgence is cleansed in the blood of the nation's enemies, my enemies, the enemies of our collective spirit, the Spirit of Planting, the Spirit of Harvest, the Spirit of Inevitable History and Victory, all of which I am. Kongi is every Ismite, and Ismite . . . (*Shoots out a clenched fist.*)

BRIGADE: Is Might. . . .

(*They beat on their drums and clash cymbals deafeningly.*)

KONGI: Ismite . . .

BRIGADE: Is Might. . . .

SEGI: Now.

(*It is the signal for the feast to begin. A real feast, a genuine Harvest orgy of food and drink that permits no spectators, only celebrants. The dancing, the singing are only part of it, the centre is the heart and stomach of a good feast.*)

Ijo mo ko w'aiye o
Ipasan ni.
Ijo mo ko w'aiye o
Ipasan ni
Igi lehin were o
Kunmo lehin were o
Aiye akowa
Ade egun ni o
Aiye akowa
Ade egun ni o
Iso lo g'aka m'ogi
Iso lo g'aka m'ogi

Mo ti d'ade egun
Pere gungun maja gungun pere
Mo ti d'ade egun
Pere gungun maja gungun pere
Omije osa
Pere gungun maja gungun pere
Won tu'to pami
Pere gungun maja gungun pere
Kelebe adete
Pere gungun maja gungun pere

Mo gbe'gi k'ari
Pere gungun maja gungun pere
Mo g'oke abuke
Pere gungun maja gungun pere
Isu o won n'ile o
Isu o won n'ile o
Won gb'ori akobi le le
Won fi gun'yan
Igi o won n'ile e
Igi o won n'ile e
Egun itan akobi o
No won fi da'na

Adeyin wa o
Igba ikore ni
Aiye erinkeji
Iyan ni mo wa je
Aiye ti mo tun wa
Iyan ni mo waje
Iyan yi kari
  Ire a kari
Iyan yi kari
  Ayo a b'ori
Etu l'ara mi
  Ire akari
Aiya ni mo wa fe
  Ayo a b'ori
Aiye erin ni mo wa
  Ayo a b'ori
Emu ni mo wa mu
  Ire a kari
Ata ni mo wa ya
  Ayo a bori
Aiye eso eso
  Eso ni baba
  Eso ni baba

The rhythm of pounding emerges triumphant, the dance grows frenzied. Above it all on the dais, KONGI, *getting progressively inspired, harangues his audience in words drowned in the bacchanal. He exhorts, declaims, reviles, cajoles, damns, curses, vilifies, excommunicates, execrates until he is a demonic mass of sweat and foam at the lips.*

SEGI *returns, disappears into the area of pestles. A copper salver is raised suddenly high; it passes from hands to hands above the women's heads; they dance with it on their heads; it is thrown from one to the other until at last it reaches Kongi's table and* SEGI *throws open the lid. In it, the head of an old man. In the ensuing scramble, no one is left but* KONGI *and the head,* KONGI*'s mouth wide open in speechless terror. A sudden blackout on both.*

HANGOVER

Again Kongi Square. It is near dawn. The square is littered with the debris and the panic of last night's feast. Enter SECRETARY, *a bundle over his shoulder, dragging his tired body by the feet. Sitting seemingly lost beside the road,* DENDE; *the* SECRETARY *does not immediately recognise him.*

SECRETARY: Good friend, how far is it
To the border? What! Well, well,
If it isn't my bold lion of Isma.
And what, may I ask, happened to
The Carpenters' Brigade? Did they
Receive my last instructions?
Not that there was anything of a genuine
Battle, if you get my meaning; nonetheless
It was time to apply
The ultimate reality of war—
For their own sakes mind you—
I hope you made that very plain
To them. I know the ropes.

To be there at all at that disgraceful
Exhibition is to be guilty of treasonable
Conspiracy et cetera, et cetera.

DENDE: There was no one to take my message
They had all anticipated
Your instructions.

SECRETARY: They lack discipline. A good soldier
Awaits starter's orders. And you?
What's happened to your Boy Scout movement?
I thought I ordered you to remove
Your carcass far from the scene of crime.

DENDE: I don't know where to go.

SECRETARY: If you don't find somewhere soon
There are those who might assist you.
And their hospitality, believe me,
Is not to be recommended. I say,
Is your problem by any chance
Shortage of funds?

DENDE: Oh no, I spend nothing on myself and
I carry all my savings with me
Everywhere—as a precaution.
As Kabiyesi himself would say . . .

SECRETARY: Oh? A quiet millionaire, are you?
Turn out your pockets.

DENDE: My pockets? What for?

SECRETARY: Don't blow your lungs, boy. When a man
Cannot even call briefly home to say
Good-bye to his native land, then hope
Remains his last luxury. Turn out
Your pockets. As your late commander
It is my duty to play censor
To your battle kit. Come on, come on,

Let's see what keepsakes and
Protection charms you wear to war. . . .
Aha, what's this? You haven't been
Despoiling fallen warriors, have you now?

DENDE: Those are rejected bits and pieces
From the things we made for the king
To take to harvest.

SECRETARY: I see . . . a kick-back artist, eh?
And starting out so young. Hm,
You carry quite a few trinkets around
With you. Saving up for a bride-price
I bet. Well, well, myself I am partial
To silver, but I'll keep the copper bangle
Till your situation improves. Really,
You astonish me. A runner travels
Light, you are lucky you arrived
Unlooted from the battle front,
It seems there is one lesson of war
Your rogue king failed to teach you—Never
Carry your own ransom on your person—
Never!

(*Enter* DANLOLA, *furtively. He is also bundled with his emergency possessions.*)

DANLOLA: Ah, my son-in-politics, is the Big Ear
Of His Immortality still flapping high
In Kongi's breath?

(SECRETARY *quickly releases* DENDE, *recovers from his astonishment at seeing* DANLOLA.)

SECRETARY: Kabiyesi, don't mock a ruined man.

DANLOLA: If you are headed in that direction,
Then that way leads to the border.

SECRETARY: Do you suggest I am running away?

DANLOLA: Not I. Just the same, I'll be glad
To keep you company. If any man exists
Who wisely has prepared for such a day
It would be you. . . . Oh ho, is that not my Dende?

SECRETARY: Hold nothing against him. Few half-wits
Can resist a uniform.

DANLOLA: I hope he proved useful.

SECRETARY: The man is a philosopher. We have
Exchanged many areas of wisdom. Right now
He is my travelling companion.

DANLOLA: I don't see that you have anything
To fear. After all, no one could
Predict that surprise gift. The show
Was well organised, I mean, until that
Sudden business, all went well.

SECRETARY: I hope I shall live long enough
To make good use of your testimonial.
Went well! That is quite a mouthful!

DANLOLA: But it did go well. Well, as a hurricane
Blows well. As a bushfire on dry
Corn stalks burns well, and with a fine
Crackle of northern wind behind it.
As a mat dances well when the man
Is full of peppers and, with the last
Guest departed, leaps upon
The trembling bride. As I ran well
When I took a final look at Kongi
And began a rapid dialogue with my legs.

SECRETARY: And me. I never thought I had so much
Motion between my legs.

DANLOLA: The others? What did the others do?

SECRETARY: I was by then too far away. Kabiyesi,
It was no time to take notes for posterity.

DANLOLA: What happens now? The hornets' nest
Is truly stirred. What happens to
The sleeping world?

SECRETARY (*sinking down*): Oh, I wish I was the mindless smile
On the face of a contented sow. Of a fat
Contented sow. Fat I am, and uncharitable
Tongues have labelled me a sow. But
Contented? That is one uneasy crown
Which still eludes my willing head.

(*Leaps up suddenly.*)

What are we doing still sitting here?

DANLOLA: For now this is the safest spot to wait
And Sarumi should join me soon—
I hope. He's gone with some twelve toughs—
All volunteers—from among
Daodu's own farmers. If he's not already
In Kongi's hands, they'll abduct him
Forcibly and parcel him across the border.
And that woman of his.

SECRETARY: He is mad. And that woman, they're both
Roadside lunatics. Even away from here—
Take my advice, have them restrained.

DANLOLA: The strange thing is, I think
Myself I drank from the stream of madness
For a little while.

SECRETARY (*looks up anxiously*): It's getting light.

DANLOLA: I'll go and hurry them. You will . . . wait?
Don't leave us behind, I beg of you.

When Providence guides my feet to a man
Of your resourcefulness, I know
Our safety is assured.

SECRETARY: Not Providence, Kabiyesi, but provisions.
I only paused to glean a few emergency
Rations from our young philosopher.
But you are wrong—this idea you have
Of travelling together, most imprudent.
An entourage like that would be suicidally
Conspicuous. Split, then meet once across
The border—that would be my strategy.

DANLOLA: Of course, of course. You see, never would I
Have thought of that.

SECRETARY: You'll learn, Kabiyesi, you'll learn.
Survival turns the least adaptable of us
To night chameleons.

DANLOLA: Very true, son. Well, I shall delay you
No further. I hope Sarumi has been delayed
By no worse than Daodu's stubbornness.

SECRETARY: Good luck, sir. I shall precede you
On active service, nonstop until
I am safe beyond the frontier. Oh,
What of this failed carpenter? Shall I
Take him with me—that is, if you don't mind?

DANLOLA: Oh, let him be. He's bound to do much
As the wind directs him, and anyway,
He is in no danger. He may even join
Our Royal Household Cavalry—in exile—
If we can find him a uniform.

SECRETARY (*undecided*): Oh, well . . . I was only thinking . . . I mean
I could use a . . . yes, he could sort of

Earn his keep carrying this load for me. . . .
No, he'd only be a nuisance. I'm off.
Better hurry yourself, obstreperous old lecher,
I would wish you a speedy restoration
And a long and happy reign, but it would sound
Like mockery. See you at the border.

(*As he leaves,* DANLOLA *shakes his head in sad amusement.*)

DANLOLA: Safe journey. If I know you
The frontier fence will lose its barbs
At one touch of your purse;
There is already less corruption
In the air, even though your rear
Is turned.

(*He starts briskly back in the opposite direction. A mixture of the royal music and the anthem rises loudly, plays for a short while, comes to an abrupt halt as the iron grating descends and hits the ground with a loud, final clang.*)

BLACKOUT

Translations of Yoruba Songs

[146]
Don't pound the king's yam
In a small mortar
Small as the spice is
It cannot be swallowed whole
A shilling's vegetable must appease
A halfpenny spice.

[147]
The king is
He who chews on the haunch from an offering
The king is a god.

The king is
He who anoints the head's pulse centre
With the oil of sacrifice
The king is a god.

[148]
Ogun did not seek the throne
Ogun did not seek the throne
Quietly retired, minding his own business
The nobles brought the crown of Ire
To the ancestor of all hunters
Ogun did not seek the throne

White nut from the offering
Pulse of the Oba's head

[148–149]
Be not angry my king with me
As the rainbow, full of wrath at the root
Drew away, pulled apart
And settled halfway to heaven

Be not angry my king with me
As Sango was angered by the people of earth
Till only with the language of lightning
Does he now hold converse with man

Be not angry with me my king
As the palm ghommid, in anger at the wine-tapper
Plucked the lizard down to earth
As a man scratches scabs from his head.

The king is not for treading on
As a man steps on dried leaves
If the elephant does not warily step
He will tread on a thorn
And hobble like a pair of stilts

The king is not to be shaken off
As a man may brush off cobwebs
A king's beard is an awesome net
A king's wisdom is awesome measure
Whatever fly cuts a careless caper
Around the scent of sacrifice
Will worship down the spider's throat.

[174–175]
At my first coming
Scourges all the way
At my first coming
Whips to my skin
Cudgels on the madman's back.

At my first coming
A crown of thorns
At my first coming

A crown of thorns
The foolhardy hedgehog
Was spread-eagled on nails.

I have borne the thorned crown
Shed tears as the sea
I was spat upon
A leper's spittle
A burden of logs
Climbed the hunchback hill
There was no dearth of yam
But the head of the firstborn
Was pounded for yam
There was no dearth of wood
Yet the thigh of the firstborn
Lost its bone for fuel.

Now this second coming
Is time for harvest
This second coming
Is for pounding of yams
The mortar spills over
Goodness abundant
My body is balm
I have come wife-seeking
I am borne on laughter
I have come palm wine thirsting
My rheum is from sweet peppers
Contentment is earth's
Ease for her portion
Peace is triumphant.

Interpretive Questions for Discussion

Why does Soyinka portray both Danlola and Kongi, the two rivals for Isma's leadership, as vain, self-serving, and autocratic?

1. Why is the struggle for power between Danlola and Kongi played out through the Festival of the New Yam? Why does Kongi long to be known as the "Spirit of the Harvest"? (103, 123)

2. Why is Danlola depicted as lecherous in contrast to Kongi, whose Spartan discipline is regarded as fanatical by everyone around him?

3. Why do the Obas sing that, although they were taught to abandon the "monster child," "the mother in us" allowed him to live? Are we meant to blame the Obas for allowing Kongi, "the monster child," to gain power? (91)

4. Why are we told that "kingship is a role" for both Danlola and Kongi? (128) Does neither of them care about good governance?

5. Why does Danlola feel "life resurrected" within him when he dances to Sarumi's song of praise? (150)

6. Why does Sarumi sing that although the Obas profited by their rule, they never went too far—that while they used much silk for the royal canopy, they "never ate the silkworm," and though they ate the first of the new yams, they "drew the poison from the root"? (89)

7. Why do both Kongi and Danlola need their Aweri? Why don't Kongi's Aweri, the sophistic disputants, respect their leader in the way that Danlola's retinue respects him? (85, 92–94, 120–121)

8. Why do Danlola and Sarumi repeatedly warn, "Don't pound the king's yam / In a small mortar" or "with a small pestle"? (83, 91, 146 [183])

9. Why is Kongi shown to be easily manipulated by his clever Secretary, while no one can manipulate Danlola? (115)

10. Why are we told that in Oba Danlola's palace his sons "speak out their minds"? (147)

11. After the failed attempt to unseat Kongi, why does Danlola interrupt his flight to the border and start briskly back to rejoin Sarumi and Daodu?

12. Are we meant to think that neither Kongi nor Danlola should rule in Isma? Why does Kongi prevail as Isma's leader even though Danlola commands more respect and is wiser and more subtle than Kongi?

Suggested textual analysis
Pages 82–92 (Hemlock)

Why can the Secretary and Daodu—the go-betweens—reach agreement and become allies, while Kongi and Danlola cannot?

1. Why is the Secretary the only person in the play who moves between the opposing worlds of Kongi's retreat and Segi's lively club? Why are we shown the Secretary drinking beer and enjoying music at Segi's club while Kongi's other advisers, his Aweri, are starving?

2. Why is Daodu able to win the admiration of the Secretary by improving upon his slogan for Kongi's rallies?

3. Why is Daodu reluctant to be "a mere antithesis" to Kongi, the "Messiah of Pain"? (134)

4. Why does Daodu abruptly stop the solemn dance of Sarumi and Danlola, a taboo act that Danlola says splits "the gut of our make-believe"? Why does Danlola say that the world has run amok, leaving Daodu "alone and sane"? (150)

5. Why does Daodu insist on Danlola's participation in the Harvest Festival even though Kongi has retracted the amnesty for the escaped prisoners? Why does Daodu say that his wish to have Danlola give Kongi the New Yam "concerns us, your children," and call Danlola's submittal to Kongi a triviality? (151–152)

6. Why does Daodu dismiss Kongi's call for the return of the escaped prisoner dead or alive as meaning "nothing"? Why do Daodu and Danlola disagree about the significance of Kongi's proclamation? (152)

7. Why does Kongi seem not to hear Daodu's disrespectful speech, while he does hear the gunshots that kill Segi's father? (170–171)

8. Why does Daodu feel defeated by the death of Segi's father and require Segi's urging to go on with their plan? (172–173)

9. Why does the Secretary assert that Daodu and Segi are "roadside lunatics" for having opposed Kongi's rule? Why does Danlola reply, "The strange thing is, I think / Myself I drank from the stream of madness / For a little while"? (180)

10. Why are we left not knowing what happens to Daodu, the "exceptional" and "democratic" prince? (105)

Suggested textual analyses

Pages 149–154: beginning, "DANLOLA, *totally swelled,*" and ending, "(*He sweeps out, the others hurrying after him.*)"

Pages 169–176: beginning, "(*An orchestra strikes up the national anthem,*" to the end of the Second Part.

Why is the mysterious, sexual "being of Segi" the greatest threat to Kongi's power?

1. Why does Soyinka make Segi Daodu's lover and Kongi's former mistress?
2. Why does Daodu say that "men know nothing of Segi"? (140) Why do the men in Segi's club sing that she is beautiful, tender, and deadly? (98–100, 117–119)
3. Why is the otherwise cool and calculating Secretary disturbed by Segi and the atmosphere of her club? (97–98, 116–117, 129)
4. Why does Segi call Daodu "my Spirit of Harvest"? Why does wearing Segi's robe make Daodu feel like "the prince of orgies . . . some decadent deity"? (132–133)
5. Why does Daodu want to preach hatred when he tries on Segi's Harvest robe, while Segi implores him to "preach life" instead? Why does Segi insist that erecting a pulpit of love and life against Kongi, "even for one moment," will be "enough"? (133–134)
6. Why does Danlola call Segi a "right cannibal of the female species"? Why does Segi frighten a seasoned old womanizer like Danlola? (140)
7. Why does Danlola agree to participate in the ceremony of the New Yam only when he learns that Segi, the daughter of the escaped prisoner, wants the festival to go on? (153)
8. Why, even after the death of her father, does Segi urge Daodu to celebrate "what earth has fattened, not what has withered within it"? (173) Why does Soyinka call for a "genuine Harvest orgy of food and drink that permits no spectators, only celebrants"? (174)
9. Why does Segi avenge her father's death by presenting Kongi with the head of her father during the Harvest orgy of food and drink?

10. Why does Segi's revenge cause Kongi to react with "speechless terror"? (176) Why does Segi's revenge result in Danlola and the Secretary fleeing for their lives?

Suggested textual analyses

Pages 97–101: beginning, "(*Looks slowly round.*)" and ending, "Well, here's to duty."

Pages 130–135: beginning, "Oh! yes, it's all clear now," and ending, "I'll be waiting."

For Further Reflection

1. Is there a correlation between being a successful politician and having a strong sexual drive?
2. Are most political leaders motivated by self-love? By their desire to be loved?
3. How can nations move from strongman dictatorships to democracy?
4. Is American politics, like Ismaland's, dominated by "isms" and empty disputations?
5. Is a government progressing or declining when it divorces itself from its people's religious roots?
6. Do you see human sexuality as the source of creativity and productivity?

The Melian Dialogue

Thucydides

THUCYDIDES (460?–400? B.C.) was a young man when the Peloponnesian War (431–404 B.C.) broke out between Athens and Sparta. From the beginning he recognized that the conflict was going to be "a great war and more worth writing about than any of those which had taken place in the past," and he made extensive notes as events unfolded. In 424 B.C., he was appointed a general and charged to defend Athenian colonies. When he failed to save the city of Amphipolis from Spartan forces, Thucydides was sent into an exile that lasted close to twenty years. During this time, Thucydides acquired firsthand information for his life's work, *History of the Peloponnesian War,* probably traveling to Sparta and Sicily in the course of his investigations. Thucydides, who is generally regarded as the first scholarly historian, presented his carefully researched facts in language meant to be read, not recited, a mode that differed from previous histories. "The Melian Dialogue" took place in 416 B.C., in the sixteenth year of the war.

THE NEXT SUMMER the Athenians made an expedition against the isle of Melos. The Melians are a colony of Lacedaemon[1] that would not submit to the Athenians like the other islanders, and at first remained neutral and took no part in the struggle, but afterwards, upon the Athenians using violence and plundering their territory, assumed an attitude of open hostility. The Athenian generals encamped in their territory with their army, and before doing any harm to their land sent envoys to negotiate. These the Melians did not bring before the people, but told them to state the object of their mission to the magistrates and the council; the Athenian envoys then said:

ATHENIANS: As we are not to speak to the people, for fear that if we made a single speech without interruption we might deceive them with attractive arguments to which there was no chance of replying—we realize that this is the meaning of our being brought before your ruling body—we suggest that you

1. [Sparta.]

who sit here should make security doubly sure. Let us have no long speeches from you either, but deal separately with each point, and take up at once any statement of which you disapprove, and criticize it.

MELIANS: We have no objection to your reasonable suggestion that we should put our respective points of view quietly to each other, but the military preparations which you have already made seem inconsistent with it. We see that you have come to be yourselves the judges of the debate, and that its natural conclusion for us will be slavery if you convince us, and war if we get the better of the argument and therefore refuse to submit.

ATHENIANS: If you have met us in order to make surmises about the future, or for any other purpose than to look existing facts in the face and to discuss the safety of your city on this basis, we will break off the conversations; otherwise, we are ready to speak.

MELIANS: In our position it is natural and excusable to explore many ideas and arguments. But the problem that has brought us here is our security, so, if you think fit, let the discussion follow the line you propose.

ATHENIANS: Then we will not make a long and unconvincing speech, full of fine phrases, to prove that our victory over Persia justifies our empire, or that we are now attacking you because you have wronged us, and we ask you not to expect to convince us by saying that you have not injured us, or that, though a colony of Lacedaemon, you did not join her. Let each of us say what we really think and reach a practical agreement. You know and we know, as practical men, that the question of justice arises only between parties equal in strength, and that the strong do what they can, and the weak submit.

MELIANS: As you ignore justice and have made self-interest the basis of discussion, we must take the same ground, and we say that in our opinion it is in your interest to maintain a principle which is for the good of all—that anyone in danger should have just and equitable treatment and any advantage, even if not strictly his due, which he can secure by persuasion. This is your interest as much as ours, for your fall would involve you in a crushing punishment that would be a lesson to the world.

ATHENIANS: We have no apprehensions about the fate of our empire, if it did fall; those who rule other peoples, like the Lacedaemonians, are not formidable to a defeated enemy. Nor is it the Lacedaemonians with whom we are now contending: the danger is from subjects who of themselves may attack and conquer their rulers. But leave that danger to us to face. At the moment we shall prove that we have come in the interest of our empire and that in what we shall say we are seeking the safety of your state; for we wish you to become our subjects with least trouble to ourselves, and we would like you to survive in our interests as well as your own.

MELIANS: It may be your interest to be our masters: how can it be ours to be your slaves?

ATHENIANS: By submitting you would avoid a terrible fate, and we should gain by not destroying you.

MELIANS: Would you not agree to an arrangement under which we should keep out of the war, and be your friends instead of your enemies, but neutral?

ATHENIANS: No: your hostility injures us less than your friendship. That, to our subjects, is an illustration of our weakness, while your hatred exhibits our power.

MELIANS: Is this the construction which your subjects put on it? Do they not distinguish between states in which you have no concern, and peoples who are most of them your colonies, and some conquered rebels?

ATHENIANS: They think that one nation has as good rights as another, but that some survive because they are strong and we are afraid to attack them. So, apart from the addition to our empire, your subjection would give us security: the fact that you are islanders (and weaker than others) makes it the more important that you should not get the better of the mistress of the sea.

MELIANS: But do you see no safety in our neutrality? You debar us from the plea of justice and press us to submit to your interests, so we must expound our own, and try to convince you, if the two happen to coincide. Will you not make enemies of all neutral powers when they see your conduct and reflect that some day you will attack them? Will not your action strengthen your existing opponents, and induce those who would otherwise never be your enemies to become so against their will?

ATHENIANS: No. The mainland states, secure in their freedom, will be slow to take defensive measures against us, and we do not consider them so formidable as independent island powers like yourselves, or subjects already smarting under our yoke. These are most likely to take a thoughtless step and bring themselves and us into obvious danger.

MELIANS: Surely then, if you are ready to risk so much to maintain your empire, and the enslaved peoples so much to escape from it, it would be criminal cowardice in us, who are still free, not to take any and every measure before submitting to slavery?

ATHENIANS: No, if you reflect calmly: for this is not a competition in heroism between equals, where your honor is at stake, but a question of self-preservation, to save you from a struggle with a far stronger power.

MELIANS: Still, we know that in war fortune is more impartial than the disproportion in numbers might lead one to expect. If we submit at once, our position is desperate; if we fight, there is still a hope that we shall stand secure.

ATHENIANS: Hope encourages men to take risks; men in a strong position may follow her without ruin, if not without loss. But when they stake all that they have to the last coin (for she is a spendthrift), she reveals her real self in the hour of failure, and when her nature is known she leaves them without means of self-protection. You are weak, your future hangs on a turn of the scales; avoid the mistake most men make, who might save themselves by human means, and then, when visible hopes desert them, in their extremity turn to the invisible—prophecies and oracles and all those things which delude men with hopes, to their destruction.

MELIANS: We too, you can be sure, realize the difficulty of struggling against your power and against Fortune if she is not impartial. Still we trust that Heaven will not allow us to be worsted by Fortune, for in this quarrel we are right and you are wrong. Besides, we expect the support of Lacedaemon to supply the deficiencies in our strength, for she is bound to help us as her kinsmen, if for no other reason, and from a sense of honor. So our confidence is not entirely unreasonable.

ATHENIANS: As for divine favor, we think that we can count on it as much as you, for neither our claims nor our actions are inconsistent with what men believe about Heaven or desire for themselves. We believe that Heaven, and we know that men, by a natural law, always rule where they are stronger. We did not make that law nor were we the first to act on it; we found it existing, and it will exist forever, after we are gone; and we know that you and anyone else as strong as we are would do as we do. As to your expectations from Lacedaemon and your belief that she will help you from a sense of honor, we congratulate you on your innocence but we do not admire your folly. So far as they themselves and their national traditions are concerned, the Lacedaemonians are a highly virtuous people; as for their behavior to others, much might be said, but we can put it shortly by saying that, most obviously of all people we know, they identify their interests with justice and the pleasantest course with honor. Such principles do not favor your present irrational hopes of deliverance.

MELIANS: That is the chief reason why we have confidence in them now; in their own interest they will not wish to betray their own colonists and so help their enemies and destroy the confidence that their friends in Greece feel in them.

ATHENIANS: Apparently you do not realize that safety and self-interest go together, while the path of justice and honor is dangerous; and danger is a risk which the Lacedaemonians are little inclined to run.

MELIANS: Our view is that they would be more likely to run a risk in our case, and would regard it as less hazardous, because our nearness to Peloponnese makes it easier for them to act and our kinship gives them more confidence in us than in others.

ATHENIANS: Yes, but an intending ally looks not to the good will of those who invoke his aid but to marked superiority of real power, and of none is this truer than of the Lacedaemonians. They mistrust their own resources and attack their neighbors only when they have numerous allies, so it is not likely that, while we are masters of the sea, they would cross it to an island.

MELIANS: They might send others. The sea of Crete is large, and this will make it more difficult for its masters to capture hostile ships than for these to elude them safely. If they failed by sea, they would attack your country and those of your allies whom Brasidas did not reach; and then you will have to fight not against a country in which you have no concern, but for your own country and your allies' lands.

ATHENIANS: Here experience may teach you like others, and you will learn that Athens has never abandoned a siege from fear of another foe. You said that you proposed to discuss the safety of your city, but we observe that in all your speeches you have never said a word on which any reasonable expectation of it could be founded. Your strength lies in deferred hopes; in comparison with the forces now arrayed against you, your resources are too small for any hope of success. You will show a great want of judgment if you do not come to a more reasonable decision after we have withdrawn. Surely you will not fall back on the idea of honor, which has been the ruin of so many when danger and disgrace were staring them in the face. How often, when men have seen the fate to which they were tending, have they been enslaved by a phrase and drawn by the power of this seductive word to fall of their own free will into irreparable disaster, bringing on themselves by their folly a greater dishonor than fortune could inflict! If you are wise, you will avoid that fate. The greatest of cities makes you a fair offer, to keep your own land and become her tributary ally: there is no dishonor in that. The choice between war and safety is given you; do not obstinately take the worse alternative. The most successful people are those who stand up to their equals, behave properly to their superiors, and treat their inferiors fairly. Think it over when we withdraw, and reflect once and again that you have only one country, and that its prosperity or ruin depends on one decision.

The Athenians now withdrew from the conference; and the Melians, left to themselves, came to a decision corresponding with what they had maintained in the discussion, and answered, "Our resolution, Athenians, is unaltered. We will not in a moment deprive of freedom a city that has existed for seven hundred years; we put our trust in the fortune by which the gods have preserved it until now, and in the help of men, that is, of the Lacedaemonians; and so we will try and save ourselves. Meanwhile we invite you to allow us to be friends to you and foes to neither party, and to retire from our country after making such a treaty as shall seem fit to us both."

Such was the answer of the Melians. The Athenians broke up the conference saying, "To judge from your decision, you are unique in regarding the future as more certain than the present and in allowing your wishes to convert the unseen into reality; and as you have staked most on, and trusted most in, the Lacedaemonians, your fortune, and your hopes, so will you be most completely deceived."

The Athenian envoys now returned to the army; and as the Melians showed no signs of yielding, the generals at once began hostilities, and drew a line of circumvallation round the Melians, dividing the work among the different states. Subsequently the Athenians returned with most of their army, leaving behind them a certain number of their own citizens and of the allies to keep guard by land and sea. The force thus left stayed on and besieged the place.

Meanwhile the Athenians at Pylos took so much plunder from the Lacedaemonians that the latter, although they still refrained from breaking off the treaty and going to war with Athens, proclaimed that any of their people that chose might plunder the Athenians. The Corinthians also commenced hostilities with the Athenians for private quarrels of their own; but the rest of the Peloponnesians stayed quiet. Meanwhile the Melians in a night attack took the part of the Athenian lines opposite the market, killed some of its garrison, and brought in corn and as many useful stores as they could. Then, retiring, they remained inactive, while the Athenians took measures to keep better guard in future.

Summer was now over. The next winter the Lacedaemonians intended to invade the Argive territory, but on arriving at the frontier found the sacrifices for crossing unfavorable, and went back again. This intention of theirs made the Argives suspicious of certain of their fellow citizens, some of whom they arrested; others, however, escaped them. About the same time the Melians again took another part of the Athenian lines which were but feebly garrisoned. In consequence reinforcements were sent from Athens, and the siege was now pressed vigorously; there was some treachery in the town, and the Melians surrendered at discretion[2] to the Athenians, who put to death all the grown men whom they took, and sold the women and children for slaves; subsequently they sent out five hundred settlers and colonized the island. ~

2. [Surrendered unconditionally.]

INTERPRETIVE QUESTIONS FOR DISCUSSION

According to Thucydides, are the Melians fools or heroes for refusing the Athenian offer?

1. Why do the Melians decide to risk the annihilation of their 700-year-old city rather than accept the "fair offer" of becoming a tributary state of Athens? (201)

2. Why don't the Melian leaders allow the Athenian envoy to speak before the people?

3. Why are the Melians convinced that they would be guilty of "criminal cowardice" should they submit to the Athenians' superior strength? (198)

4. Why do the Melians place their hopes in the rightness of their cause as well as in the Spartan sense of honor?

5. Why do the Athenians know better than the Melians that Sparta will not come to the aid of their kinsmen? Why do the Melians suffer the misconception that it would be in Sparta's self-interest to come to their aid?

6. Do the Melians have a keener sense of honor than the Athenians, or are they only using honor as a ploy for getting out of a difficult situation?

Suggested textual analysis
Pages 200–201: beginning, "ATHENIANS: Here experience may teach you like others," and ending, "be most completely deceived."

Why do the Athenians give the Melians a chance to avoid a battle?

1. Why do the Athenians make clear from the beginning that they do not want to speak of justice? (196)
2. Why do the Athenians try to convince the Melians that might makes right, rather than just threaten them with their power? (196, 199)
3. Why do the Athenians desire a practical dialogue with the Melians, rather than long speeches with fine phrases? (196)
4. Why do the Athenians state that "this is not a competition in heroism between equals"? (198)
5. Are the Melians exaggerating, or are they correct when they say that the Athenians are only offering them slavery? (196, 198, 201)
6. Are we meant to accept the Athenians' argument that weak island states that might take a "thoughtless step" pose a greater threat to their empire than strong mainland states? (198)
7. Do the Athenians not allow the Melians to remain neutral because they do not trust the Melians?

Suggested textual analysis
Pages 196–198: beginning, "ATHENIANS: Then we will not make a long and unconvincing speech," and ending, "with a far stronger power."

Why do the Athenians wipe out the Melians altogether, rather than merely subdue them?

1. Are the Melians or the Athenians more responsible for the devastation of the Melians?
2. Why do the Athenians believe they will fare better if their subjects fear them rather than trust them?

3. Why do the Athenians suggest that being defeated by their own subjects is a worse fate than being defeated by a foreign power? (197)

4. Why do the Athenians destroy the Melians if they believe that the "most successful people . . . treat their inferiors fairly"? (201)

5. Why are we told that treachery from within the city of Melos led to the unconditional surrender of the Melians? (202)

6. Are we intended to see the Athenians as ruthless barbarians, or as doing what is necessary to survive in a dangerous, dog-eat-dog world?

Suggested textual analysis
Pages 198–200: beginning, "ATHENIANS: Hope encourages men to take risks;" and ending, "they would cross it to an island."

For Further Reflection

1. Should the Melians have accepted the Athenian offer?

2. Which is more important—freedom or survival? Is honor more important than life itself?

3. Is it prudent or impractical to remain a pacifist in a violent world?

4. Does the "natural law" that the strong always rule over the weak apply in a democracy?

5. Practically speaking, does the question of justice arise only between people of equal power?

6. Are the standards of justice for nations different than those for individuals? Among countries, if not in our personal relationships, does might make right?

7. Do you want your leaders to be motivated by the realpolitik of the Athenian generals, or by the sense of fair play and regard for justice argued for by the Melians?

Julius Caesar

William Shakespeare

WILLIAM SHAKESPEARE (1564–1616) was born in Stratford-upon-Avon, England. Although many details of Shakespeare's life are unknown or contested, we know that his father was a shopkeeper, glover, and prominent local citizen who served as alderman and bailiff for Stratford. William Shakespeare was educated only at the local grammar school, where he studied Latin and most likely read the plays of Terence and Plautus. It is unclear when and how Shakespeare went to London and began working in the theater, but by 1594 he had joined the Lord Chamberlain's Men acting company as an actor, playwright, and shareholder. *Julius Caesar* was probably first performed in the autumn of 1599. It represents a turning point in the dramatist's career, as Shakespeare moved away from English history and happy romantic comedy to embark upon his great tragedies.

Characters

Julius Caesar	
Octavius Caesar Mark Antony M. Aemilius Lepidus	triumvirs after the death of Julius Caesar
Cicero Publius Popilius Lena	senators
Marcus Brutus Cassius Casca Trebonius Caius Ligarius Decius Brutus Metellus Cimber Cinna	conspirators against Julius Caesar
Flavius and Marullus	tribunes
Artemidorus of Cnidos	a teacher of rhetoric
Soothsayer	
Cinna	a poet

Another POET

LUCILIUS TITINIUS MESSALA YOUNG CATO VOLUMNIUS FLAVIUS	officers under Brutus and Cassius
VARRO CLITUS CLAUDIUS DARDANIUS	soldiers in Brutus' army
STRATO LUCIUS	servants and slaves to Brutus
PINDARUS	servant and slave to Cassius
CALPURNIA	wife to Caesar
PORTIA	wife to Brutus
SENATORS, CITIZENS, GUARDS, ATTENDANTS, etc.	

[SCENE: *Rome; the neighborhood of Sardis; the neighborhood of Philippi.*]

Act I

[Scene I: *A street in Rome.*]

Enter Flavius, Marullus, *and certain* Commoners *over the stage.*

Flavius: Hence! Home, you idle creatures, get you home!
Is this a holiday? What, know you not,
Being mechanical,[1] you ought not walk
Upon a laboring day without the sign
Of your profession? Speak, what trade art thou?

Carpenter: Why, sir, a carpenter.

Marullus: Where is thy leather apron and thy rule?
What dost thou with thy best apparel on?
You, sir, what trade are you?

Cobbler: Truly, sir, in respect of a fine workman, I am but, as you would say, a cobbler.[2]

Marullus: But what trade art thou? Answer me directly.

Cobbler: A trade, sir, that I hope I may use with a safe conscience, which is indeed, sir, a mender of bad soles.

Flavius: What trade, thou knave? Thou naughty knave, what trade?

Cobbler: Nay, I beseech you, sir, be not out with me. Yet if you be out, sir, I can mend you.

Flavius: What mean'st thou by that? Mend me, thou saucy fellow?

Cobbler: Why, sir, cobble you.

---

1. [*mechanical:* workers.]
2. [*cobbler:* shoemaker, but also "bungler."]

FLAVIUS: Thou art a cobbler, art thou?

COBBLER: Truly, sir, all that I live by is with the awl. I meddle with no tradesman's matters, nor women's matters; but withal I am indeed, sir, a surgeon to old shoes. When they are in great danger, I recover them. As proper men as ever trod upon neat's leather have gone upon my handiwork.

FLAVIUS: But wherefore art not in thy shop today?
Why dost thou lead these men about the streets?

COBBLER: Truly, sir, to wear out their shoes, to get myself into more work. But indeed, sir, we make holiday to see Caesar and to rejoice in his triumph.

MARULLUS: Wherefore rejoice? What conquest brings he home?
What tributaries follow him to Rome,
To grace in captive bonds his chariot wheels?
You blocks, you stones, you worse than senseless things!
O you hard hearts, you cruel men of Rome,
Knew you not Pompey?[3] Many a time and oft
Have you climb'd up to walls and battlements,
To tow'rs and windows, yea, to chimney tops,
Your infants in your arms, and there have sat
The livelong day, with patient expectation,
To see great Pompey pass the streets of Rome.
And when you saw his chariot but appear,
Have you not made an universal shout,
That Tiber trembled underneath her banks
To hear the replication of your sounds
Made in her concave shores?
And do you now put on your best attire?
And do you now cull out a holiday?
And do you now strew flowers in his way
That comes in triumph over Pompey's blood?
Be gone!

3. [A great soldier and former triumvir; defeated by Caesar and later murdered.]

Run to your houses, fall upon your knees,
Pray to the gods to intermit the plague
That needs must light on this ingratitude.

FLAVIUS: Go, go, good countrymen, and, for this fault,
Assemble all the poor men of your sort;
Draw them to Tiber banks, and weep your tears
Into the channel, till the lowest stream
Do kiss the most exalted shores of all.

Exeunt all the COMMONERS.

See whe'er their basest mettle be not mov'd.
They vanish tongue-tied in their guiltiness.
Go you down that way towards the Capitol;
This way will I. Disrobe the images
If you do find them deck'd with ceremonies.

MARULLUS: May we do so?
You know it is the feast of Lupercal.

FLAVIUS: It is no matter. Let no images
Be hung with Caesar's trophies. I'll about,
And drive away the vulgar from the streets.
So do you too, where you perceive them thick.
These growing feathers pluck'd from Caesar's wing
Will make him fly an ordinary pitch,
Who else would soar above the view of men
And keep us all in servile fearfulness.

Exeunt.

[Scene II: *A public place.*]

Enter CAESAR; ANTONY, *for the course;* CALPURNIA, PORTIA, DECIUS, CICERO, BRUTUS, CASSIUS, CASCA, *a* SOOTHSAYER; *after them,* MARULLUS *and* FLAVIUS.

CAESAR: Calpurnia!

CASCA: Peace, ho! Caesar speaks.

CAESAR: Calpurnia!

CALPURNIA: Here, my lord.

CAESAR: Stand you directly in Antonius' way,
When he doth run his course. Antonius!

ANTONY: Caesar, my lord?

CAESAR: Forget not, in your speed, Antonius,
To touch Calpurnia; for our elders say,
The barren, touched in this holy chase,
Shake off their sterile curse.

ANTONY: I shall remember.
When Caesar says, "Do this," it is perform'd.

CAESAR: Set on, and leave no ceremony out.

[*Flourish.*]

SOOTHSAYER: Caesar!

CAESAR: Ha? Who calls?

CASCA: Bid every noise be still. Peace yet again!

[*Music ceases.*]

CAESAR: Who is it in the press that calls on me?
I hear a tongue, shriller than all the music,
Cry "Caesar!" Speak. Caesar is turn'd to hear.

SOOTHSAYER: Beware the ides of March.

CAESAR: What man is that?

BRUTUS: A soothsayer bids you beware the ides of March.

CAESAR: Set him before me; let me see his face.

CASSIUS: Fellow, come from the throng. [*The* SOOTHSAYER *comes forward.*] Look upon Caesar.

CAESAR: What say'st thou to me now? Speak once again.

SOOTHSAYER: Beware the ides of March.

CAESAR: He is a dreamer. Let us leave him. Pass.

Sennet. Exeunt. Mane[n]t BRUTUS *and* CASSIUS.

CASSIUS: Will you go see the order of the course?

BRUTUS: Not I.

CASSIUS: I pray you, do.

BRUTUS: I am not gamesome. I do lack some part
Of that quick spirit that is in Antony.
Let me not hinder, Cassius, your desires;
I'll leave you.

CASSIUS: Brutus, I do observe you now of late.
I have not from your eyes that gentleness
And show of love as I was wont to have.
You bear too stubborn and too strange a hand
Over your friend that loves you.

BRUTUS: Cassius,
Be not deceiv'd. If I have veil'd my look,
I turn the trouble of my countenance
Merely upon myself. Vexed I am
Of late with passions of some difference,
Conceptions only proper to myself,
Which give some soil, perhaps, to my behaviors.
But let not therefore my good friends be griev'd—
Among which number, Cassius, be you one—
Nor construe any further my neglect,
Than that poor Brutus, with himself at war,
Forgets the shows of love to other men.

CASSIUS: Then, Brutus, I have much mistook your passion,
By means whereof this breast of mine hath buried
Thoughts of great value, worthy cogitations.
Tell me, good Brutus, can you see your face?

BRUTUS: No, Cassius, for the eye sees not itself
But by reflection, by some other things.

CASSIUS: 'Tis just.
And it is very much lamented, Brutus,
That you have no such mirrors as will turn
Your hidden worthiness into your eye,
That you might see your shadow. I have heard
Where many of the best respect in Rome,
Except immortal Caesar, speaking of Brutus
And groaning underneath this age's yoke,
Have wish'd that noble Brutus had his eyes.

BRUTUS: Into what dangers would you lead me, Cassius,
That you would have me seek into myself
For that which is not in me?

CASSIUS: Therefore, good Brutus, be prepar'd to hear;
And since you know you cannot see yourself
So well as by reflection, I, your glass,
Will modestly discover to yourself
That of yourself which you yet know not of.
And be not jealous on[4] me, gentle Brutus.
Were I a common laughter,[5] or did use
To stale with ordinary oaths my love
To every new protester; if you know
That I do fawn on men and hug them hard
And after scandal them, or if you know
That I profess myself in banqueting
To all the rout, then hold me dangerous.

Flourish, and shout.

---

4. [*jealous on:* suspicious of.]

5. [*laughter:* object of ridicule.]

BRUTUS: What means this shouting? I do fear the people
Choose Caesar for their king.

CASSIUS: Ay, do you fear it?
Then must I think you would not have it so.

BRUTUS: I would not, Cassius, yet I love him well.
But wherefore do you hold me here so long?
What is it that you would impart to me?
If it be aught toward the general good,
Set honor in one eye and death i' th' other,
And I will look on both indifferently;
For let the gods so speed me as I love
The name of honor more than I fear death.

CASSIUS: I know that virtue to be in you, Brutus,
As well as I do know your outward favor.
Well, honor is the subject of my story.
I cannot tell what you and other men
Think of this life; but, for my single self,
I had as lief not be as live to be
In awe of such a thing as I myself.
I was born free as Caesar; so were you.
We both have fed as well, and we can both
Endure the winter's cold as well as he.
For once, upon a raw and gusty day,
The troubled Tiber chafing with her shores,
Caesar said to me, "Dar'st thou, Cassius, now
Leap in with me into this angry flood,
And swim to yonder point?" Upon the word,
Accoutred as I was, I plunged in
And bade him follow; so indeed he did.
The torrent roar'd, and we did buffet it,
With lusty sinews throwing it aside
And stemming it with hearts of controversy;
But ere we could arrive the point propos'd,

Caesar cried, "Help me, Cassius, or I sink!"
Ay, as Aeneas, our great ancestor,
Did from the flames of Troy upon his shoulder
The old Anchises bear, so from the waves of Tiber
Did I the tired Caesar. And this man
Is now become a god, and Cassius is
A wretched creature and must bend his body
If Caesar carelessly but nod on him.
He had a fever when he was in Spain,
And when the fit was on him, I did mark
How he did shake. 'Tis true, this god did shake.
His coward lips did from their color fly,
And that same eye whose bend doth awe the world
Did lose his luster. I did hear him groan.
Ay, and that tongue of his that bade the Romans
Mark him and write his speeches in their books,
"Alas," it cried, "give me some drink, Titinius,"
As a sick girl. Ye gods, it doth amaze me
A man of such a feeble temper should
So get the start of the majestic world
And bear the palm alone.

Shout. Flourish.

BRUTUS: Another general shout?
I do believe that these applauses are
For some new honors that are heap'd on Caesar.

CASSIUS: Why, man, he doth bestride the narrow world
Like a Colossus, and we petty men
Walk under his huge legs and peep about
To find ourselves dishonorable graves.
Men at some time are masters of their fates.
The fault, dear Brutus, is not in our stars,
But in ourselves, that we are underlings.
Brutus and Caesar. What should be in that "Caesar"?
Why should that name be sounded more than yours?

Write them together, yours is as fair a name;
Sound them, it doth become the mouth as well;
Weigh them, it is as heavy; conjure with 'em,
"Brutus" will start a spirit as soon as "Caesar."
Now, in the names of all the gods at once,
Upon what meat doth this our Caesar feed
That he is grown so great? Age, thou art sham'd!
Rome, thou hast lost the breed of noble bloods!
When went there by an age, since the great flood,
But it was fam'd with more than with one man?
When could they say, till now, that talk'd of Rome,
That her wide walks encompassed but one man?
Now is it Rome indeed and room enough,
When there is in it but one only man.
O, you and I have heard our fathers say
There was a Brutus[6] once that would have brook'd
Th' eternal devil to keep his state in Rome
As easily as a king.

BRUTUS: That you do love me, I am nothing jealous.
What you would work me to, I have some aim.
How I have thought of this, and of these times,
I shall recount hereafter. For this present,
I would not, so with love I might entreat you,
Be any further mov'd. What you have said
I will consider; what you have to say
I will with patience hear, and find a time
Both meet to hear and answer such high things.
Till then, my noble friend, chew upon this:
Brutus had rather be a villager
Than to repute himself a son of Rome
Under these hard conditions as this time
Is like to lay upon us.

---

6. [Lucius Junius Brutus, who expelled the Tarquins and founded the Roman Republic in 509 B.C.]

CASSIUS: I am glad that my weak words
Have struck but thus much show of fire from Brutus.

Enter CAESAR *and his* TRAIN.

BRUTUS: The games are done and Caesar is returning.

CASSIUS: As they pass by, pluck Casca by the sleeve,
And he will, after his sour fashion, tell you
What hath proceeded worthy note today.

BRUTUS: I will do so. But, look you, Cassius,
The angry spot doth glow on Caesar's brow,
And all the rest look like a chidden train.
Calpurnia's cheek is pale, and Cicero
Looks with such ferret and such fiery eyes
As we have seen him in the Capitol,
Being cross'd in conference by some senators.

CASSIUS: Casca will tell us what the matter is.

CAESAR: Antonius!

ANTONY: Caesar?

CAESAR: Let me have men about me that are fat,
Sleek-headed men, and such as sleep o' nights.
Yond Cassius has a lean and hungry look.
He thinks too much. Such men are dangerous.

ANTONY: Fear him not, Caesar; he's not dangerous.
He is a noble Roman, and well given.

CAESAR: Would he were fatter! But I fear him not.
Yet if my name were liable to fear,
I do not know the man I should avoid
So soon as that spare Cassius. He reads much,
He is a great observer, and he looks
Quite through the deeds of men. He loves no plays,
As thou dost, Antony; he hears no music.

Seldom he smiles, and smiles in such a sort
As if he mock'd himself and scorn'd his spirit
That could be mov'd to smile at anything.
Such men as he be never at heart's ease
Whiles they behold a greater than themselves,
And therefore are they very dangerous.
I rather tell thee what is to be fear'd
Than what I fear; for always I am Caesar.
Come on my right hand, for this ear is deaf,
And tell me truly what thou think'st of him.

Sennet. Exeunt CAESAR *and his* TRAIN. [*Manet* CASCA.]

CASCA: You pull'd me by the cloak. Would you speak with me?

BRUTUS: Ay, Casca. Tell us what hath chanc'd today,
That Caesar looks so sad.

CASCA: Why, you were with him, were you not?

BRUTUS: I should not then ask Casca what had chanc'd.

CASCA: Why, there was a crown offer'd him, and being offer'd him, he put it by with the back of his hand, thus; and then the people fell a-shouting.

BRUTUS: What was the second noise for?

CASCA: Why, for that too.

CASSIUS: They shouted thrice. What was the last cry for?

CASCA: Why, for that too.

BRUTUS: Was the crown offer'd him thrice?

CASCA: Ay, marry, was't, and he put it by thrice, every time gentler than other, and at every putting-by mine honest neighbors shouted.

CASSIUS: Who offer'd him the crown?

CASCA: Why, Antony.

BRUTUS: Tell us the manner of it, gentle Casca.

CASCA: I can as well be hang'd as tell the manner of it. It was mere foolery; I did not mark it. I saw Mark Antony offer him a crown—yet 'twas not a crown neither, 'twas one of these coronets[7]—and, as I told you, he put it by once; but, for all that, to my thinking, he would fain have had it. Then he offer'd it to him again; then he put it by again; but, to my thinking, he was very loath to lay his fingers off it. And then he offer'd it the third time. He put it the third time by, and still as he refus'd it, the rabblement hooted and clapp'd their chopp'd hands, and threw up their sweaty nightcaps, and utter'd such a deal of stinking breath because Caesar refus'd the crown that it had almost chok'd Caesar, for he swounded and fell down at it. And for mine own part I durst not laugh, for fear of opening my lips and receiving the bad air.

CASSIUS: But, soft, I pray you. What, did Caesar swoon?

CASCA: He fell down in the marketplace, and foam'd at mouth, and was speechless.

BRUTUS: 'Tis very like. He hath the falling sickness.[8]

CASSIUS: No, Caesar hath it not, but you and I,
And honest Casca, we have the falling sickness.

CASCA: I know not what you mean by that, but I am sure Caesar fell down. If the tag-rag people did not clap him and hiss him, according as he pleas'd and displeas'd them, as they use to do the players in the theatre, I am no true man.

BRUTUS: What said he when he came unto himself?

CASCA: Marry, before he fell down, when he perceiv'd the com-

7. [*coronets:* garlands.]

8. [*falling sickness:* epilepsy.]

mon herd was glad he refus'd the crown, he pluck'd me ope his doublet and offer'd them his throat to cut. An I had been a man of any occupation, if I would not have taken him at a word, I would I might go to hell among the rogues. And so he fell. When he came to himself again, he said, if he had done or said anything amiss, he desir'd their worships to think it was his infirmity. Three or four wenches, where I stood, cried, "Alas, good soul!" and forgave him with all their hearts. But there's no heed to be taken of them. If Caesar had stabb'd their mothers, they would have done no less.

BRUTUS: And after that, he came thus sad away?

CASCA: Ay.

CASSIUS: Did Cicero say anything?

CASCA: Ay, he spoke Greek.

CASSIUS: To what effect?

CASCA: Nay, an I tell you that, I'll ne'er look you i' th' face again. But those that understood him smil'd at one another and shook their heads; but, for mine own part, it was Greek to me. I could tell you more news too. Marullus and Flavius, for pulling scarfs off Caesar's images, are put to silence.[9] Fare you well. There was more foolery yet, if I could remember it.

CASSIUS: Will you sup with me tonight, Casca?

CASCA: No, I am promis'd forth.

CASSIUS: Will you dine with me tomorrow?

CASCA: Ay, if I be alive, and your mind hold, and your dinner worth the eating.

9. [*put to silence:* dismissed from office.]

CASSIUS: Good. I will expect you.

CASCA: Do so. Farewell, both.

Exit.

BRUTUS: What a blunt fellow is this grown to be!
He was quick mettle when he went to school.

CASSIUS: So is he now in execution
Of any bold or noble enterprise,
However he puts on this tardy form.
This rudeness is a sauce to his good wit,
Which gives men stomach to disgest his words
With better appetite.

BRUTUS: And so it is. For this time I will leave you.
Tomorrow, if you please to speak with me,
I will come home to you; or, if you will,
Come home to me, and I will wait for you.

CASSIUS: I will do so. Till then, think of the world.

Exit BRUTUS.

Well, Brutus, thou art noble. Yet I see
Thy honorable mettle may be wrought
From that it is dispos'd. Therefore it is meet
That noble minds keep ever with their likes;
For who so firm that cannot be seduc'd?
Caesar doth bear me hard, but he loves Brutus.
If I were Brutus now and he were Cassius,
He should not humor me. I will this night,
In several hands, in at his windows, throw,
As if they came from several citizens,
Writings, all tending to the great opinion
That Rome holds of his name, wherein obscurely
Caesar's ambition shall be glanced at.

And after this let Caesar seat him sure,
For we will shake him, or worse days endure.

Exit.

[SCENE III: *A street.*]

Thunder and lightning. Enter[*, meeting,*] CASCA [*with his sword drawn*] *and* CICERO.

CICERO: Good even, Casca. Brought you Caesar home?
Why are you breathless? And why stare you so?

CASCA: Are not you mov'd, when all the sway of earth
Shakes like a thing unfirm? O Cicero,
I have seen tempests when the scolding winds
Have riv'd the knotty oaks, and I have seen
Th' ambitious ocean swell and rage and foam
To be exalted with the threat'ning clouds;
But never till tonight, never till now,
Did I go through a tempest dropping fire.
Either there is a civil strife in heaven,
Or else the world, too saucy with the gods,
Incenses them to send destruction.

CICERO: Why, saw you anything more wonderful?

CASCA: A common slave—you know him well by sight—
Held up his left hand, which did flame and burn
Like twenty torches join'd, and yet his hand,
Not sensible of fire, remain'd unscorch'd.
Besides—I ha' not since put up my sword—
Against the Capitol I met a lion,
Who glaz'd upon me, and went surly by
Without annoying me. And there were drawn
Upon a heap a hundred ghastly women,
Transformed with their fear, who swore they saw
Men, all in fire, walk up and down the streets.

And yesterday the bird of night did sit
Even at noonday upon the marketplace,
Hooting and shrieking. When these prodigies
Do so conjointly meet, let not men say
"These are their reasons, they are natural,"
For I believe they are portentous things
Unto the climate that they point upon.

CICERO: Indeed, it is a strange-disposed time.
But men may construe things after their fashion,
Clean from the purpose of the things themselves.
Comes Caesar to the Capitol tomorrow?

CASCA: He doth; for he did bid Antonius
Send word to you he would be there tomorrow.

CICERO: Good night then, Casca. This disturbed sky
Is not to walk in.

CASCA: Farewell, Cicero.

Exit CICERO.

Enter CASSIUS.

CASSIUS: Who's there?

CASCA: A Roman.

CASSIUS: Casca, by your voice.

CASCA: Your ear is good. Cassius, what night is this!

CASSIUS: A very pleasing night to honest men.

CASCA: Who ever knew the heavens menace so?

CASSIUS: Those that have known the earth so full of faults.
For my part, I have walk'd about the streets,
Submitting me unto the perilous night,
And, thus unbraced, Casca, as you see,
Have bar'd my bosom to the thunder-stone;

And when the cross blue lightning seem'd to open
The breast of heaven, I did present myself
Even in the aim and very flash of it.

CASCA: But wherefore did you so much tempt the heavens?
It is the part of men to fear and tremble,
When the most mighty gods by tokens send
Such dreadful heralds to astonish us.

CASSIUS: You are dull, Casca, and those sparks of life
That should be in a Roman you do want,
Or else you use not. You look pale, and gaze,
And put on fear, and cast yourself in wonder,
To see the strange impatience of the heavens.
But if you would consider the true cause
Why all these fires, why all these gliding ghosts,
Why birds and beasts from quality and kind,
Why old men, fools, and children calculate,
Why all these things change from their ordinance,
Their natures, and preformed faculties,
To monstrous quality—why, you shall find
That heaven hath infus'd them with these spirits
To make them instruments of fear and warning
Unto some monstrous state.
Now could I, Casca, name to thee a man
Most like this dreadful night,
That thunders, lightens, opens graves, and roars
As doth the lion in the Capitol—
A man no mightier than thyself or me
In personal action, yet prodigious grown
And fearful, as these strange eruptions are.

CASCA: 'Tis Caesar that you mean, is it not, Cassius?

CASSIUS: Let it be who it is. For Romans now
Have thews and limbs like to their ancestors;
But, woe the while, our fathers' minds are dead,

And we are govern'd with our mothers' spirits.
Our yoke and sufferance show us womanish.

CASCA: Indeed, they say the senators tomorrow
Mean to establish Caesar as a king,
And he shall wear his crown by sea and land,
In every place, save here in Italy.

CASSIUS: I know where I will wear this dagger then;
Cassius from bondage will deliver Cassius.
Therein, ye gods, you make the weak most strong;
Therein, ye gods, you tyrants do defeat.
Nor stony tower, nor walls of beaten brass,
Nor airless dungeon, nor strong links of iron,
Can be retentive to the strength of spirit;
But life, being weary of these worldly bars,
Never lacks power to dismiss itself.
If I know this, know all the world besides,
That part of tyranny that I do bear
I can shake off at pleasure.

Thunder still.

CASCA: So can I.
So every bondman in his own hand bears
The power to cancel his captivity.

CASSIUS: And why should Caesar be a tyrant then?
Poor man, I know he would not be a wolf,
But that he sees the Romans are but sheep;
He were no lion, were not Romans hinds.
Those that with haste will make a mighty fire
Begin it with weak straws. What trash is Rome,
What rubbish and what offal, when it serves
For the base matter to illuminate
So vile a thing as Caesar! But, O grief,
Where hast thou led me? I perhaps speak this
Before a willing bondman; then I know

My answer must be made. But I am arm'd,
And dangers are to me indifferent.

CASCA: You speak to Casca, and to such a man
That is no fleering telltale. Hold, my hand.
Be factious for redress of all these griefs,
And I will set this foot of mine as far
As who goes farthest.

[*They shake hands.*]

CASSIUS: There's a bargain made.
Now know you, Casca, I have mov'd already
Some certain of the noblest-minded Romans
To undergo with me an enterprise
Of honorable-dangerous consequence;
And I do know, by this, they stay for me
In Pompey's porch. For now, this fearful night,
There is no stir or walking in the streets,
And the complexion of the element
In favor's like the work we have in hand,
Most bloody, fiery, and most terrible.

Enter CINNA.

CASCA: Stand close awhile, for here comes one in haste.

CASSIUS: 'Tis Cinna; I do know him by his gait.
He is a friend.—Cinna, where haste you so?

CINNA: To find out you. Who's that? Metellus Cimber?

CASSIUS: No, it is Casca; one incorporate
To our attempts. Am I not stay'd for, Cinna?

CINNA: I am glad on't. What a fearful night is this!
There's two or three of us have seen strange sights.

CASSIUS: Am I not stay'd for? Tell me.

CINNA: Yes, you are. O Cassius, if you could
But win the noble Brutus to our party—

CASSIUS: Be you content. Good Cinna, take this paper,

[*Gives papers.*]

And look you lay it in the praetor's chair,[10]
Where Brutus may but find it. And throw this
In at his window. Set this up with wax
Upon old Brutus' statue. All this done,
Repair to Pompey's porch, where you shall find us.
Is Decius Brutus and Trebonius there?

CINNA: All but Metellus Cimber; and he's gone
To seek you at your house. Well, I will hie,
And so bestow these papers as you bade me.

CASSIUS: That done, repair to Pompey's theatre.

Exit CINNA.

Come, Casca, you and I will yet ere day
See Brutus at his house. Three parts of him
Is ours already, and the man entire
Upon the next encounter yields him ours.

CASCA: O, he sits high in all the people's hearts;
And that which would appear offense in us,
His countenance, like richest alchemy,
Will change to virtue and to worthiness.

CASSIUS: Him and his worth, and our great need of him,
You have right well conceited.[11] Let us go,
For it is after midnight; and ere day
We will awake him and be sure of him.

Exeunt.

10. [*praetor's chair:* official seat of the highest-ranking judicial magistrate, at that time Brutus.]

11. [*conceited:* conceived.]

Act II

[Scene I: *Brutus' garden (orchard).*]

Enter Brutus *in his orchard.*

Brutus: What, Lucius, ho!
I cannot, by the progress of the stars,
Give guess how near to day. Lucius, I say!
I would it were my fault to sleep so soundly.
When, Lucius, when? Awake, I say! What, Lucius!

Enter Lucius.

Lucius: Call'd you, my lord?

Brutus: Get me a taper in my study, Lucius.
When it is lighted, come and call me here.

Lucius: I will, my lord.

Exit.

Brutus: It must be by his death. And, for my part,
I know no personal cause to spurn at him,
But for the general. He would be crown'd.
How that might change his nature, there's the question.
It is the bright day that brings forth the adder,
And that craves wary walking. Crown him that,
And then I grant we put a sting in him
That at his will he may do danger with.
Th' abuse of greatness is when it disjoins
Remorse from power. And, to speak truth of Caesar,
I have not known when his affections sway'd
More than his reason. But 'tis a common proof
That lowliness[12] is young ambition's ladder,
Whereto the climber-upward turns his face;
But when he once attains the upmost round,

12. [*lowliness:* affected humility.]

He then unto the ladder turns his back,
Looks in the clouds, scorning the base degrees
By which he did ascend. So Caesar may.
Then, lest he may, prevent. And, since the quarrel
Will bear no color for the thing he is,
Fashion it thus: that what he is, augmented,
Would run to these and these extremities.
And therefore think him as a serpent's egg
Which, hatch'd, would, as his kind, grow mischievous,
And kill him in the shell.

Enter LUCIUS.

LUCIUS: The taper burneth in your closet, sir.
Searching the window for a flint, I found
This paper, thus seal'd up, and I am sure
It did not lie there when I went to bed.

Gives him the letter.

BRUTUS: Get you to bed again. It is not day.
Is not tomorrow, boy, the ides of March?

LUCIUS: I know not, sir.

BRUTUS: Look in the calendar, and bring me word.

LUCIUS: I will, sir.

Exit.

BRUTUS: The exhalations whizzing in the air
Give so much light that I may read by them.

Opens the letter and reads.

"Brutus, thou sleep'st; awake, and see thyself!
Shall Rome, etc. Speak, strike, redress!
Brutus, thou sleep'st; awake!"
Such instigations have been often dropp'd

Where I have took them up.
"Shall Rome, etc." Thus must I piece it out:
Shall Rome stand under one man's awe? What, Rome?
My ancestors did from the streets of Rome
The Tarquin drive, when he was call'd a king.
"Speak, strike, redress!" Am I entreated
To speak and strike? O Rome, I make thee promise,
If the redress will follow, thou receivest
Thy full petition at the hand of Brutus!

Enter LUCIUS.

LUCIUS: Sir, March is wasted fifteen days.

Knock within.

BRUTUS: 'Tis good. Go to the gate; somebody knocks.

[*Exit* LUCIUS.]

Since Cassius first did whet me against Caesar,
I have not slept.
Between the acting of a dreadful thing
And the first motion, all the interim is
Like a phantasma, or a hideous dream.
The Genius and the mortal instruments[13]
Are then in council; and the state of man,
Like to a little kingdom, suffers then
The nature of an insurrection.

Enter LUCIUS.

LUCIUS: Sir, 'tis your brother Cassius at the door,
Who doth desire to see you.

BRUTUS: Is he alone?

LUCIUS: No, sir, there are moe with him.

13. [*Genius and the mortal instruments:* one's spirit and one's intellectual and emotional faculties.]

BRUTUS: Do you know them?

LUCIUS: No, sir; their hats are pluck'd about their ears,
And half their faces buried in their cloaks,
That by no means I may discover them
By any mark of favor.

BRUTUS: Let 'em enter.

[*Exit* LUCIUS.]

They are the faction. O conspiracy,
Sham'st thou to show thy dang'rous brow by night,
When evils are most free? O, then by day
Where wilt thou find a cavern dark enough
To mask thy monstrous visage? Seek none, conspiracy!
Hide it in smiles and affability;
For if thou path, thy native semblance on,
Not Erebus itself were dim enough
To hide thee from prevention.

Enter the conspirators, CASSIUS, CASCA, DECIUS,
CINNA, METELLUS [CIMBER], *and* TREBONIUS.

CASSIUS: I think we are too bold upon your rest.
Good morrow, Brutus. Do we trouble you?

BRUTUS: I have been up this hour, awake all night.
Know I these men that come along with you?

CASSIUS: Yes, every man of them, and no man here
But honors you; and every one doth wish
You had but that opinion of yourself
Which every noble Roman bears of you.
This is Trebonius.

BRUTUS: He is welcome hither.

CASSIUS: This, Decius Brutus.

BRUTUS: He is welcome too.

CASSIUS: This, Casca; this, Cinna; and this, Metellus Cimber.

BRUTUS: They are all welcome.
What watchful cares do interpose themselves
Betwixt your eyes and night?

CASSIUS: Shall I entreat a word?

They [BRUTUS *and* CASSIUS] *whisper.*

DECIUS: Here lies the east. Doth not the day break here?

CASCA: No.

CINNA: O, pardon, sir, it doth; and yon gray lines
That fret the clouds are messengers of day.

CASCA: You shall confess that you are both deceiv'd.
Here, as I point my sword, the sun arises,
Which is a great way growing on the south,
Weighing the youthful season of the year.
Some two months hence, up higher toward the north
He first presents his fire; and the high east
Stands, as the Capitol, directly here.

BRUTUS: Give me your hands all over, one by one.

CASSIUS: And let us swear our resolution.

BRUTUS: No, not an oath. If not the face of men,
The sufferance of our souls, the time's abuse—
If these be motives weak, break off betimes,
And every man hence to his idle bed;
So let high-sighted[14] tyranny range on,
Till each man drop by lottery. But if these,
As I am sure they do, bear fire enough
To kindle cowards and to steel with valor

---

14. [*high-sighted:* arrogant.]

The melting spirits of women, then, countrymen,
What need we any spur but our own cause
To prick us to redress? What other bond
Than secret Romans, that have spoke the word,
And will not palter? And what other oath
Than honesty to honesty engag'd
That this shall be, or we will fall for it?
Swear priests and cowards, and men cautelous,[15]
Old feeble carrions, and such suffering souls
That welcome wrongs; unto bad causes swear
Such creatures as men doubt; but do not stain
The even virtue of our enterprise,
Nor th' insuppressive mettle of our spirits,
To think that or our cause or our performance
Did need an oath; when every drop of blood
That every Roman bears, and nobly bears,
Is guilty of a several bastardy
If he do break the smallest particle
Of any promise that hath pass'd from him.

CASSIUS: But what of Cicero? Shall we sound him?
I think he will stand very strong with us.

CASCA: Let us not leave him out.

CINNA: No, by no means.

METELLUS: O, let us have him, for his silver hairs
Will purchase us a good opinion
And buy men's voices to commend our deeds.
It shall be said his judgment rul'd our hands;
Our youths and wildness shall no whit appear,
But all be buried in his gravity.

BRUTUS: O, name him not. Let us not break with him;
For he will never follow anything
That other men begin.

15. [*cautelous:* deceitful.]

CASSIUS: Then leave him out.

CASCA: Indeed he is not fit.

DECIUS: Shall no man else be touch'd but only Caesar?

CASSIUS: Decius, well urg'd. I think it is not meet
Mark Antony, so well belov'd of Caesar,
Should outlive Caesar. We shall find of him
A shrewd contriver; and you know, his means,
If he improve them, may well stretch so far
As to annoy us all. Which to prevent,
Let Antony and Caesar fall together.

BRUTUS: Our course will seem too bloody, Caius Cassius,
To cut the head off and then hack the limbs,
Like wrath in death and envy afterwards;
For Antony is but a limb of Caesar.
Let's be sacrificers, but not butchers, Caius.
We all stand up against the spirit of Caesar,
And in the spirit of men there is no blood.
O, that we then could come by Caesar's spirit,
And not dismember Caesar! But, alas,
Caesar must bleed for it. And, gentle friends,
Let's kill him boldly, but not wrathfully;
Let's carve him as a dish fit for the gods,
Not hew him as a carcass fit for hounds.
And let our hearts, as subtle masters do,
Stir up their servants to an act of rage,
And after seem to chide 'em. This shall make
Our purpose necessary, and not envious;
Which so appearing to the common eyes,
We shall be call'd purgers, not murderers.
And for Mark Antony, think not of him;
For he can do no more than Caesar's arm
When Caesar's head is off.

CASSIUS: Yet I fear him,
For in the ingrafted love he bears to Caesar—

BRUTUS: Alas, good Cassius, do not think of him.
If he love Caesar, all that he can do
Is to himself—take thought and die for Caesar.
And that were much he should, for he is given
To sports, to wildness, and much company.

TREBONIUS: There is no fear in him. Let him not die,
For he will live, and laugh at this hereafter.

Clock strikes.

BRUTUS: Peace! Count the clock.

CASSIUS: The clock hath stricken three.

TREBONIUS: 'Tis time to part.

CASSIUS: But it is doubtful yet
Whether Caesar will come forth today, or no;
For he is superstitious grown of late,
Quite from the main opinion he held once
Of fantasy, of dreams, and ceremonies.
It may be these apparent prodigies,
The unaccustomed terror of this night,
And the persuasion of his augurers
May hold him from the Capitol today.

DECIUS: Never fear that. If he be so resolv'd,
I can o'ersway him; for he loves to hear
That unicorns may be betray'd with trees,
And bears with glasses, elephants with holes,
Lions with toils, and men with flatterers;
But when I tell him he hates flatterers,
He says he does, being then most flattered.
Let me work;
For I can give his humor the true bent,
And I will bring him to the Capitol.

CASSIUS: Nay, we will all of us be there to fetch him.

BRUTUS: By the eighth hour. Is that the uttermost?

CINNA: Be that the uttermost, and fail not then.

METELLUS: Caius Ligarius doth bear Caesar hard,
Who rated him for speaking well of Pompey.
I wonder none of you have thought of him.

BRUTUS: Now, good Metellus, go along by him.
He loves me well, and I have given him reasons;
Send him but hither, and I'll fashion him.

CASSIUS: The morning comes upon's. We'll leave you, Brutus.
And, friends, disperse yourselves; but all remember
What you have said, and show yourselves true Romans.

BRUTUS: Good gentlemen, look fresh and merrily;
Let not our looks put on our purposes,
But bear it as our Roman actors do,
With untir'd spirits and formal constancy.
And so good morrow to you every one.

Exeunt. Manet BRUTUS.

Boy! Lucius! Fast asleep? It is no matter.
Enjoy the honey-heavy dew of slumber.
Thou hast no figures nor no fantasies
Which busy care draws in the brains of men;
Therefore thou sleep'st so sound.

Enter PORTIA.

PORTIA: Brutus, my lord!

BRUTUS: Portia, what mean you? Wherefore rise you now?
It is not for your health thus to commit
Your weak condition to the raw cold morning.

PORTIA: Nor for yours neither. Y' have ungently, Brutus,
Stole from my bed. And yesternight, at supper,

You suddenly arose, and walk'd about,
Musing and sighing, with your arms across,
And when I ask'd you what the matter was,
You star'd upon me with ungentle looks.
I urg'd you further; then you scratch'd your head,
And too impatiently stamp'd with your foot.
Yet I insisted, yet you answer'd not,
But, with an angry wafture of your hand,
Gave sign for me to leave you. So I did,
Fearing to strengthen that impatience
Which seem'd too much enkindled, and withal
Hoping it was but an effect of humor,
Which sometime hath his hour with every man.
It will not let you eat, nor talk, nor sleep,
And could it work so much upon your shape
As it hath much prevailed on your condition,
I should not know you Brutus. Dear my lord,
Make me acquainted with your cause of grief.

BRUTUS: I am not well in health, and that is all.

PORTIA: Brutus is wise, and, were he not in health
He would embrace the means to come by it.

BRUTUS: Why, so I do. Good Portia, go to bed.

PORTIA: Is Brutus sick? And is it physical
To walk unbraced and suck up the humors
Of the dank morning? What, is Brutus sick,
And will he steal out of his wholesome bed
To dare the vile contagion of the night,
And tempt the rheumy and unpurged air
To add unto his sickness? No, my Brutus,
You have some sick offense within your mind,
Which by the right and virtue of my place [*Kneels.*]
I ought to know of. And, upon my knees,
I charm you, by my once-commended beauty,
By all your vows of love, and that great vow

Which did incorporate and make us one,
That you unfold to me, your self, your half,
Why you are heavy, and what men tonight
Have had resort to you; for here have been
Some six or seven, who did hide their faces
Even from darkness.

BRUTUS: Kneel not, gentle Portia.

[*Raises her.*]

PORTIA: I should not need, if you were gentle Brutus.
Within the bond of marriage, tell me, Brutus,
Is it excepted I should know no secrets
That appertain to you? Am I yourself
But, as it were, in sort or limitation,
To keep with you at meals, comfort your bed,
And talk to you sometimes? Dwell I but in the suburbs
Of your good pleasure? If it be no more,
Portia is Brutus' harlot, not his wife.

BRUTUS: You are my true and honorable wife,
As dear to me as are the ruddy drops
That visit my sad heart.

PORTIA: If this were true, then should I know this secret.
I grant I am a woman, but withal
A woman that Lord Brutus took to wife.
I grant I am a woman, but withal
A woman well-reputed, Cato's[16] daughter.
Think you I am no stronger than my sex,
Being so father'd and so husbanded?
Tell me your counsels, I will not disclose 'em.
I have made strong proof of my constancy,
Giving myself a voluntary wound

16. [Cato of Utica, famous for his integrity, fought with Pompey against Caesar and committed suicide to avoid submission to Caesar; he was Brutus' uncle as well as his father-in-law.]

Here, in the thigh. Can I bear that with patience,
And not my husband's secrets?

BRUTUS: O ye gods,
Render me worthy of this noble wife!

Knock [*within*].

Hark, hark! One knocks. Portia, go in awhile,
And by and by thy bosom shall partake
The secrets of my heart.
All my engagements I will construe to thee,
All the charactery of my sad brows.
Leave me with haste.

Exit PORTIA.

Lucius, who's that knocks?

Enter LUCIUS *and* [CAIUS] LIGARIUS [*wearing a kerchief*].

LUCIUS: Here is a sick man that would speak with you.

BRUTUS: Caius Ligarius, that Metellus spake of.
Boy, stand aside.

[*Exit* LUCIUS.]

Caius Ligarius, how?

LIGARIUS: Vouchsafe good morrow from a feeble tongue.

BRUTUS: O, what a time have you chose out, brave Caius,
To wear a kerchief! Would you were not sick!

LIGARIUS: I am not sick, if Brutus have in hand
Any exploit worthy the name of honor.

BRUTUS: Such an exploit have I in hand, Ligarius,
Had you a healthful ear to hear of it.

LIGARIUS: By all the gods that Romans bow before,
I here discard my sickness! Soul of Rome!

[*Throws off his kerchief.*]

Brave son, deriv'd from honorable loins!
Thou, like an exorcist, hast conjur'd up
My mortified spirit. Now bid me run,
And I will strive with things impossible,
Yea, get the better of them. What's to do?

BRUTUS: A piece of work that will make sick men whole.

LIGARIUS: But are not some whole that we must make sick?

BRUTUS: That must we also. What it is, my Caius,
I shall unfold to thee as we are going
To whom it must be done.

LIGARIUS: Set on your foot,
And with a heart new-fir'd I follow you,
To do I know not what; but it sufficeth
That Brutus leads me on.

Thunder.

BRUTUS: Follow me, then.

Exeunt.

[SCENE II: *Caesar's house.*]

Thunder and lightning. Enter JULIUS CAESAR, *in his nightgown.*

CAESAR: Nor heaven nor earth have been at peace tonight.
Thrice hath Calpurnia in her sleep cried out,
"Help, ho, they murder Caesar!" Who's within?

Enter a SERVANT.

SERVANT: My lord?

CAESAR: Go bid the priests do present sacrifice
And bring me their opinions of success.

SERVANT: I will, my lord.

Exit.

Enter CALPURNIA.

CALPURNIA: What mean you, Caesar? Think you to walk forth?
You shall not stir out of your house today.

CAESAR: Caesar shall forth. The things that threaten'd me
Ne'er look'd but on my back. When they shall see
The face of Caesar, they are vanished.

CALPURNIA: Caesar, I never stood on ceremonies,[17]
Yet now they fright me. There is one within,
Besides the things that we have heard and seen,
Recounts most horrid sights seen by the watch.
A lioness hath whelped in the streets,
And graves have yawn'd and yielded up their dead;
Fierce fiery warriors fight upon the clouds,
In ranks and squadrons and right form of war,
Which drizzled blood upon the Capitol;
The noise of battle hurtled in the air,
Horses did neigh, and dying men did groan,
And ghosts did shriek and squeal about the streets.
O Caesar, these things are beyond all use,
And I do fear them.

CAESAR: What can be avoided
Whose end is purpos'd by the mighty gods?
Yet Caesar shall go forth; for these predictions
Are to the world in general as to Caesar.

CALPURNIA: When beggars die, there are no comets seen;
The heavens themselves blaze forth the death of princes.

CAESAR: Cowards die many times before their deaths;
The valiant never taste of death but once.

17. [*stood on ceremonies:* heeded omens.]

Of all the wonders that I yet have heard,
It seems to me most strange that men should fear,
Seeing that death, a necessary end,
Will come when it will come.

Enter a SERVANT.

What say the augurers?

SERVANT: They would not have you to stir forth today.
Plucking the entrails of an offering forth,
They could not find a heart within the beast.

CAESAR: The gods do this in shame of cowardice.
Caesar should be a beast without a heart,
If he should stay at home today for fear.
No, Caesar shall not. Danger knows full well
That Caesar is more dangerous than he.
We are two lions litter'd in one day,
And I the elder and more terrible;
And Caesar shall go forth.

CALPURNIA: Alas, my lord,
Your wisdom is consum'd in confidence.
Do not go forth today! Call it my fear
That keeps you in the house, and not your own.
We'll send Mark Antony to the Senate-house,
And he shall say you are not well today.
Let me, upon my knee, prevail in this.

[*Kneels.*]

CAESAR: Mark Antony shall say I am not well,
And for thy humor I will stay at home.

Enter DECIUS.

Here's Decius Brutus. He shall tell them so.

DECIUS: Caesar, all hail! Good morrow, worthy Caesar.
I come to fetch you to the Senate-house.

CAESAR: And you are come in very happy time
To bear my greeting to the senators
And tell them that I will not come today.
Cannot, is false, and that I dare not, falser;
I will not come today. Tell them so, Decius.

CALPURNIA: Say he is sick.

CAESAR: Shall Caesar send a lie?
Have I in conquest stretch'd mine arm so far,
To be afeard to tell graybeards the truth?
Decius, go tell them Caesar will not come.

DECIUS: Most mighty Caesar, let me know some cause,
Lest I be laugh'd at when I tell them so.

CAESAR: The cause is in my will. I will not come;
That is enough to satisfy the Senate.
But for your private satisfaction,
Because I love you, I will let you know.
Calpurnia here, my wife, stays me at home.
She dreamt tonight she saw my statue,
Which, like a fountain with an hundred spouts,
Did run pure blood; and many lusty Romans
Came smiling, and did bathe their hands in it.
And these does she apply for warnings and portents
And evils imminent, and on her knee
Hath begg'd that I will stay at home today.

DECIUS: This dream is all amiss interpreted;
It was a vision fair and fortunate.
Your statue spouting blood in many pipes,
In which so many smiling Romans bath'd,
Signifies that from you great Rome shall suck
Reviving blood, and that great men shall press
For tinctures, stains, relics, and cognizance.
This by Calpurnia's dream is signified.

CAESAR: And this way have you well expounded it.

DECIUS: I have, when you have heard what I can say;
And know it now. The Senate have concluded
To give this day a crown to mighty Caesar.
If you shall send them word you will not come,
Their minds may change. Besides, it were a mock
Apt to be render'd, for some one to say,
"Break up the Senate till another time
When Caesar's wife shall meet with better dreams."
If Caesar hide himself, shall they not whisper
"Lo, Caesar is afraid"?
Pardon me, Caesar, for my dear dear love
To your proceeding bids me tell you this;
And reason to my love is liable.

CAESAR: How foolish do your fears seem now, Calpurnia!
I am ashamed I did yield to them.
Give me my robe, for I will go.

Enter BRUTUS, LIGARIUS, METELLUS, CASCA,
TREBONIUS, CINNA, *and* PUBLIUS.

And look where Publius is come to fetch me.

PUBLIUS: Good morrow, Caesar.

CAESAR: Welcome, Publius.
What, Brutus, are you stirr'd so early too?
Good morrow, Casca. Caius Ligarius,
Caesar was ne'er so much your enemy
As that same ague which hath made you lean.
What is't o'clock?

BRUTUS: Caesar, 'tis strucken eight.

CAESAR: I thank you for your pains and courtesy.

Enter ANTONY.

See, Antony, that revels long o' nights,
Is notwithstanding up. Good morrow, Antony.

ANTONY: So to most noble Caesar.

CAESAR: Bid them prepare within.
I am to blame to be thus waited for.
Now, Cinna. Now, Metellus. What, Trebonius!
I have an hour's talk in store for you;
Remember that you call on me today.
Be near me, that I may remember you.

TREBONIUS: Caesar, I will. [*Aside.*] And so near will I be
That your best friends shall wish I had been further.

CAESAR: Good friends, go in, and taste some wine with me,
And we, like friends, will straightway go together.

BRUTUS [*aside*]: That every like is not the same, O Caesar,
The heart of Brutus earns[18] to think upon!

Exeunt.

[SCENE III: *A street near the Capitol.*]

Enter ARTEMIDORUS [*reading a paper*].

ARTEMIDORUS: "Caesar, beware of Brutus; take heed of Cassius; come not near Casca; have an eye to Cinna; trust not Trebonius; mark well Metellus Cimber; Decius Brutus loves thee not; thou hast wrong'd Caius Ligarius. There is but one mind in all these men, and it is bent against Caesar. If thou beest not immortal, look about you. Security gives way to conspiracy. The mighty gods defend thee! Thy lover,[19]
Artemidorus."

18. [*earns:* grieves.]

19. [*lover:* dear friend.]

Here will I stand till Caesar pass along,
And as a suitor[20] will I give him this.
My heart laments that virtue cannot live
Out of the teeth of emulation.[21]
If thou read this, O Caesar, thou mayest live;
If not, the Fates with traitors do contrive.

Exit.

[SCENE IV: *Before the house of Brutus.*]

Enter PORTIA *and* LUCIUS.

PORTIA: I prithee, boy, run to the Senate-house.
Stay not to answer me, but get thee gone.
Why dost thou stay?

LUCIUS: To know my errand, madam.

PORTIA: I would have had thee there and here again
Ere I can tell thee what thou shouldst do there.—
[*Aside.*] O constancy, be strong upon my side,
Set a huge mountain 'tween my heart and tongue!
I have a man's mind, but a woman's might.
How hard it is for women to keep counsel!—
Art thou here yet?

LUCIUS: Madam, what should I do?
Run to the Capitol, and nothing else?
And so return to you, and nothing else?

PORTIA: Yes, bring me word, boy, if thy lord look well,
For he went sickly forth; and take good note
What Caesar doth, what suitors press to him.
Hark, boy, what noise is that?

20. [*suitor:* petitioner.]

21. [*emulation:* envious rivalry.]

LUCIUS: I hear none, madam.

PORTIA: Prithee, listen well.
I heard a bustling rumor, like a fray,
And the wind brings it from the Capitol.

LUCIUS: Sooth, madam, I hear nothing.

Enter the SOOTHSAYER.

PORTIA: Come hither, fellow. Which way hast thou been?

SOOTHSAYER: At mine own house, good lady.

PORTIA: What is't o'clock?

SOOTHSAYER: About the ninth hour, lady.

PORTIA: Is Caesar yet gone to the Capitol?

SOOTHSAYER: Madam, not yet. I go to take my stand,
To see him pass on to the Capitol.

PORTIA: Thou hast some suit to Caesar, hast thou not?

SOOTHSAYER: That I have, lady, if it will please Caesar
To be so good to Caesar as to hear me:
I shall beseech him to befriend himself.

PORTIA: Why, know'st thou any harm's intended towards him?

SOOTHSAYER: None that I know will be, much that I fear may chance.
Good morrow to you. Here the street is narrow.
The throng that follows Caesar at the heels,
Of senators, of praetors, common suitors,
Will crowd a feeble man almost to death.
I'll get me to a place more void, and there
Speak to great Caesar as he comes along.

Exit.

PORTIA: I must go in. Ay me, how weak a thing
The heart of woman is! O Brutus,
The heavens speed thee in thine enterprise!
Sure, the boy heard me.—Brutus hath a suit
That Caesar will not grant.—O, I grow faint.—
Run, Lucius, and commend me to my lord;
Say I am merry. Come to me again,
And bring me word what he doth say to thee.

Exeunt [*severally*].

ACT III

[SCENE I: *Before the Capitol.*]

Flourish. Enter CAESAR, BRUTUS, CASSIUS, CASCA, DECIUS, METELLUS [CIMBER], TREBONIUS, CINNA, ANTONY, LEPIDUS, ARTEMIDORUS, PUBLIUS, [POPILIUS,] *and the* SOOTHSAYER.

CAESAR [*to the* SOOTHSAYER]: The ides of March are come.

SOOTHSAYER: Ay, Caesar, but not gone.

ARTEMIDORUS: Hail, Caesar! Read this schedule.

DECIUS: Trebonius doth desire you to o'er-read,
At your best leisure, this his humble suit.

ARTEMIDORUS: O Caesar, read mine first, for mine's a suit
That touches Caesar nearer. Read it, great Caesar.

CAESAR: What touches us ourself shall be last serv'd.

ARTEMIDORUS: Delay not, Caesar, read it instantly.

CAESAR: What, is the fellow mad?

PUBLIUS: Sirrah, give place.

CASSIUS: What, urge you your petitions in the street?
Come to the Capitol.

[CAESAR *goes to the Capitol, the rest following.*]

POPILIUS [*to* CASSIUS]: I wish your enterprise today may thrive.

CASSIUS: What enterprise, Popilius?

POPILIUS: Fare you well.

[*Advances to* CAESAR.]

BRUTUS: What said Popilius Lena?

CASSIUS: He wish'd today our enterprise might thrive.
I fear our purpose is discovered.

BRUTUS: Look, how he makes to Caesar. Mark him.

CASSIUS: Casca, be sudden, for we fear prevention.
Brutus, what shall be done? If this be known,
Cassius or Caesar never shall turn back,
For I will slay myself.

BRUTUS: Cassius, be constant.
Popilius Lena speaks not of our purposes;
For look, he smiles, and Caesar doth not change.

CASSIUS: Trebonius knows his time; for look you, Brutus,
He draws Mark Antony out of the way.

[*Exeunt* ANTONY *and* TREBONIUS.]

DECIUS: Where is Metellus Cimber? Let him go
And presently prefer his suit to Caesar.

BRUTUS: He is address'd. Press near and second him.

CINNA: Casca, you are the first that rears your hand.

[*They press near* CAESAR.]

CAESAR: Are we all ready? What is now amiss
That Caesar and his Senate must redress?

METELLUS: Most high, most mighty, and most puissant Caesar,
Metellus Cimber throws before thy seat
An humble heart—

[*Kneeling.*]

CAESAR: I must prevent thee, Cimber.
These couchings and these lowly courtesies
Might fire the blood of ordinary men,
And turn preordinance and first decree
Into the law of children. Be not fond
To think that Caesar bears such rebel blood
That will be thaw'd from the true quality
With that which melteth fools—I mean, sweet words,
Low-crooked curtsies, and base spaniel fawning.
Thy brother by decree is banished.
If thou dost bend and pray and fawn for him,
I spurn thee like a cur out of my way.
Know, Caesar doth not wrong, nor without cause
Will he be satisfied.

METELLUS: Is there no voice more worthy than my own,
To sound more sweetly in great Caesar's ear
For the repealing of my banish'd brother?

BRUTUS [*kneeling*]: I kiss thy hand, but not in flattery, Caesar,
Desiring thee that Publius Cimber may
Have an immediate freedom of repeal.

CAESAR: What, Brutus?

CASSIUS [*kneeling*]: Pardon, Caesar! Caesar, pardon!
As low as to thy foot doth Cassius fall,
To beg enfranchisement for Publius Cimber.

CAESAR: I could be well mov'd, if I were as you;
If I could pray to move, prayers would move me.
But I am constant as the northern star,
Of whose true-fix'd and resting quality

There is no fellow in the firmament.
The skies are painted with unnumb'red sparks,
They are all fire and every one doth shine,
But there's but one in all doth hold his place.
So in the world: 'tis furnish'd well with men,
And men are flesh and blood, and apprehensive;
Yet in the number I do know but one
That unassailable holds on his rank,
Unshak'd of motion. And that I am he,
Let me a little show it, even in this—
That I was constant Cimber should be banish'd,
And constant do remain to keep him so.

CINNA: O Caesar—

CAESAR: Hence! Wilt thou lift up Olympus?

DECIUS: Great Caesar—

CAESAR: Doth not Brutus bootless[22] kneel?

CASCA: Speak, hands, for me!

They stab CAESAR [CASCA *first,* BRUTUS *last*].

CAESAR: *Et tu, Brutè?* Then fall, Caesar!

CINNA: Liberty! Freedom! Tyranny is dead!
Run hence, proclaim, cry it about the streets.

CASSIUS: Some to the common pulpits, and cry out
"Liberty, freedom, and enfranchisement!"

BRUTUS: People and senators, be not affrighted.
Fly not; stand still. Ambition's debt is paid.

CASCA: Go to the pulpit, Brutus.

DECIUS: And Cassius too.

22. [*bootless:* in vain.]

BRUTUS: Where's Publius?

CINNA: Here, quite confounded with this mutiny.

METELLUS: Stand fast together, lest some friend of Caesar's
Should chance—

BRUTUS: Talk not of standing. Publius, good cheer.
There is no harm intended to your person,
Nor to no Roman else. So tell them, Publius.

CASSIUS: And leave us, Publius, lest that the people,
Rushing on us, should do your age some mischief.

BRUTUS: Do so, and let no man abide this deed
But we the doers.

[*Exeunt all but the* CONSPIRATORS.]

Enter TREBONIUS.

CASSIUS: Where is Antony?

TREBONIUS: Fled to his house amaz'd.
Men, wives, and children stare, cry out, and run
As it were doomsday.

BRUTUS: Fates, we will know your pleasures.
That we shall die, we know; 'tis but the time,
And drawing days out, that men stand upon.

CASCA: Why, he that cuts off twenty years of life
Cuts off so many years of fearing death.

BRUTUS: Grant that, and then is death a benefit.
So are we Caesar's friends, that have abridg'd
His time of fearing death. Stoop, Romans, stoop,
And let us bathe our hands in Caesar's blood
Up to the elbows, and besmear our swords.
Then walk we forth, even to the marketplace,
And, waving our red weapons o'er our heads,

Let's all cry, "Peace, freedom, and liberty!"

CASSIUS: Stoop, then, and wash.

[*They bathe their hands and weapons.*]

How many ages hence
Shall this our lofty scene be acted over
In states unborn and accents yet unknown!

BRUTUS: How many times shall Caesar bleed in sport,
That now on Pompey's basis lies along[23]
No worthier than the dust!

CASSIUS: So oft as that shall be,
So often shall the knot of us be call'd
The men that gave their country liberty.

DECIUS: What, shall we forth?

CASSIUS: Ay, every man away.
Brutus shall lead, and we will grace his heels
With the most boldest and best hearts of Rome.

Enter a SERVANT.

BRUTUS: Soft, who comes here? A friend of Antony's.

SERVANT [*kneeling*]: Thus, Brutus, did my master bid me kneel,
Thus did Mark Antony bid me fall down.
And, being prostrate, thus he bade me say:
Brutus is noble, wise, valiant, and honest;
Caesar was mighty, bold, royal, and loving.
Say I love Brutus, and I honor him;
Say I fear'd Caesar, honor'd him, and lov'd him.
If Brutus will vouchsafe that Antony
May safely come to him, and be resolv'd
How Caesar hath deserv'd to lie in death,
Mark Antony shall not love Caesar dead

23. [*on Pompey's basis lies along:* lies prostrate at the pedestal of Pompey's statue.]

So well as Brutus living, but will follow
The fortunes and affairs of noble Brutus
Thorough the hazards of this untrod state
With all true faith. So says my master Antony.

BRUTUS: Thy master is a wise and valiant Roman;
I never thought him worse.
Tell him, so please him come unto this place,
He shall be satisfied and, by my honor,
Depart untouch'd.

SERVANT: I'll fetch him presently.

Exit SERVANT.

BRUTUS: I know that we shall have him well to friend.

CASSIUS: I wish we may. But yet have I a mind
That fears him much; and my misgiving still
Falls shrewdly to the purpose.

Enter ANTONY.

BRUTUS: But here comes Antony.—Welcome, Mark Antony.

ANTONY: O mighty Caesar! Dost thou lie so low?
Are all thy conquests, glories, triumphs, spoils,
Shrunk to this little measure? Fare thee well.—
I know not, gentlemen, what you intend,
Who else must be let blood, who else is rank;
If I myself, there is no hour so fit
As Caesar's death's hour, nor no instrument
Of half that worth as those your swords, made rich
With the most noble blood of all this world.
I do beseech ye, if you bear me hard,
Now, whilst your purpled hands do reek and smoke,
Fulfill your pleasure. Live a thousand years,
I shall not find myself so apt to die;
No place will please me so, no mean of death,

As here by Caesar, and by you cut off,
The choice and master spirits of this age.

BRUTUS: O Antony, beg not your death of us.
Though now we must appear bloody and cruel,
As by our hands and this our present act
You see we do, yet see you but our hands
And this the bleeding business they have done.
Our hearts you see not. They are pitiful;
And pity to the general wrong of Rome—
As fire drives out fire, so pity pity—
Hath done this deed on Caesar. For your part,
To you our swords have leaden points, Mark Antony.
Our arms in strength of malice, and our hearts
Of brothers' temper, do receive you in
With all kind love, good thoughts, and reverence.

CASSIUS: Your voice shall be as strong as any man's
In the disposing of new dignities.[24]

BRUTUS: Only be patient till we have appeas'd
The multitude, beside themselves with fear,
And then we will deliver you the cause
Why I, that did love Caesar when I struck him,
Have thus proceeded.

ANTONY: I doubt not of your wisdom.
Let each man render me his bloody hand.
First, Marcus Brutus, will I shake with you;
Next, Caius Cassius, do I take your hand;
Now, Decius Brutus, yours; now yours, Metellus;
Yours, Cinna; and, my valiant Casca, yours;
Though last, not least in love, yours, good Trebonius.
Gentlemen all—alas, what shall I say?
My credit now stands on such slippery ground
That one of two bad ways you must conceit me,

24. [*dignities:* offices of state.]

Either a coward or a flatterer.
That I did love thee, Caesar, O, 'tis true!
If then thy spirit look upon us now,
Shall it not grieve thee dearer than thy death
To see thy Antony making his peace,
Shaking the bloody fingers of thy foes—
Most noble!—in the presence of thy corse?
Had I as many eyes as thou hast wounds,
Weeping as fast as they stream forth thy blood,
It would become me better than to close
In terms of friendship with thine enemies.
Pardon me, Julius! Here wast thou bay'd, brave hart,
Here didst thou fall, and here thy hunters stand,
Sign'd in thy spoil,[25] and crimson'd in thy lethe.[26]
O world, thou wast the forest to this hart,
And this, indeed, O world, the heart of thee!
How like a deer, strucken by many princes,
Dost thou here lie!

CASSIUS: Mark Antony—

ANTONY: Pardon me, Caius Cassius.
The enemies of Caesar shall say this;
Then, in a friend, it is cold modesty.[27]

CASSIUS: I blame you not for praising Caesar so,
But what compact mean you to have with us?
Will you be prick'd in number of our friends,
Or shall we on, and not depend on you?

ANTONY: Therefore I took your hands, but was indeed
Sway'd from the point by looking down on Caesar.
Friends am I with you all, and love you all,

---

25. [*Sign'd in thy spoil:* marked with the tokens of your slaughter.]

26. [*lethe:* river of oblivion in the underworld, here associated with Caesar's lifeblood.]

27. [*modesty:* moderation.]

Upon this hope, that you shall give me reasons
Why and wherein Caesar was dangerous.

BRUTUS: Or else were this a savage spectacle.
Our reasons are so full of good regard
That were you, Antony, the son of Caesar,
You should be satisfied.

ANTONY: That's all I seek,
And am moreover suitor that I may
Produce his body to the marketplace,
And in the pulpit, as becomes a friend,
Speak in the order of his funeral.

BRUTUS: You shall, Mark Antony.

CASSIUS: Brutus, a word with you.
[*Aside to* BRUTUS.] You know not what you do. Do not consent
That Antony speak in his funeral.
Know you how much the people may be mov'd
By that which he will utter?

BRUTUS [*aside to* CASSIUS]: By your pardon;
I will myself into the pulpit first,
And show the reason of our Caesar's death.
What Antony shall speak, I will protest
He speaks by leave and by permission,
And that we are contented Caesar shall
Have all true rites and lawful ceremonies.
It shall advantage more than do us wrong.

CASSIUS [*aside to* BRUTUS]: I know not what may fall; I like it not.

BRUTUS: Mark Antony, here, take you Caesar's body.
You shall not in your funeral speech blame us,
But speak all good you can devise of Caesar,
And say you do't by our permission.
Else shall you not have any hand at all
About his funeral. And you shall speak

In the same pulpit whereto I am going,
After my speech is ended.

ANTONY: Be it so.
I do desire no more.

BRUTUS: Prepare the body then, and follow us.

Exeunt. Manet ANTONY.

ANTONY: O, pardon me, thou bleeding piece of earth,
That I am meek and gentle with these butchers!
Thou art the ruins of the noblest man
That ever lived in the tide of times.
Woe to the hand that shed this costly blood!
Over thy wounds now do I prophesy—
Which, like dumb mouths, do ope their ruby lips
To beg the voice and utterance of my tongue—
A curse shall light upon the limbs of men;
Domestic fury and fierce civil strife
Shall cumber all the parts of Italy;
Blood and destruction shall be so in use
And dreadful objects so familiar
That mothers shall but smile when they behold
Their infants quartered with the hands of war,
All pity chok'd with custom of fell deeds;
And Caesar's spirit, ranging for revenge,
With Ate[28] by his side come hot from hell,
Shall in these confines with a monarch's voice
Cry "Havoc!"[29] and let slip the dogs of war,
That this foul deed shall smell above the earth
With carrion men, groaning for burial.

Enter Octavius' SERVANT.

You serve Octavius Caesar, do you not?

28. [Goddess of discord and destruction.]

29. [*Havoc:* the signal for unlimited plunder and slaughter.]

SERVANT: I do, Mark Antony.

ANTONY: Caesar did write for him to come to Rome.

SERVANT: He did receive his letters, and is coming,
And bid me say to you by word of mouth—
O Caesar!—

[*Seeing the body.*]

ANTONY: Thy heart is big. Get thee apart and weep.
Passion, I see, is catching, for mine eyes,
Seeing those beads of sorrow stand in thine,
Began to water. Is thy master coming?

SERVANT: He lies tonight within seven leagues of Rome.

ANTONY: Post back with speed, and tell him what hath chanc'd.
Here is a mourning Rome, a dangerous Rome,
No Rome of safety for Octavius yet;
Hie hence, and tell him so. Yet, stay awhile.
Thou shalt not back till I have borne this corse
Into the marketplace. There shall I try,
In my oration, how the people take
The cruel issue of these bloody men,
According to the which thou shalt discourse
To young Octavius of the state of things.
Lend me your hand.

Exeunt [*with* CAESAR*'s body*].

[SCENE II: *The Forum.*]

Enter BRUTUS *and* [*presently*] *goes into the pulpit, and* CASSIUS, *with the* PLEBEIANS.

PLEBEIANS: We will be satisfi'd! Let us be satisfi'd!

BRUTUS: Then follow me, and give me audience, friends.
Cassius, go you into the other street,

And part the numbers.
Those that will hear me speak, let 'em stay here;
Those that will follow Cassius, go with him;
And public reasons shall be rendered
Of Caesar's death.

FIRST PLEBEIAN: I will hear Brutus speak.

SECOND PLEBEIAN: I will hear Cassius, and compare their reasons,
When severally we hear them rendered.

[*Exit* CASSIUS, *with some of the* PLEBEIANS.]

THIRD PLEBEIAN: The noble Brutus is ascended. Silence!

BRUTUS: Be patient till the last.

Romans, countrymen, and lovers, hear me for my cause, and be silent, that you may hear. Believe me for mine honor, and have respect to mine honor, that you may believe. Censure[30] me in your wisdom, and awake your senses, that you may the better judge. If there be any in this assembly, any dear friend of Caesar's, to him I say, that Brutus' love to Caesar was no less than his. If then that friend demand why Brutus rose against Caesar, this is my answer: Not that I lov'd Caesar less, but that I lov'd Rome more. Had you rather Caesar were living and die all slaves, than that Caesar were dead, to live all free men? As Caesar lov'd me, I weep for him; as he was fortunate, I rejoice at it; as he was valiant, I honor him; but, as he was ambitious, I slew him. There is tears for his love; joy for his fortune; honor for his valor; and death for his ambition. Who is here so base that would be a bondman? If any, speak, for him have I offended. Who is here so rude[31] that would not be a Roman? If any, speak, for him have I offended. Who is here so vile that will not love his country? If any, speak, for him have I offended. I pause for a reply.

30. [*Censure:* judge.]

31. [*rude:* barbarous.]

ALL: None, Brutus, none!

BRUTUS: Then none have I offended. I have done no more to Caesar than you shall do to Brutus. The question of his death is enroll'd in the Capitol; his glory not extenuated, wherein he was worthy, nor his offenses enforc'd, for which he suffer'd death.

Enter MARK ANTONY [*and others*] *with* CAESAR'*s body.*

Here comes his body, mourn'd by Mark Antony, who, though he had no hand in his death, shall receive the benefit of his dying, a place in the commonwealth, as which of you shall not? With this I depart, that, as I slew my best lover for the good of Rome, I have the same dagger for myself, when it shall please my country to need my death.

ALL: Live, Brutus, live, live!

FIRST PLEBEIAN: Bring him with triumph home unto his house.

SECOND PLEBEIAN: Give him a statue with his ancestors.

THIRD PLEBEIAN: Let him be Caesar.

FOURTH PLEBEIAN: Caesar's better parts
Shall be crown'd in Brutus.

FIRST PLEBEIAN: We'll bring him to his house with shouts and clamors.

BRUTUS: My countrymen—

SECOND PLEBEIAN: Peace, silence! Brutus speaks.

FIRST PLEBEIAN: Peace, ho!

BRUTUS: Good countrymen, let me depart alone,
And, for my sake, stay here with Antony.
Do grace to Caesar's corpse, and grace his speech
Tending to Caesar's glories, which Mark Antony,
By our permission, is allow'd to make.

I do entreat you, not a man depart,
Save I alone, till Antony have spoke.

Exit.

FIRST PLEBEIAN: Stay, ho, and let us hear Mark Antony.

THIRD PLEBEIAN: Let him go up into the public chair.
We'll hear him. Noble Antony, go up.

ANTONY: For Brutus' sake, I am beholding to you.

[*Goes into the pulpit.*]

FOURTH PLEBEIAN: What does he say of Brutus?

THIRD PLEBEIAN: He says, for Brutus' sake
He finds himself beholding to us all.

FOURTH PLEBEIAN: 'Twere best he speak no harm of Brutus here.

FIRST PLEBEIAN: This Caesar was a tyrant.

THIRD PLEBEIAN: Nay, that's certain.
We are blest that Rome is rid of him.

SECOND PLEBEIAN: Peace! Let us hear what Antony can say.

ANTONY: You gentle Romans—

ALL: Peace, ho! Let us hear him.

ANTONY: Friends, Romans, countrymen, lend me your ears.
I come to bury Caesar, not to praise him.
The evil that men do lives after them;
The good is oft interred with their bones.
So let it be with Caesar. The noble Brutus
Hath told you Caesar was ambitious.
If it were so, it was a grievous fault,
And grievously hath Caesar answer'd it.
Here, under leave of Brutus and the rest—

For Brutus is an honorable man;
So are they all, all honorable men—
Come I to speak in Caesar's funeral.
He was my friend, faithful and just to me;
But Brutus says he was ambitious,
And Brutus is an honorable man.
He hath brought many captives home to Rome,
Whose ransoms did the general coffers fill.
Did this in Caesar seem ambitious?
When that the poor have cried, Caesar hath wept;
Ambition should be made of sterner stuff.
Yet Brutus says he was ambitious,
And Brutus is an honorable man.
You all did see that on the Lupercal
I thrice presented him a kingly crown,
Which he did thrice refuse. Was this ambition?
Yet Brutus says he was ambitious,
And, sure, he is an honorable man.
I speak not to disprove what Brutus spoke,
But here I am to speak what I do know.
You all did love him once, not without cause.
What cause withholds you then, to mourn for him?
O judgment! Thou art fled to brutish beasts,
And men have lost their reason. Bear with me;
My heart is in the coffin there with Caesar,
And I must pause till it come back to me.

[*He weeps.*]

FIRST PLEBEIAN: Methinks there is much reason in his sayings.

SECOND PLEBEIAN: If thou consider rightly of the matter,
Caesar has had great wrong.

THIRD PLEBEIAN: Has he, masters?
I fear there will a worse come in his place.

FOURTH PLEBEIAN: Mark'd ye his words? He would not take the crown;
Therefore 'tis certain he was not ambitious.

FIRST PLEBEIAN: If it be found so, some will dear abide it.

SECOND PLEBEIAN: Poor soul! His eyes are red as fire with weeping.

THIRD PLEBEIAN: There's not a nobler man in Rome than Antony.

FOURTH PLEBEIAN: Now mark him, he begins again to speak.

ANTONY: But yesterday the word of Caesar might
Have stood against the world. Now lies he there,
And none so poor to do him reverence.
O masters! If I were dispos'd to stir
Your hearts and minds to mutiny and rage,
I should do Brutus wrong, and Cassius wrong,
Who, you all know, are honorable men.
I will not do them wrong; I rather choose
To wrong the dead, to wrong myself and you,
Than I will wrong such honorable men.
But here's a parchment with the seal of Caesar;
I found it in his closet, 'tis his will.

[*Shows the will.*]

Let but the commons hear this testament—
Which, pardon me, I do not mean to read—
And they would go and kiss dead Caesar's wounds
And dip their napkins in his sacred blood,
Yea, beg a hair of him for memory,
And, dying, mention it within their wills,
Bequeathing it as a rich legacy
Unto their issue.

FOURTH PLEBEIAN: We'll hear the will! Read it, Mark Antony.

ALL: The will, the will! We will hear Caesar's will.

ANTONY: Have patience, gentle friends, I must not read it.
It is not meet you know how Caesar lov'd you.
You are not wood, you are not stones, but men;
And, being men, hearing the will of Caesar,
It will inflame you, it will make you mad.
'Tis good you know not that you are his heirs,
For, if you should, O, what would come of it?

FOURTH PLEBEIAN: Read the will! We'll hear it, Antony.
You shall read us the will, Caesar's will.

ANTONY: Will you be patient? Will you stay awhile?
I have o'ershot myself to tell you of it.
I fear I wrong the honorable men
Whose daggers have stabb'd Caesar; I do fear it.

FOURTH PLEBEIAN: They were traitors. Honorable men!

ALL: The will! The testament!

SECOND PLEBEIAN: They were villains, murderers. The will! Read the will!

ANTONY: You will compel me then to read the will?
Then make a ring about the corpse of Caesar,
And let me show you him that made the will.
Shall I descend? And will you give me leave?

ALL: Come down.

SECOND PLEBEIAN: Descend.

THIRD PLEBEIAN: You shall have leave.

[ANTONY *comes down. They gather around* CAESAR.]

FOURTH PLEBEIAN: A ring; stand round.

FIRST PLEBEIAN: Stand from the hearse, stand from the body.

SECOND PLEBEIAN: Room for Antony, most noble Antony.

ANTONY: Nay, press not so upon me. Stand far off.

ALL: Stand back! Room! Bear back!

ANTONY: If you have tears, prepare to shed them now.
You all do know this mantle. I remember
The first time ever Caesar put it on;
'Twas on a summer's evening, in his tent,
That day he overcame the Nervii.
Look, in this place ran Cassius' dagger through.
See what a rent the envious Casca made.
Through this the well-beloved Brutus stabb'd,
And, as he pluck'd his cursed steel away,
Mark how the blood of Caesar followed it,
As rushing out of doors to be resolv'd
If Brutus so unkindly knock'd or no;
For Brutus, as you know, was Caesar's angel.
Judge, O you gods, how dearly Caesar lov'd him!
This was the most unkindest cut of all;
For when the noble Caesar saw him stab,
Ingratitude, more strong than traitors' arms,
Quite vanquish'd him. Then burst his mighty heart,
And, in his mantle muffling up his face,
Even at the base of Pompey's statue,
Which all the while ran blood, great Caesar fell.
O, what a fall was there, my countrymen!
Then I, and you, and all of us fell down,
Whilst bloody treason flourish'd over us.
O, now you weep, and I perceive you feel
The dint of pity. These are gracious drops.
Kind souls, what weep you when you but behold
Our Caesar's vesture wounded? Look you here,
Here is himself, marr'd, as you see, with traitors.

[*He lifts Caesar's mantle.*]

FIRST PLEBEIAN: O piteous spectacle!

SECOND PLEBEIAN: O noble Caesar!

THIRD PLEBEIAN: O woeful day!

FOURTH PLEBEIAN: O traitors, villains!

FIRST PLEBEIAN: O most bloody sight!

SECOND PLEBEIAN: We will be reveng'd.

ALL: Revenge! About! Seek! Burn! Fire! Kill! Slay! Let not a traitor live!

ANTONY: Stay, countrymen.

FIRST PLEBEIAN: Peace there! Hear the noble Antony.

SECOND PLEBEIAN: We'll hear him, we'll follow him, we'll die with him!

ANTONY: Good friends, sweet friends, let me not stir you up
To such a sudden flood of mutiny.
They that have done this deed are honorable.
What private griefs[32] they have, alas, I know not,
That made them do it. They are wise and honorable,
And will no doubt with reasons answer you.
I come not, friends, to steal away your hearts.
I am no orator, as Brutus is,
But, as you know me all, a plain blunt man,
That love my friend; and that they know full well
That gave me public leave to speak of him.
For I have neither wit, nor words, nor worth,
Action, nor utterance, nor the power of speech
To stir men's blood. I only speak right on.
I tell you that which you yourselves do know,
Show you sweet Caesar's wounds, poor poor dumb mouths,

32. [*griefs:* grievances.]

And bid them speak for me. But were I Brutus,
And Brutus Antony, there were an Antony
Would ruffle up your spirits, and put a tongue
In every wound of Caesar that should move
The stones of Rome to rise and mutiny.

ALL: We'll mutiny.

FIRST PLEBEIAN: We'll burn the house of Brutus.

THIRD PLEBEIAN: Away, then! Come, seek the conspirators.

ANTONY: Yet hear me, countrymen. Yet hear me speak.

ALL: Peace, ho! Hear Antony. Most noble Antony!

ANTONY: Why, friends, you go to do you know not what.
Wherein hath Caesar thus deserv'd your loves?
Alas, you know not! I must tell you, then,
You have forgot the will I told you of.

ALL: Most true. The will! Let's stay and hear the will.

ANTONY: Here is the will, and under Caesar's seal.
To every Roman citizen he gives,
To every several man, seventy-five drachmas.

SECOND PLEBEIAN: Most noble Caesar! We'll revenge his death.

THIRD PLEBEIAN: O royal Caesar!

ANTONY: Hear me with patience.

ALL: Peace, ho!

ANTONY: Moreover, he hath left you all his walks,
His private arbors and new-planted orchards,
On this side Tiber; he hath left them you,
And to your heirs forever—common pleasures,[33]
To walk abroad and recreate yourselves.
Here was a Caesar! When comes such another?

33. [*common pleasures:* public parks.]

FIRST PLEBEIAN: Never, never! Come, away, away!
We'll burn his body in the holy place,
And with the brands fire the traitors' houses.
Take up the body.

SECOND PLEBEIAN: Go fetch fire.

THIRD PLEBEIAN: Pluck down benches.

FOURTH PLEBEIAN: Pluck down forms, windows, anything.

Exeunt PLEBEIANS [*with the body*].

ANTONY: Now let it work. Mischief, thou art afoot,
Take thou what course thou wilt!

Enter SERVANT.

How now, fellow?

SERVANT: Sir, Octavius is already come to Rome.

ANTONY: Where is he?

SERVANT: He and Lepidus are at Caesar's house.

ANTONY: And thither will I straight to visit him.
He comes upon a wish. Fortune is merry,
And in this mood will give us anything.

SERVANT: I heard him say, Brutus and Cassius
Are rid like madmen through the gates of Rome.

ANTONY: Belike they had some notice of the people,
How I had mov'd them. Bring me to Octavius.

Exeunt.

[SCENE III: *A street.*]

Enter CINNA *the poet, and after him the* PLEBEIANS.

CINNA: I dreamt tonight that I did feast with Caesar,
And things unluckily charge my fantasy.[34]
I have no will to wander forth of doors,
Yet something leads me forth.

FIRST PLEBEIAN: What is your name?

SECOND PLEBEIAN: Whither are you going?

THIRD PLEBEIAN: Where do you dwell?

FOURTH PLEBEIAN: Are you a married man or a bachelor?

SECOND PLEBEIAN: Answer every man directly.

FIRST PLEBEIAN: Ay, and briefly.

FOURTH PLEBEIAN: Ay, and wisely.

THIRD PLEBEIAN: Ay, and truly, you were best.

CINNA: What is my name? Whither am I going? Where do I dwell? Am I a married man or a bachelor? Then, to answer every man directly and briefly, wisely and truly: wisely I say, I am a bachelor.

SECOND PLEBEIAN: That's as much as to say, they are fools that marry. You'll bear me a bang for that, I fear. Proceed directly.

CINNA: Directly, I am going to Caesar's funeral.

FIRST PLEBEIAN: As a friend or an enemy?

CINNA: As a friend.

SECOND PLEBEIAN: That matter is answer'd directly.

FOURTH PLEBEIAN: For your dwelling—briefly.

CINNA: Briefly, I dwell by the Capitol.

THIRD PLEBEIAN: Your name, sir, truly.

34. [*things unluckily charge my fantasy*: what has happened fills me with foreboding.]

CINNA: Truly, my name is Cinna.

FIRST PLEBEIAN: Tear him to pieces! He's a conspirator!

CINNA: I am Cinna the poet, I am Cinna the poet!

FOURTH PLEBEIAN: Tear him for his bad verses, tear him for his bad verses!

CINNA: I am not Cinna the conspirator.

FOURTH PLEBEIAN: It is no matter, his name's Cinna. Pluck but his name out of his heart, and turn him going.

THIRD PLEBEIAN: Tear him, tear him! Come, brands, ho! Firebrands! To Brutus', to Cassius'; burn all! Some to Decius' house, and some to Casca's; some to Ligarius'. Away, go!

Exeunt all the PLEBEIANS [*dragging off* CINNA].

ACT IV

[SCENE I: *Antony's house.*]

Enter ANTONY [*with a list*], OCTAVIUS, *and* LEPIDUS.

ANTONY: These many, then, shall die. Their names are prick'd.

OCTAVIUS: Your brother too must die. Consent you, Lepidus?

LEPIDUS: I do consent—

OCTAVIUS: Prick him down, Antony.

LEPIDUS: Upon condition Publius shall not live,
Who is your sister's son, Mark Antony.

ANTONY: He shall not live. Look, with a spot I damn him.
But, Lepidus, go you to Caesar's house.
Fetch the will hither, and we shall determine

How to cut off some charge[35] in legacies.

LEPIDUS: What, shall I find you here?

OCTAVIUS: Or here, or at the Capitol.

[*Exit* LEPIDUS.]

ANTONY: This is a slight unmeritable man,
Meet to be sent on errands. Is it fit,
The threefold world divided, he should stand
One of the three to share it?

OCTAVIUS: So you thought him,
And took his voice who should be prick'd to die
In our black sentence and proscription.[36]

ANTONY: Octavius, I have seen more days than you;
And though we lay these honors on this man,
To ease ourselves of divers sland'rous loads,
He shall but bear them as the ass bears gold,
To groan and sweat under the business,
Either led or driven, as we point the way;
And having brought our treasure where we will,
Then take we down his load, and turn him off,
Like to the empty ass, to shake his ears
And graze in commons.

OCTAVIUS: You may do your will;
But he's a tried and valiant soldier.

ANTONY: So is my horse, Octavius, and for that
I do appoint him store of provender.
It is a creature that I teach to fight,
To wind, to stop, to run directly on,
His corporal motion govern'd by my spirit.
And, in some taste, is Lepidus but so.

35. [*cut off some charge:* reduce the outlay (by altering the will).]

36. [*proscription:* condemnation to death or exile.]

He must be taught, and train'd, and bid go forth—
A barren-spirited fellow, one that feeds
On objects, arts, and imitations,
Which, out of use and stal'd by other men,
Begin his fashion. Do not talk of him
But as a property. And now, Octavius,
Listen great things. Brutus and Cassius
Are levying powers. We must straight make head.[37]
Therefore let our alliance be combin'd,
Our best friends made, our means stretch'd;
And let us presently go sit in council
How covert matters may be best disclos'd,
And open perils surest answered.

OCTAVIUS: Let us do so, for we are at the stake,
And bay'd about with many enemies;
And some that smile have in their hearts, I fear,
Millions of mischiefs.

Exeunt.

[SCENE II: *The camp near Sardis, in Asia Minor. Before Brutus' tent.*]

Drum. Enter BRUTUS, LUCILIUS, [LUCIUS,] *and the army;* TITINIUS *and* PINDARUS *meet them.*

BRUTUS: Stand, ho!

LUCILIUS: Give the word, ho! And stand.

BRUTUS: What now, Lucilius, is Cassius near?

LUCILIUS: He is at hand, and Pindarus is come
To do you salutation from his master.

BRUTUS: He greets me well. Your master, Pindarus,

37. [*straight make head:* immediately raise an army.]

In his own change, or by ill officers,
Hath given me some worthy cause to wish
Things done, undone; but, if he be at hand,
I shall be satisfied.

PINDARUS: I do not doubt
But that my noble master will appear
Such as he is, full of regard and honor.

BRUTUS: He is not doubted. A word, Lucilius,
How he receiv'd you; let me be resolv'd.

LUCILIUS: With courtesy and with respect enough,
But not with such familiar instances,
Nor with such free and friendly conference,
As he hath us'd of old.

BRUTUS: Thou hast describ'd
A hot friend cooling. Ever note, Lucilius,
When love begins to sicken and decay,
It useth an enforced ceremony.
There are no tricks in plain and simple faith.
But hollow men, like horses hot at hand,
Make gallant show and promise of their mettle;

Low march within.

But when they should endure the bloody spur,
They fall their crests, and, like deceitful jades,
Sink in the trial. Comes his army on?

LUCILIUS: They mean this night in Sardis to be quarter'd.
The greater part, the horse in general,
Are come with Cassius.

Enter CASSIUS *and his powers.*

BRUTUS: Hark, he is arriv'd.
March gently on to meet him.

CASSIUS: Stand, ho!

BRUTUS: Stand, ho! Speak the word along.

FIRST SOLDIER: Stand!

SECOND SOLDIER: Stand!

THIRD SOLDIER: Stand!

CASSIUS: Most noble brother, you have done me wrong.

BRUTUS: Judge me, you gods! Wrong I mine enemies?
And, if not so, how should I wrong a brother?

CASSIUS: Brutus, this sober form of yours hides wrongs;
And when you do them—

BRUTUS: Cassius, be content;
Speak your griefs softly. I do know you well.
Before the eyes of both our armies here,
Which should perceive nothing but love from us,
Let us not wrangle. Bid them move away.
Then in my tent, Cassius, enlarge your griefs,
And I will give you audience.

CASSIUS: Pindarus,
Bid our commanders lead their charges off
A little from this ground.

BRUTUS: Lucius, do you the like, and let no man
Come to our tent till we have done our conference.
Let Lucilius and Titinius guard our door.

Exeunt. Mane[n]t BRUTUS *and* CASSIUS.
[LUCILIUS *and* TITINIUS *stand guard at the door.*]

[SCENE III: *Within Brutus' tent.*]

CASSIUS: That you have wrong'd me doth appear in this:
You have condemn'd and noted Lucius Pella

For taking bribes here of the Sardians,
Wherein my letters, praying on his side,
Because I knew the man, was slighted off.

BRUTUS: You wrong'd yourself to write in such a case.

CASSIUS: In such a time as this it is not meet
That every nice offense should bear his comment.

BRUTUS: Let me tell you, Cassius, you yourself
Are much condemn'd to have an itching palm,
To sell and mart your offices for gold
To undeservers.

CASSIUS: I an itching palm?
You know that you are Brutus that speaks this,
Or, by the gods, this speech were else your last.

BRUTUS: The name of Cassius honors this corruption,
And chastisement doth therefore hide his head.

CASSIUS: Chastisement?

BRUTUS: Remember March, the ides of March remember.
Did not great Julius bleed for justice' sake?
What villain touch'd his body that did stab
And not for justice? What, shall one of us,
That struck the foremost man of all this world
But for supporting robbers, shall we now
Contaminate our fingers with base bribes,
And sell the mighty space of our large honors
For so much trash as may be grasped thus?
I had rather be a dog, and bay the moon,
Than such a Roman.

CASSIUS: Brutus, bait not me!
I'll not endure it. You forget yourself
To hedge me in. I am a soldier, I,
Older in practice, abler than yourself
To make conditions.

BRUTUS: Go to! You are not, Cassius.

CASSIUS: I am.

BRUTUS: I say you are not.

CASSIUS: Urge me no more, I shall forget myself.
Have mind upon your health. Tempt me no farther.

BRUTUS: Away, slight man!

CASSIUS: Is't possible?

BRUTUS: Hear me, for I will speak.
Must I give way and room to your rash choler?
Shall I be frighted when a madman stares?

CASSIUS: O ye gods, ye gods! Must I endure all this?

BRUTUS: All this? Ay, more. Fret till your proud heart break.
Go show your slaves how choleric you are,
And make your bondmen tremble. Must I budge?
Must I observe you? Must I stand and crouch
Under your testy humor? By the gods,
You shall digest the venom of your spleen
Though it do split you; for, from this day forth,
I'll use you for my mirth, yea, for my laughter,
When you are waspish.

CASSIUS: Is it come to this?

BRUTUS: You say you are a better soldier.
Let it appear so; make your vaunting true,
And it shall please me well. For mine own part,
I shall be glad to learn of noble men.

CASSIUS: You wrong me every way! You wrong me, Brutus.
I said, an elder soldier, not a better.
Did I say "better"?

BRUTUS: If you did, I care not.

CASSIUS: When Caesar liv'd, he durst not thus have mov'd me.

BRUTUS: Peace, peace! You durst not so have tempted him.

CASSIUS: I durst not?

BRUTUS: No.

CASSIUS: What, durst not tempt him?

BRUTUS: For your life you durst not.

CASSIUS: Do not presume too much upon my love.
I may do that I shall be sorry for.

BRUTUS: You have done that you should be sorry for.
There is no terror, Cassius, in your threats,
For I am arm'd so strong in honesty
That they pass by me as the idle wind,
Which I respect not. I did send to you
For certain sums of gold—which you denied me—
For I can raise no money by vile means.
By heaven, I had rather coin my heart
And drop my blood for drachmas than to wring
From the hard hands of peasants their vile trash
By any indirection. I did send
To you for gold to pay my legions,
Which you denied me. Was that done like Cassius?
Should I have answer'd Caius Cassius so?
When Marcus Brutus grows so covetous
To lock such rascal counters from his friends,
Be ready, gods, with all your thunderbolts;
Dash him to pieces!

CASSIUS: I denied you not.

BRUTUS: You did.

CASSIUS: I did not. He was but a fool that brought
My answer back. Brutus hath riv'd my heart.

A friend should bear his friend's infirmities,
But Brutus makes mine greater than they are.

BRUTUS: I do not, till you practice them on me.

CASSIUS: You love me not.

BRUTUS: I do not like your faults.

CASSIUS: A friendly eye could never see such faults.

BRUTUS: A flatterer's would not, though they do appear
As huge as high Olympus.

CASSIUS: Come, Antony, and young Octavius, come,
Revenge yourselves alone on Cassius,
For Cassius is aweary of the world;
Hated by one he loves, brav'd by his brother,
Check'd like a bondman, all his faults observ'd,
Set in a notebook, learn'd, and conn'd by rote,
To cast into my teeth. O, I could weep
My spirit from mine eyes! There is my dagger,

[*Offers his unsheathed dagger.*]

And here my naked breast; within, a heart
Dearer than Pluto's mine, richer than gold.
If that thou be'st a Roman, take it forth.
I, that denied thee gold, will give my heart.
Strike, as thou didst at Caesar; for I know,
When thou didst hate him worst, thou lovedst him better
Than ever thou lovedst Cassius.

BRUTUS: Sheathe your dagger.
Be angry when you will, it shall have scope;
Do what you will, dishonor shall be humor.[38]
O Cassius, you are yoked with a lamb
That carries anger as the flint bears fire,

38. [*dishonor shall be humor:* i.e., I shall think of your insults as stemming from your hot temper.]

Who, much enforced, shows a hasty spark,
And straight is cold again.

CASSIUS: Hath Cassius liv'd
To be but mirth and laughter to his Brutus,
When grief and blood ill-temper'd vexeth him?

BRUTUS: When I spoke that, I was ill-temper'd too.

CASSIUS: Do you confess so much? Give me your hand.

BRUTUS: And my heart too.

[*They embrace.*]

CASSIUS: O Brutus!

BRUTUS: What's the matter?

CASSIUS: Have not you love enough to bear with me,
When that rash humor which my mother gave me
Makes me forgetful?

BRUTUS: Yes, Cassius; and, from henceforth,
When you are over-earnest with your Brutus,
He'll think your mother chides, and leave you so.

Enter a POET [*followed by* LUCILIUS *and* TITINIUS, *who have been standing guard at the door*].

POET: Let me go in to see the generals.
There is some grudge between 'em, 'tis not meet
They be alone.

LUCILIUS: You shall not come to them.

POET: Nothing but death shall stay me.

CASSIUS: How now? What's the matter?

POET: For shame, you generals! What do you mean?
Love and be friends, as two such men should be;
For I have seen more years, I'm sure, than ye.

CASSIUS: Ha, ha, how vilely doth this cynic rhyme!

BRUTUS: Get you hence, sirrah. Saucy fellow, hence!

CASSIUS: Bear with him, Brutus. 'Tis his fashion.

BRUTUS: I'll know his humor, when he knows his time.
What should the wars do with these jigging fools?
Companion, hence!

CASSIUS: Away, away, be gone!

Exit POET.

BRUTUS: Lucilius and Titinius, bid the commanders
Prepare to lodge their companies tonight.

CASSIUS: And come yourselves, and bring Messala with you
Immediately to us.

[*Exeunt* LUCILIUS *and* TITINIUS.]

BRUTUS [*to* LUCIUS *within*]: Lucius, a bowl of wine!

CASSIUS: I did not think you could have been so angry.

BRUTUS: O Cassius, I am sick of many griefs.

CASSIUS: Of your philosophy you make no use,
If you give place to accidental evils.

BRUTUS: No man bears sorrow better. Portia is dead.

CASSIUS: Ha? Portia?

BRUTUS: She is dead.

CASSIUS: How scap'd I killing when I cross'd you so?
O insupportable and touching loss!
Upon what sickness?

BRUTUS: Impatient of my absence,
And grief that young Octavius with Mark Antony
Have made themselves so strong—for with her death

That tidings came—with this she fell distract,
And, her attendants absent, swallow'd fire.

CASSIUS: And died so?

BRUTUS: Even so.

CASSIUS: O ye immortal gods!

Enter Boy [LUCIUS] *with wine and tapers.*

BRUTUS: Speak no more of her. Give me a bowl of wine.
In this I bury all unkindness, Cassius.

Drinks.

CASSIUS: My heart is thirsty for that noble pledge.
Fill, Lucius, till the wine o'erswell the cup;
I cannot drink too much of Brutus' love.

[*Drinks. Exit* LUCIUS.]

Enter TITINIUS *and* MESSALA.

BRUTUS: Come in, Titinius! Welcome, good Messala.
Now sit we close about this taper here,
And call in question our necessities.

[*They sit.*]

CASSIUS: Portia, art thou gone?

BRUTUS: No more, I pray you.
Messala, I have here received letters
That young Octavius and Mark Antony
Come down upon us with a mighty power,
Bending their expedition toward Philippi.

[*Shows letters.*]

MESSALA: Myself have letters of the selfsame tenor.

BRUTUS: With what addition?

MESSALA: That by proscription and bills of outlawry
Octavius, Antony, and Lepidus
Have put to death an hundred senators.

BRUTUS: Therein our letters do not well agree;
Mine speak of seventy senators that died
By their proscriptions, Cicero being one.

CASSIUS: Cicero one?

MESSALA: Cicero is dead,
And by that order of proscription.
Had you your letters from your wife, my lord?

BRUTUS: No, Messala.

MESSALA: Nor nothing in your letters writ of her?

BRUTUS: Nothing, Messala.

MESSALA: That, methinks, is strange.

BRUTUS: Why ask you? Hear you aught of her in yours?

MESSALA: No, my lord.

BRUTUS: Now, as you are a Roman, tell me true.

MESSALA: Then like a Roman bear the truth I tell:
For certain she is dead, and by strange manner.

BRUTUS: Why, farewell, Portia.[39] We must die, Messala.
With meditating that she must die once,
I have the patience to endure it now.

MESSALA: Even so great men great losses should endure.

CASSIUS: I have as much of this in art as you,
But yet my nature could not bear it so.

---

39. [It is not clear whether Shakespeare intended two announcements of Portia's death or whether one is a later revision.]

BRUTUS: Well, to our work alive. What do you think
Of marching to Philippi presently?

CASSIUS: I do not think it good.

BRUTUS: Your reason?

CASSIUS: This it is:
'Tis better that the enemy seek us.
So shall he waste his means, weary his soldiers,
Doing himself offense; whilst we, lying still,
Are full of rest, defense, and nimbleness.

BRUTUS: Good reasons must of force give place to better.
The people 'twixt Philippi and this ground
Do stand but in a forc'd affection,
For they have grudg'd us contribution.
The enemy, marching along by them,
By them shall make a fuller number up,
Come on refresh'd, new-added, and encourag'd;
From which advantage shall we cut him off
If at Philippi we do face him there,
These people at our back.

CASSIUS: Hear me, good brother.

BRUTUS: Under your pardon. You must note beside
That we have tried the utmost of our friends,
Our legions are brimfull, our cause is ripe.
The enemy increaseth every day;
We, at the height, are ready to decline.
There is a tide in the affairs of men,
Which, taken at the flood, leads on to fortune;
Omitted, all the voyage of their life
Is bound in shallows and in miseries.
On such a full sea are we now afloat,
And we must take the current when it serves,
Or lose our ventures.

CASSIUS: Then, with your will, go on.
We'll along ourselves, and meet them at Philippi.

BRUTUS: The deep of night is crept upon our talk,
And nature must obey necessity,
Which we will niggard with a little rest.
There is no more to say?

CASSIUS: No more. Good night.
Early tomorrow will we rise, and hence.

BRUTUS: Lucius! (*Enter* LUCIUS.) My gown. [*Exit* LUCIUS.]
Farewell, good Messala.
Good night, Titinius. Noble, noble Cassius,
Good night, and good repose.

CASSIUS: O my dear brother!
This was an ill beginning of the night.
Never come such division 'tween our souls!
Let it not, Brutus.

Enter LUCIUS *with the gown.*

BRUTUS: Everything is well.

CASSIUS: Good night, my lord.

BRUTUS: Good night, good brother.

TITINIUS, MESSALA: Good night, Lord Brutus.

BRUTUS: Farewell, everyone.

Exeunt [*all but* BRUTUS *and* LUCIUS].

Give me the gown. Where is thy instrument?

LUCIUS: Here in the tent.

BRUTUS: What, thou speak'st drowsily?
Poor knave, I blame thee not; thou art o'erwatch'd.
Call Claudius and some other of my men;
I'll have them sleep on cushions in my tent.

LUCIUS: Varro and Claudius!

Enter VARRO *and* CLAUDIUS.

VARRO: Calls my lord?

BRUTUS: I pray you, sirs, lie in my tent and sleep.
It may be I shall raise you by and by
On business to my brother Cassius.

VARRO: So please you, we will stand and watch your pleasure.

BRUTUS: I will not have it so. Lie down, good sirs.
It may be I shall otherwise bethink me.

[VARRO *and* CLAUDIUS *lie down.*]

Look, Lucius, here's the book I sought for so;
I put it in the pocket of my gown.

LUCIUS: I was sure your lordship did not give it me.

BRUTUS: Bear with me, good boy, I am much forgetful.
Canst thou hold up thy heavy eyes awhile,
And touch thy instrument a strain or two?

LUCIUS: Ay, my lord, an't please you.

BRUTUS: It does, my boy.
I trouble thee too much, but thou art willing.

LUCIUS: It is my duty, sir.

BRUTUS: I should not urge thy duty past thy might;
I know young bloods look for a time of rest.

LUCIUS: I have slept, my lord, already.

BRUTUS: It was well done; and thou shalt sleep again;
I will not hold thee long. If I do live,
I will be good to thee.

Music, and a song. [LUCIUS *falls asleep.*]

This is a sleepy tune. O murd'rous slumber,
Layest thou thy leaden mace upon my boy,
That plays thee music? Gentle knave, good night;
I will not do thee so much wrong to wake thee.
If thou dost nod, thou break'st thy instrument;
I'll take it from thee. And, good boy, good night.

[*He removes* LUCIUS' *instrument, and begins to read.*]

Let me see, let me see; is not the leaf turn'd down
Where I left reading? Here it is, I think.

Enter the GHOST OF CAESAR.

How ill this taper burns! Ha! Who comes here?
I think it is the weakness of mine eyes
That shapes this monstrous apparition.
It comes upon me. Art thou any thing?
Art thou some god, some angel, or some devil,
That mak'st my blood cold and my hair to stare?
Speak to me what thou art.

GHOST: Thy evil spirit, Brutus.

BRUTUS: Why com'st thou?

GHOST: To tell thee thou shalt see me at Philippi.

BRUTUS: Well; then I shall see thee again?

GHOST: Ay, at Philippi.

BRUTUS: Why, I will see thee at Philippi, then.

[*Exit* GHOST.]

Now I have taken heart thou vanishest.
Ill spirit, I would hold more talk with thee.

Boy, Lucius! Varro! Claudius! Sirs, awake!
Claudius!

LUCIUS: The strings, my lord, are false.

BRUTUS: He thinks he still is at his instrument.
Lucius, awake!

LUCIUS: My lord?

BRUTUS: Didst thou dream, Lucius, that thou so criedst out?

LUCIUS: My lord, I do not know that I did cry.

BRUTUS: Yes, that thou didst. Didst thou see anything?

LUCIUS: Nothing, my lord.

BRUTUS: Sleep again, Lucius. Sirrah Claudius!
[*To* VARRO.] Fellow thou, awake!

VARRO: My lord?

CLAUDIUS: My lord?

[*They get up.*]

BRUTUS: Why did you so cry out, sirs, in your sleep?

VARRO, CLAUDIUS: Did we, my lord?

BRUTUS: Ay. Saw you anything?

VARRO: No, my lord, I saw nothing.

CLAUDIUS: Nor I, my lord.

BRUTUS: Go and commend me to my brother Cassius.
Bid him set on his pow'rs betimes before,
And we will follow.

VARRO, CLAUDIUS: It shall be done, my lord.

ACT V

[SCENE I: *The plains of Philippi, in Macedonia.*]

Enter OCTAVIUS, ANTONY, *and their army.*

OCTAVIUS: Now, Antony, our hopes are answered.
You said the enemy would not come down,
But keep the hills and upper regions.
It proves not so. Their battles are at hand;
They mean to warn us at Philippi here,
Answering before we do demand of them.

ANTONY: Tut, I am in their bosoms, and I know
Wherefore they do it. They could be content
To visit other places, and come down
With fearful bravery, thinking by this face
To fasten in our thoughts that they have courage;
But 'tis not so.

Enter a MESSENGER.

MESSENGER: Prepare you, generals.
The enemy comes on in gallant show;
Their bloody sign of battle is hung out,
And something to be done immediately.

ANTONY: Octavius, lead your battle softly on
Upon the left hand of the even field.

OCTAVIUS: Upon the right hand I; keep thou the left.

ANTONY: Why do you cross me in this exigent?

OCTAVIUS: I do not cross you; but I will do so.

March.

Drum. Enter BRUTUS, CASSIUS, *and their army* [*with* LUCILIUS, TITINIUS, MESSALA, *and others*].

BRUTUS: They stand, and would have parley.

CASSIUS: Stand fast, Titinius. We must out and talk.

OCTAVIUS: Mark Antony, shall we give sign of battle?

ANTONY: No, Caesar, we will answer on their charge.
Make forth. The generals would have some words.

OCTAVIUS: Stir not until the signal.

BRUTUS: Words before blows. Is it so, countrymen?

OCTAVIUS: Not that we love words better, as you do.

BRUTUS: Good words are better than bad strokes, Octavius.

ANTONY: In your bad strokes, Brutus, you give good words.
Witness the hole you made in Caesar's heart,
Crying "Long live! Hail, Caesar!"

CASSIUS: Antony,
The posture of your blows are yet unknown;
But for your words, they rob the Hybla bees,
And leave them honeyless.

ANTONY: Not stingless too?

BRUTUS: O, yes, and soundless too.
For you have stol'n their buzzing, Antony,
And very wisely threat before you sting.

ANTONY: Villains! You did not so, when your vile daggers
Hack'd one another in the sides of Caesar.
You show'd your teeth like apes, and fawn'd like hounds,
And bow'd like bondmen, kissing Caesar's feet,
Whilst damned Casca, like a cur, behind
Struck Caesar on the neck. O you flatterers!

CASSIUS: Flatterers? Now, Brutus, thank yourself!
This tongue had not offended so today
If Cassius might have rul'd.

OCTAVIUS: Come, come, the cause. If arguing make us sweat,
The proof of it will turn to redder drops.
Look, [*He draws.*]
I draw a sword against conspirators.
When think you that the sword goes up again?
Never, till Caesar's three and thirty wounds
Be well aveng'd, or till another Caesar
Have added slaughter to the sword of traitors.

BRUTUS: Caesar, thou canst not die by traitors' hands,
Unless thou bring'st them with thee.

OCTAVIUS: So I hope.
I was not born to die on Brutus' sword.

BRUTUS: O, if thou wert the noblest of thy strain,
Young man, thou couldst not die more honorable.

CASSIUS: A peevish schoolboy, worthless of such honor,
Join'd with a masker and a reveler!

ANTONY: Old Cassius still.

OCTAVIUS: Come, Antony, away!
Defiance, traitors, hurl we in your teeth.
If you dare fight today, come to the field;
If not, when you have stomachs.

Exeunt OCTAVIUS, ANTONY, *and army.*

CASSIUS: Why, now, blow wind, swell billow, and swim bark!
The storm is up, and all is on the hazard.

BRUTUS: Ho, Lucilius! Hark, a word with you.

LUCILIUS (*stands forth*): My lord?

[BRUTUS *and* LUCILIUS *converse apart.*]

CASSIUS: Messala!

MESSALA (*stands forth*): What says my general?

CASSIUS: Messala,
This is my birthday; as this very day
Was Cassius born. Give me thy hand, Messala.
Be thou my witness that against my will,
As Pompey was, am I compell'd to set
Upon one battle all our liberties.
You know that I held Epicurus strong
And his opinion. Now I change my mind,
And partly credit things that do presage.
Coming from Sardis, on our former ensign
Two mighty eagles fell, and there they perch'd,
Gorging and feeding from our soldiers' hands,
Who to Philippi here consorted us.
This morning are they fled away and gone,
And in their steads do ravens, crows, and kites
Fly o'er our heads, and downward look on us,
As we were sickly prey. Their shadows seem
A canopy most fatal, under which
Our army lies, ready to give up the ghost.

MESSALA: Believe not so.

CASSIUS: I but believe it partly,
For I am fresh of spirit, and resolv'd
To meet all perils very constantly.

BRUTUS: Even so, Lucilius.

CASSIUS: Now, most noble Brutus,
The gods today stand friendly, that we may,
Lovers in peace, lead on our days to age!
But since the affairs of men rest still incertain,
Let's reason with the worst that may befall.
If we do lose this battle, then is this
The very last time we shall speak together.
What are you then determined to do?

BRUTUS: Even by the rule of that philosophy
By which I did blame Cato for the death
Which he did give himself—I know not how,
But I do find it cowardly and vile,
For fear of what might fall, so to prevent[40]
The time of life—arming myself with patience
To stay the providence of some high powers
That govern us below.

CASSIUS: Then, if we lose this battle,
You are contented to be led in triumph
Thorough the streets of Rome?

BRUTUS: No, Cassius, no. Think not, thou noble Roman,
That ever Brutus will go bound to Rome;
He bears too great a mind. But this same day
Must end that work the ides of March begun;
And whether we shall meet again I know not.
Therefore our everlasting farewell take.
For ever, and for ever, farewell, Cassius!
If we do meet again, why, we shall smile;
If not, why then this parting was well made.

CASSIUS: For ever, and for ever, farewell, Brutus!
If we do meet again, we'll smile indeed;
If not, 'tis true this parting was well made.

BRUTUS: Why, then, lead on. O, that a man might know
The end of this day's business ere it come!
But it sufficeth that the day will end,
And then the end is known. Come, ho! Away!

Exeunt.

[SCENE II: *The battlefield.*]

Alarum. Enter BRUTUS *and* MESSALA.

40. [*prevent:* cut short.]

BRUTUS: Ride, ride, Messala, ride, and give these bills[41]
Unto the legions on the other side.

[*Gives written orders.*]
Loud alarum.

Let them set on at once; for I perceive
But cold demeanor in Octavius' wing,
And sudden push gives them the overthrow.
Ride, ride, Messala! Let them all come down.

Exeunt.

[SCENE III: *Another part of the battlefield.*]

Alarums. Enter CASSIUS[, *carrying a standard,*] *and* TITINIUS.

CASSIUS: O, look, Titinius, look, the villains fly!
Myself have to mine own turn'd enemy.
This ensign here of mine was turning back;
I slew the coward, and did take it from him.

TITINIUS: O Cassius, Brutus gave the word too early,
Who, having some advantage on Octavius,
Took it too eagerly. His soldiers fell to spoil,[42]
Whilst we by Antony are all enclos'd.

Enter PINDARUS.

PINDARUS: Fly further off, my lord, fly further off!
Mark Antony is in your tents, my lord.
Fly, therefore, noble Cassius, fly far off.

CASSIUS: This hill is far enough. Look, look, Titinius!
Are those my tents where I perceive the fire?

TITINIUS: They are, my lord.

---

41. [*bills:* written orders.]

42. [*spoil:* looting.]

CASSIUS: Titinius, if thou lovest me,
Mount thou my horse, and hide thy spurs in him,
Till he have brought thee up to yonder troops
And here again, that I may rest assur'd
Whether yond troops are friend or enemy.

TITINIUS: I will be here again, even with a thought.

Exit.

CASSIUS: Go, Pindarus, get higher on that hill.
My sight was ever thick. Regard Titinius,
And tell me what thou not'st about the field.

[PINDARUS *goes up.*]

This day I breathed first. Time is come round,
And where I did begin, there shall I end.
My life is run his compass. Sirrah, what news?

PINDARUS (*above*): O my lord!

CASSIUS: What news?

PINDARUS (*above*): Titinius is enclosed round about
With horsemen, that make to him on the spur;
Yet he spurs on. Now they are almost on him.
Now, Titinius! Now some light. O, he
Lights too. He's ta'en. (*Shout.*) And, hark! They shout for joy.

CASSIUS: Come down, behold no more.
O, coward that I am, to live so long,
To see my best friend ta'en before my face!

Enter PINDARUS [*from above*].

Come hither, sirrah.
In Parthia did I take thee prisoner;
And then I swore thee, saving of thy life,
That whatsoever I did bid thee do,
Thou shouldst attempt it. Come now, keep thine oath.

Now be a freeman, and with this good sword,
That ran through Caesar's bowels, search this bosom.
Stand not to answer. Here, take thou the hilts;
And, when my face is cover'd, as 'tis now,
Guide thou the sword.

[PINDARUS *does so.*]

Caesar, thou art reveng'd,
Even with the sword that kill'd thee.

[*Dies.*]

PINDARUS: So, I am free; yet would not so have been,
Durst I have done my will. O Cassius!
Far from this country Pindarus shall run,
Where never Roman shall take note of him.

[*Exit.*]

Enter TITINIUS *and* MESSALA.

MESSALA: It is but change, Titinius; for Octavius
Is overthrown by noble Brutus' power,
As Cassius' legions are by Antony.

TITINIUS: These tidings will well comfort Cassius.

MESSALA: Where did you leave him?

TITINIUS: All disconsolate,
With Pindarus his bondman, on this hill.

MESSALA: Is not that he that lies upon the ground?

TITINIUS: He lies not like the living. O my heart!

MESSALA: Is not that he?

TITINIUS: No, this was he, Messala,
But Cassius is no more. O setting sun,
As in thy red rays thou dost sink to night,
So in his red blood Cassius' day is set!

The sun of Rome is set. Our day is gone;
Clouds, dews, and dangers come; our deeds are done!
Mistrust of my success hath done this deed.

MESSALA: Mistrust of good success hath done this deed.
O hateful error, melancholy's child,
Why dost thou show to the apt thoughts of men
The things that are not? O error, soon conceiv'd,
Thou never com'st unto a happy birth,
But kill'st the mother that engend'red thee!

TITINIUS: What, Pindarus! Where art thou, Pindarus?

MESSALA: Seek him, Titinius, whilst I go to meet
The noble Brutus, thrusting this report
Into his ears. I may say "thrusting" it;
For piercing steel and darts envenomed
Shall be as welcome to the ears of Brutus
As tidings of this sight.

TITINIUS: Hie you, Messala,
And I will seek for Pindarus the while.

[*Exit* MESSALA.]

Why didst thou send me forth, brave Cassius?
Did I not meet thy friends? And did not they
Put on my brows this wreath of victory,
And bid me give it thee? Didst thou not hear their shouts?
Alas, thou hast misconstrued everything!
But, hold thee, take this garland on thy brow.

[*He places a garland on* CASSIUS' *brow.*]

Thy Brutus bid me give it thee, and I
Will do his bidding. Brutus, come apace,
And see how I regarded Caius Cassius.
By your leave, gods!—This is a Roman's part.

Come, Cassius' sword, and find Titinius' heart.

[*Stabs himself and*] *dies.*

Alarum. Enter BRUTUS, MESSALA, *young* CATO, STRATO, VOLUMNIUS, *and* LUCILIUS.

BRUTUS: Where, where, Messala, doth his body lie?

MESSALA: Lo, yonder, and Titinius mourning it.

BRUTUS: Titinius' face is upward.

CATO: He is slain.

BRUTUS: O Julius Caesar, thou art mighty yet!
Thy spirit walks abroad, and turns our swords
In our own proper entrails.

Low alarums.

CATO: Brave Titinius!
Look whe'er he have not crown'd dead Cassius!

BRUTUS: Are yet two Romans living such as these?
The last of all the Romans, fare thee well!
It is impossible that ever Rome
Should breed thy fellow. Friends, I owe moe tears
To this dead man than you shall see me pay.
I shall find time, Cassius, I shall find time.
Come, therefore, and to Thasos send his body.
His funerals shall not be in our camp,
Lest it discomfort us. Lucilius, come,
And come, young Cato, let us to the field.
Labeo and Flavius set our battles on.
'Tis three o'clock; and, Romans, yet ere night
We shall try fortune in a second fight.

Exeunt.

[SCENE IV: *Another part of the battlefield.*]

Alarum. Enter BRUTUS, MESSALA, [*young*] CATO, LUCILIUS, *and* FLAVIUS.

BRUTUS: Yet, countrymen, O, yet hold up your heads!

[*Exit, followed by* MESSALA *and* FLAVIUS.]

CATO: What bastard doth not? Who will go with me?
I will proclaim my name about the field:
I am the son of Marcus Cato, ho!
A foe to tyrants, and my country's friend.
I am the son of Marcus Cato, ho!

Enter SOLDIERS *and fight.*

LUCILIUS: And I am Brutus, Marcus Brutus I!
Brutus, my country's friend! Know me for Brutus!

[*Young* CATO *is slain by* ANTONY*'s men.*]

O young and noble Cato, art thou down?
Why, now thou diest as bravely as Titinius,
And mayst be honor'd, being Cato's son.

FIRST SOLDIER: Yield, or thou diest.

LUCILIUS: Only I yield to die.
There is so much that thou wilt kill me straight;
Kill Brutus, and be honor'd in his death.

FIRST SOLDIER: We must not. A noble prisoner!

SECOND SOLDIER: Room, ho! Tell Antony, Brutus is ta'en.

Enter ANTONY.

FIRST SOLDIER: I'll tell the news. Here comes the general.
Brutus is ta'en, Brutus is ta'en, my lord.

ANTONY: Where is he?

LUCILIUS: Safe, Antony; Brutus is safe enough.
I dare assure thee that no enemy
Shall ever take alive the noble Brutus.
The gods defend him from so great a shame!
When you do find him, or alive or dead,
He will be found like Brutus, like himself.

ANTONY: This is not Brutus, friend, but, I assure you,
A prize no less in worth. Keep this man safe;
Give him all kindness. I had rather have
Such men my friends than enemies. Go on,
And see whe'er Brutus be alive or dead;
And bring us word unto Octavius' tent
How every thing is chanc'd.

Exeunt [*severally*].

[SCENE V: *Another part of the battlefield.*]

Enter BRUTUS, DARDANIUS, CLITUS, STRATO, *and* VOLUMNIUS.

BRUTUS: Come, poor remains of friends, rest on this rock.

[*Sits.*]

CLITUS: Statilius show'd the torchlight, but, my lord,
He came not back. He is or ta'en or slain.

BRUTUS: Sit thee down, Clitus. Slaying is the word.
It is a deed in fashion. Hark thee, Clitus.

[*Whispers.*]

CLITUS: What, I, my lord? No, not for all the world.

BRUTUS: Peace then. No words.

CLITUS: I'll rather kill myself.

BRUTUS: Hark thee, Dardanius.

[*Whispers.*]

DARDANIUS: Shall I do such a deed?

[DARDANIUS *and* CLITUS *move away from* BRUTUS.]

CLITUS: O Dardanius!

DARDANIUS: O Clitus!

CLITUS: What ill request did Brutus make to thee?

DARDANIUS: To kill him, Clitus. Look, he meditates.

CLITUS: Now is that noble vessel full of grief,
That it runs over even at his eyes.

BRUTUS: Come hither, good Volumnius; list a word.

VOLUMNIUS: What say my lord?

BRUTUS: Why, this, Volumnius:
The ghost of Caesar hath appear'd to me
Two several times by night; at Sardis once,
And, this last night, here in Philippi fields.
I know my hour is come.

VOLUMNIUS: Not so, my lord.

BRUTUS: Nay, I am sure it is, Volumnius.
Thou seest the world, Volumnius, how it goes;
Our enemies have beat us to the pit.

Low alarums.

It is more worthy to leap in ourselves,
Than tarry till they push us. Good Volumnius,
Thou know'st that we two went to school together.
Even for that our love of old, I prithee,
Hold thou my sword-hilts, whilst I run on it.

VOLUMNIUS: That's not an office for a friend, my lord.

Alarum still.

CLITUS: Fly, fly, my lord! There is no tarrying here.

BRUTUS: Farewell to you; and you; and you, Volumnius.
Strato, thou hast been all this while asleep;
Farewell to thee too, Strato. Countrymen,
My heart doth joy that yet in all my life
I found no man but he was true to me.
I shall have glory by this losing day
More than Octavius and Mark Antony
By this vile conquest shall attain unto.
So fare you well at once; for Brutus' tongue
Hath almost ended his life's history.
Night hangs upon mine eyes; my bones would rest,
That have but labor'd to attain this hour.

Alarum. Cry within, "Fly, fly, fly!"

CLITUS: Fly, my lord, fly!

BRUTUS: Hence, I will follow.

[*Exeunt* CLITUS, DARDANIUS, *and* VOLUMNIUS.]

I prithee, Strato, stay thou by thy lord.
Thou art a fellow of a good respect;
Thy life hath had some smatch of honor in it.
Hold then my sword, and turn away thy face,
While I do run upon it. Wilt thou, Strato?

STRATO: Give me your hand first. Fare you well, my lord.

BRUTUS: Farewell, good Strato.

[*Runs on his sword.*]

Caesar, now be still.
I kill'd not thee with half so good a will.

Dies.

Alarum. Retreat. Enter ANTONY, OCTAVIUS;
MESSALA, LUCILIUS [*as prisoners*]; *and the army.*

OCTAVIUS: What man is that?

MESSALA: My master's man. Strato, where is thy master?

STRATO: Free from the bondage you are in, Messala.
The conquerors can but make a fire of him,
For Brutus only overcame himself,
And no man else hath honor by his death.

LUCILIUS: So Brutus should be found. I thank thee, Brutus,
That thou hast prov'd Lucilius' saying true.

OCTAVIUS: All that serv'd Brutus, I will entertain them.
Fellow, wilt thou bestow thy time with me?

STRATO: Ay, if Messala will prefer[43] me to you.

OCTAVIUS: Do so, good Messala.

MESSALA: How died my master, Strato?

STRATO: I held the sword, and he did run on it.

MESSALA: Octavius, then take him to follow thee,
That did the latest service to my master.

---

43. [*prefer:* recommend.]

ANTONY: This was the noblest Roman of them all.
All the conspirators save only he
Did that they did in envy of great Caesar;
He, only in a general honest thought
And common good to all, made one of them.
His life was gentle, and the elements
So mix'd in him that Nature might stand up
And say to all the world, "This was a man!"

OCTAVIUS: According to his virtue let us use him,
With all respect and rites of burial.
Within my tent his bones tonight shall lie,
Most like a soldier, ordered honorably.
So call the field to rest; and let's away,
To part the glories of this happy day.

Exeunt omnes.

Interpretive Questions for Discussion

Why is Brutus, who loves Caesar well, persuaded to slay Caesar for his ambition?

1. Why does Brutus brood and keep his thoughts to himself until Cassius leads him on to rebellion? (217, 221) Why does Brutus say that Cassius "whet me against Caesar"? (235)

2. Why does Cassius allow Brutus to assume leadership of the conspiracy? Why does Cassius give way and let Brutus override his good advice? (237–240; cf. 289–290)

3. Why does Brutus view the assassination of Caesar as an honorable act, rather than as cowardly treachery plotted with men who move cloaked in secrecy? Why does Brutus tell Cassius, "I love/The name of honor more than I fear death"? (219)

4. Why does Brutus believe that Caesar must be killed, not for what he already is, but for what he "may" become? (234)

5. Why does Brutus insist that the conspirators swear no oath? (237–238) Why does Brutus want the conspirators to bathe their hands in Caesar's blood before speaking to the populace? (257)

6. Why are we shown Portia, Brutus' wife, wounding herself as proof of her courage and fidelity? (243–244)

7. Why doesn't Brutus fear Mark Antony as Cassius does? (239–240, 259) Why does Brutus allow Antony to speak at Caesar's funeral and then not stay to hear what he will say? (262, 267)

8. Why is Brutus unaffected—neither tempted to accept nor fearful of the mob's fickle nature—when the plebeians call for him to be the next Caesar? (266–267)

9. Why is Brutus haunted by the ghost of Caesar? Why does the ghost vanish when Brutus reasserts his self-confidence? (292, 306)

10. Why is there a falling-out between Brutus and Cassius? Why does Brutus suspect Cassius of being a "hot friend cooling" and accuse Cassius of stealing and taking bribes in the face of Brutus' own impeccable honesty? (279, 280–285)

11. Why doesn't Brutus regret his actions, even though they lead to civil war and his own death? Why does Brutus die mistakenly believing that he will receive more glory than either Antony or Octavius? (307)

12. Are we meant to think that justice is on the side of Brutus for striking down a tyrant?

Suggested textual analyses
Pages 233–245 (Act II, scene i)

Pages 265–267: beginning, "Romans, countrymen, and lovers," and ending, "Save I alone, till Antony have spoke."

Why does Shakespeare portray Caesar, who is deified by the people and feared by the republicans for his ambition and power, as physically weak, superstitious, and vulnerable to flattery?

1. Why does the play begin with Marullus and Flavius shaming the crowd for praising Caesar and forgetting Pompey, their former hero whom Caesar had defeated? (214–215) Why are we told that the tribunes "are put to silence" for removing Caesar's trophies from the statues of Rome? (225)

2. Why does Caesar refuse the crown that Antony offers him? Why are we told by the sour-mannered Casca of Caesar's reluctance to reject the crown? (223–225)

3. Why does Caesar listen to the soothsayer's warning, but disregard his advice? (216–217) Why, despite abundant ill omens and portents, does Caesar not suspect the conspirators?

4. Why is Caesar insightful enough to distrust Cassius, but unable to recognize how truly dangerous he is? (222–223)

5. Why does Caesar insist that Decius tell the Senate merely that it is his will that he not come to the Senate that day? (248)

6. Why is the mighty Caesar vulnerable to the flattery of Decius? Why is Decius able to lure Caesar to his death by telling him that the Senate plans to offer him a crown? (248–249)

7. Why does Caesar say that he is ever Caesar, and so is not subject to fear? (223) Why does Caesar die just after he boasts that he is as fixed as the North Star? (255–256)

8. Why does Calpurnia know better than Caesar the danger that he is in?

9. Why are Caesar's last words, "*Et tu, Brutè?* Then fall, Caesar!"? (256)

10. Why doesn't the assassination of Caesar by thoughtful men with noble intentions preserve the Roman Republic?

Suggested textual analysis
Pages 245–249: beginning, "*Thunder and lightning,*" and ending, "Give me my robe, for I will go."

Are we meant to view Cassius and Antony equally as villains, responsible for the deaths of two great men?

1. Why does Cassius serve as Brutus' "glass"? Why is Cassius able to lure Brutus to seek within himself "for that which is not in me"? (218)

2. Why does Cassius tell Brutus the story of how he saved Caesar from drowning and then go on to mock Caesar's crying out like "a sick girl" when he was ill? (219–220)

3. Why does Cassius tell Brutus that the fault "is not in our stars, / But in ourselves, that we are underlings"? (220)

4. Why does Antony offer Caesar a crown?

5. Why doesn't Cassius, an able soldier and a man of courage, act against Caesar until Brutus joins the conspiracy?

6. Why does Cassius, who had wanted Antony to fall with Caesar, promise Antony that his "voice shall be as strong as any man's / In the disposing of new dignities"? (260)

7. Is Antony's vow to avenge Caesar's murder motivated by personal ambition or by regard for Caesar and hatred for his murderers? (263)

8. Why is Antony better able than Brutus to sway the populace? (265–274)

9. Why are we shown Antony speaking rudely of Lepidus and attempting to dominate Octavius? (277–278) Why are we shown Antony plotting to alter Caesar's will and coldly condemning his own nephew to death? (276–277)

10. Why is Cassius more shaken than Brutus by the news of Portia's death and the murder of one hundred senators? (288–289)

11. Why does Cassius fall just as triumph is at hand? (301) Why does Cassius forswear his allegiance to Epicureanism and embrace a belief in superstition and auguries just before the battle of Philippi? (297)

12. Why does Antony praise Brutus after his death and call him "the noblest Roman of them all"? (309)

Suggested textual analyses

Pages 217–227: beginning, "Will you go see the order of the course?" and ending, "For we will shake him, or worse days endure."

Pages 267–274: beginning, "Friends, Romans, countrymen, lend me your ears," and ending, "Take thou what course thou wilt!"

Pages 276–278: beginning, "These many, then, shall die," and ending, "Millions of mischiefs."

For Further Reflection

1. Was Brutus right to fear what Caesar would become? Can justice be served when preemptive violence is based on an idea of what "may" occur?
2. Are the qualities of intelligence, patriotism, and sincerity, such as Brutus possessed, simply not enough to lead a country in times of crisis?
3. Do great soldiers like Caesar usually make poor politicians?
4. Does the same self-confidence required to accomplish extraordinary feats also carry the seeds of its own destruction?
5. Can a charismatic and powerful leader like Caesar truly have friends or trust anybody?
6. Does *Julius Caesar* provide any insight into why Octavius eventually becomes the first emperor of Rome and rules more successfully than those who preceded him?

LONGING

Amos Oz

AMOS OZ (1939–   ) was born in Jerusalem into a family of right-wing Zionist supporters. As a teenager he went to live on a kibbutz, making it his home for much of his adult life. Oz is a veteran of the 1967 and 1973 wars in Sinai and the Golan Heights. The author of numerous novels, short stories, novellas, children's stories, essays, and articles, Oz has received many international awards, including Officer of Arts and Letters in France and the 1992 Frankfurt Peace Prize. He is a founding member of the Peace Now movement in Israel and remains a highly regarded political commentator.

From Dr. Emanuel Nussbaum to Dr. Hermine Oswald, Late of Kibbutz Tel Tomer

Malachi Street, Jerusalem
September 2, 1947

Dear Mina,

There is not much time left. You are probably in Haifa by now, perhaps packing your brassbound black leather trunk; your lips are pursed, you have just reprimanded some waiter or obsequious clerk, you are throbbing all over with efficiency and moral indignation, repeating to yourself over and over again, perhaps even aloud, the word "disgusting."

Or maybe you are not in Haifa. Perhaps you are already on board the ship bound for New York, sitting in your second-class cabin, wearing your reading glasses, digesting some uninspired article in one of your learned journals, untroubled and unexcited by the swell of the waves and the salt smell of the sea air, undistracted by the seagulls, the darkening expanse of the sea, or the strains of the tango wafting down from the ballroom. You are completely absorbed in yourself, no doubt. As always. Up to your ears in work.

I am simply guessing.

I do not know where you are at this moment. How could I know? You never answered either of the letters I wrote you two months ago, and you left no forwarding address. So, you've made up your mind to turn over a new leaf. Your gray eyes are fixed firmly on the future and on the assignments you have undertaken. You will not look back, remember, feel longing, regret. You are striding purposefully forward. Naturally, you are not entirely unacquainted with weakness of mind: after all, that is the subject of your research. But who can rival your firm resolve to turn over a new leaf from time to time? And you didn't leave me any address. I even wasted my time trying at the Kibbutz Tel Tomer office. She's through. Gone away. She's been invited to lecture in America. She may have left already. Sorry.

It is possible that eventually you will be stirred by courtesy or curiosity, and I shall suddenly receive an American postcard with a picture of colorful towers or some grandiose steel bridge. I have still not entirely given up hope, as I said to myself this morning while shaving. However, the sight of my face in the mirror almost stirs feelings of curiosity and sadness in me myself. And disgust, too. My illness has made my cheeks collapse inward, it has made my eyes so prominent that they terrify little children, and it has especially emphasized my nose, like a Nazi caricature. Symptoms. And my hair, that artistic gray mop that you used to enjoy running your fingers through for the static electricity, is all faded and thin. No more sparks. If it went on falling out at that rate for a few more months, I shouldn't have a hair left on my head. As if I had deliberately set out to make fun of the appearance of my dear father, by exaggerating it.

What have I to do with exaggeration? What have I to do with fun? I have always been, and still am, a quiet man. The happy medium, a balanced choice of words—these were always my pride. Albeit a silent pride. There were times, in our nights of love, when I would let go and a savage, pulsating side of me would temporarily take over. Now our love is finished, and I am my usual self again. I have settled back and found nothing. A salty waste. An arid plain. A few stray longings scattered here and there like thornbushes. You know. After all, inside you, too—forgive me—there is a barren desert. A different kind of desert, though. Scorched earth, a phrase I came across this morning in the paper in connection with the termination of the British Mandate.

Well, then.

Dear Mina, as I have already said, there is not much time left. War will break out here soon; almost everybody admits it now. This morning I had a few neighbors in for a kind of meeting in my study. Even my own Kerem Avraham is already forming a sort of civil-defense committee. That's how far things have gone.

What will come of this war I haven't the faintest idea. Only all sorts of hopes and fears. You will be in a safe place, far from Jerusalem, far from Galilee and the valleys you have explored so thoroughly during these last years. It goes without saying that I shall not be able to play an active part in the war, either as a doctor on the battlefield or in a hospital behind the lines. The illness is progressing toward its final phases. Not in a continuous straight line, though. It is toying with me, with cunning ploys, temporary concessions, feigned moderation, a brilliant strategy of deception and false hopes. I almost smile to myself: doesn't it realize it's dealing with a doctor, and not, say, an artist? It can't take me in. These arabesques, the alternating alarms and all-clears, the false hopes, the avoidance of a frontal assault, how unnecessary they all are when the designated target is a man like me, an experienced diagnostician, an educated man, with a modest medical library at my disposal and with German as my mother tongue.

In short, I am my usual self: in a state of calm despair. The terminal stage will begin in the winter and be over before the spring, or it may begin in the spring and continue at most until the first heat waves of 1948. I won't go into details. I trust, dear Mina, that there is no need to prove to you in writing that in the meantime I am quietly and confidently continuing with the routine of my daily life.

No news.

There's nothing much new that I can offer you in general.

I don't have much time to spare, either.

I spend most of the hours of day and night on the lookout to see what is happening in Jerusalem. Now and again I still try to make my modest patriotic contribution, such as this morning, in the meeting of the local defense committee. And I still keep up certain friendly neighborly contacts. And I am continuing my chemical experiments in my private laboratory, which may eventually render some service to the community in connection with the war effort.

Meanwhile, my observations have yielded a definite conviction that here in Jerusalem the summer is gradually, almost from day to day, relaxing its hold. There are already a few unobtrusive indications of the approach of autumn. The leaves have not begun to fall yet, of course, but there are hints of a slight change of tint, in the foliage, or in the refracted light at dawn or dusk. Or in both together: no contradiction is involved.

There is a shadow of clouds over our backyards. People speak softly and seriously. The twilight is beginning earlier, and its glow is more subdued than usual, more fantastic, a poet might add more desperate, a kind of bitter enthusiasm like a last act of love, which is full of wild abandon because it is the last and there is no more to come. At the end of the twilight, you can see a column of gray light over the western mountains and splashes of fire on the windowpanes, the towers, and the domes, and some water tank or other on a rooftop may go crazy and flare up. After this fire, the mountains are swathed in smoke. And a miracle: suddenly there is even a smell of smoke in Jerusalem.

So the lazy summer sunsets are over and gone. There is a new seriousness in the air. It is even cool outside in the early evening. Occasionally I have the feeling that there are fewer birds around. I must check this latest detail carefully, though, because common sense would indicate that autumn brings back the migrating birds.

So here I am, Mina, writing this letter to you slowly, on these small, smooth sheets of paper with my name printed at the top in Hebrew and German, which I used to use for writing prescriptions. You used to call these letters of mine "schoolboy notes." The difference is that this time, apparently, I shall not be brief. Or witty, either.

I am sitting at a table on the balcony, wearing a gray pullover but still with the peasant sandals you bought me in the Old City more than a year ago. Between the fingers that are writing to you and the toes in these sandals there seems to be a great distance now, not because I have suddenly grown taller, but because of the diseased organs in between. Dear Mina, the evening is still light enough for me to write, but I can sense the light beginning to fade. The whole city will be swathed, enfolded, district after district will attach itself to the cavalcade of night. The towers on top of the hills to the east will lead the procession, and the entire city will fall in behind, and march down into the enclosing desert. The nightly routine of Jerusalem. You have heard me say this before, and you called it all "poetic fantasy." There is nothing new. A particular pain has just started up and is almost tormenting me, as if a man like me is unlikely to take a mere hint. Very well. I shall swallow my pride and stifle the pain with an injection. Presently.

I should like to come back to the balcony and go on writing even when it is dark. The cool air is gentle and almost stimulating. I shall switch the lights on inside and try to bring the desk lamp out from the study. Will the extension cord reach? We shall see. I doubt it.

From the balcony opposite, across the neglected yard, my neighbor Mrs. Grill is questioning me:

"How are you feeling today, Dr. Emanuel, what does the radio say this evening, and when will your car be arriving?" My radio is the only one in the immediate neighborhood. Sometimes I serve as the link between the neighbors and what they call the outside world. The neighbors' boy Uri has taken to dropping in because I have permitted him to come and listen to the news, and so it was that he discovered my laboratory. As for the car, everyone here is saying that I shall soon have one of my own. The source of this rumor is apparently the boys, Uri's enemies. They know that I have stopped working as a doctor, they have somehow heard that I am doing some work for the Jewish Agency, and they have already invested me with a private car. I deny it gently. I apologize, as though I have been accused of doing something improper. Meanwhile, Mrs. Grill chuckles at me:

"Don't worry, Dr. Emanuel, we're used to keeping secrets. My husband's a veteran of the Trade Union, and as for me, I lost all my family in Lodz. You can count on us. We're not the sort to gossip."

"Perish the thought," I mutter. "It never entered my head to suggest that you . . . But the fact of the matter is that . . ." But she's already vanished: rushed back to her kitchen to save a pan of milk from boiling over or disappeared behind the linens she hangs out to dry on her balcony, among the crates and washtubs and suitcases. I am alone once more.

Let me tell you, in passing, about the Jewish Agency. I have a little cubbyhole tucked away behind my study, a storage room, a home laboratory, a darkroom. You complained once about the chemical smells that came from there and spread all over the apartment. I expect you remember. Well, I haven't given up my modest experiments. Some time ago I drew up a kind of memorandum about the possible military uses of a certain chemical of which we have relatively plentiful supplies. As a result, three weeks ago an engineer from the Jewish Agency or the Hagganah arrived in a great flurry to ask whether I would be willing to draw up an inventory of explosives that are legally stored in the Solel Boneh quarries in the mountains, and also of other explosives that are dispersed in various places in Jerusalem. And also to make a card index of useful chemicals held in Jewish factories in the city. And also to suggest all sorts of combinations and to work out what we have and what we would be short of in case of a prolonged war. We'd be short of everything, I replied; we wouldn't even have enough bread or water. My visitor smiled: he had decided I was possessed of a morbid sense of humor. "Dr. Nussbaum," he said, still smiling as he turned to leave, "everything will be all right. Just you compile the inventory. And leave the rest to us. We'll be prepared to try out any reasonable idea that occurs to you. Dushkin himself considers you one of the most brilliant minds in the field. We'll be in touch. Good-bye."

In short, I accepted. Anyway, the man didn't wait for an answer. As if he had given me an order. Ever since I had drawn up that memo, or perhaps since Dushkin had spoken to me in his usual effusive way at some meeting, someone must have been crediting me with magical powers, or expecting me to be a sort of alchemist for them. In brief, they would be very pleased but not at all surprised if I turned up tomorrow morning, tonight, clutching the formula for a powerful explosive that could be manufactured quickly, cheaply, in any kitchen, and of which a minute quantity would have a devastating effect. There is a slogan current here at the moment that is repeated every evening by the Underground on their shortwave broadcasts: "When your back's to the wall, even the incredible is possible." Admittedly, you or I could easily refute this slogan on a philosophical plane. But nevertheless, for the time being I accept it, both out of a sense of loyalty and because, with a little effort, I can discern a certain poetry in it. A crude poetry, it is true, but then, if I may so express myself, the state of affairs at the moment is crude.

A minor miracle has just occurred. I have managed despite everything to bring the desk lamp from my study out onto the balcony. The extension cord was almost long enough. A slight compromise: I moved the table a little nearer to the door. But I'm still outside, surrounded by a halo of electric light, with incredible shadows flickering on the stone wall behind me, and now what do I care if it's dark.

By the way, I have already numbered my little pages: I shall have to concentrate. On what? On the main point. Dear Mina, let me try to define just what the main point is at the moment. I shall put my empty cup down on the pages, because the wind is liable to blow up without warning, as usual here in the evening in the early autumn.

Well, then.

It has occurred to me to set down in writing various details about myself, about my immediate surroundings, certain observations about Jerusalem, and, in particular, my district, Kerem Avraham: things seen and heard. No doubt here and there cautious comparisons will emerge, and certain memories may find their way in. Don't worry, Mina: I don't intend to embellish or sully our shared memories in writing this. No chains around your new life. America, I have read, is a good and wonderful country where all eyes are constantly on the future, where even longing is directed to the future, and everybody agrees that the past is condemned to silence.

Have you arrived yet, Mina, have you discovered a quiet café among the towers and bridges where you can sit down, put on your glasses, and spread out your notes? Are you getting used to speaking Red Indian? Or are you still on the boat, on your way, just passing, say, the Azores? Does the name Sierra Madre mean something to you yet? Dear Mina, are you all right?

Perhaps it isn't too late yet.

Perhaps you are still in Haifa, packing, getting ready, and I could still catch the evening train, arrive before midnight, find you in some small boardinghouse on the Carmel, and sit with you in silence looking out over the dark water, the shadow of the Galilean hills, with British warships ablaze with lights in the bay, and one of them suddenly bursting into a plaintive moan.

I don't know.

My health isn't up to the journey, either.

And if I do come, and if I manage to find you, you're sure to say:

"Emanuel. Why have you come? And what a mess you look."

If I say that I've come to say good-bye, my voice will betray me. Or my lips will tremble. And you will remark with cold sorrow:

"That's not true."

I shall be forced into silence. There will be embarrassment, awkwardness, probably physical pains as well. I shall be a burden on you.

No journey. After all, I have no idea where you are.

I don't even know why I am writing you this long letter, what the subject is, what, as they say, is on the agenda, what I am writing to you about. I'm sorry.

It is evening now. I've already said that twice, but still the evening continues. Below me, on the sidewalk, some girls are playing hopscotch, and Uri, out of their sight, is following their skipping from his hiding place among the shrubs with a slow movement of the muzzle of his ray gun. Now he has stopped and is sunk in thought or in dreams. From where I am sitting, I can see his head and the silhouette of the gun. This child is always on guard and always seems to be asleep at his post. Soon the children will be going indoors. The cries will die away, but there will be no quiet. I have pains; one of them is particularly cruel, but I shall persist in ignoring it and concentrate on recording the place and the time. Dear Mina, please don't read these words with your patient, ironic smile; try for once to smile innocently or not at all. I hate your irony. Always effortlessly piercing the barrier of words, deciphering what lies behind them, always forgiving. How desolate. Are the birds really changing guard in the fig tree and the mulberry as the blaze of oleanders dies down in the garden? Evening has come. Barking of dogs far away, echo of bells, shooting, a raven's croak. Such simple, instant, trivial things—why do they all sound to me as though never again.

Now the moment is approaching when the light in Jerusalem is distorted. It is the light of the stone that is beginning to make itself felt, as if it were not the last traces of the sun setting behind the clouds but, rather, the walls, the ramparts, the distant towers projecting the inner light of their souls. At this point you may exhale your cigarette smoke through your nostrils, as usual, and say to yourself, "What, again."

You may, I said. Meaning, I can't prevent it.

I could never prevent anything. Whatever happened, happened because you wanted it.

You said to me once: Here we are, Emanuel and Mina, two educated people, two people with similar backgrounds, and yet there is no reason for them to establish a permanent relationship.

I agree. On the one hand, Dr. Nussbaum, a gentle man, a man beset by doubts: even when he wants something he always suspects his motives, and frequently his smile is confused, like that of a man who has finally dared to tell a story and immediately starts wondering: Is it funny, has it been understood, is it out of place. On the other, Dr. Oswald, a bitter, determined woman; even her rare compromises are almost a matter of life and death. She stubs out her cigarettes as though she were trying to bore a hole in the bottom of the ashtray.

Surely we both knew in advance it would be a mistake.

Yet even so, you saw fit to be linked to me for a while. As for me—is it proper for a man like me, a man in my condition, to say so?—I loved you. I still do.

Jerusalem
September 3, 1947

Dear Mina,

In my dreams at night you come back to me in a gray-brown dress, with knowing fingers. Quiet. Even your voice in the dreams is different, calmer, warmer.

At midnight I had a snack: a roll with olives, tomato, cucumber. I gave myself my nightly injection and took two different pain-killing tablets. In bed I read a few pages of the journal of an acute English pilgrim who visited the Holy Land eighty years ago and saw Jerusalem in a dismal light. It was O'Leary who lent me the book. Then I turned off the light and heard the distant humming of engines, probably a British military convoy making its way to Ramallah and the mountains of Samaria. Drowsily, unconcernedly, I could see in my mind's eye the desolate valleys, the miserable stone-built villages, some sacred tree wrapped in darkness among the boulders, with perhaps a fox sniffing in its shadows, and farther on the caves, embers of bonfires, ancient olive trees, the sadness of the deserted goat tracks in the night, the rustling thistles in the scented, late-summer breeze, and the column of British jeeps with dimmed headlights winding up the mountain road. A very ancient land. Then there was a whispering on the steps of the house. My father and his lawyer in the passage, arguing, chuckling, I can hardly catch the words, but the subject is apparently some fraud, some investigation that threatens me, legal arguments that can still perhaps save me from some great disgrace. I lock the study door and rush to the kitchen. I must push my father almost roughly out of there, while the lawyer bows to me sadly and tactfully. In vain I search feverishly for the source of the damp smoke. I cough and almost choke. I must hurry. Any moment now, the British police may arrive, and Uri's parents would blame me for everything. And then your brown dress on the kitchen balcony, and suddenly you. I don't try to resist. I drape my jacket carefully over the back of the chair, roll up my vest, even guide you to the line of my diaphragm and almost enjoy the sight of your knowing fingers. Unerringly, painlessly, you rip open the skin, penetrate the rib cage, seek and find the affected gland, and extract the revolting fluid from it with forceps and a fine scalpel. There is no bleeding. No pain. The nerve endings are like white worms. The muscle tissue tears with the sound of ripping cloth. And I sit and watch your fingers operating inside my body as in an illustrated textbook. Look, Emanuel, you smile, it's all over. Thank you, I whisper. And I add: I'd like to get dressed. And then the gland itself, bloated and bluish-green, looking like a gigantic tick, swollen with pus, walking insectlike on thin, hairy legs slowly down my thigh, my calf, onto the floor; I throw the tin mug at it and miss, you crush it under the toe of your shoe, and a greasy jet squirts out. Now get dressed and we'll have a drink, you say, coffee, you say, but the shrewd light glints in your eye as you change your mind: You mustn't drink coffee, Emanuel, you must make do with fresh fruit until you are a little stronger. Your hands in my hair. I feel good. I say nothing. My child, you say, how cold you are. And how pale. Now close your eyes. Stop thinking. Sleep quietly. I obey. Inside my closed eyes the kitchen fades, and there is only the jam jar on the kitchen table, swarming with wormlike glands, hairy, damp, with insect antennae, and in the bread, too, in the fruit bowl, there is even one crawling up my pajama sleeve. Never mind. I am at rest. With my eyes closed I can hear your voice, a Russian song. Where did you get this Russian, from the kibbutz in the Jezreel Valley, from the fields, take me there when my strength returns, and there I shall follow you. Dear Mina. At three o'clock, the bell of the dock tower in the Schneller Barracks pierces my sleep. I switch on the light; with a shaking hand I clutch the cup of cold tea, remove the glass saucer that covers it, have a sip, take another pill, and return to the English pilgrim and argue with him in my mind about the line of the watershed, which he unhesitatingly locates along the ridge of Mount Scopus and the Mount of Olives. With the dawn, I fall asleep again in the twilight, without turning off the light, and I hear you say that now you can reveal that you have borne me a child and lodged it in one of the kibbutzim in the valley to spare me the trouble of looking after it in my present condition. Your lips in my hair. You have not gone, Mina. No, I haven't gone. I am here. Every night I shall come to you, Emanuel, but during the day I must hide because of the searches and the curfew, until we have outwitted the enemy and the Hebrew state has gained its freedom. I fall asleep with my head in your lap and wake up to the sound of repeated bursts of sharp firing. Tonight the Irgun or the Stern Group has raided the British barracks again. Perhaps the first tentative engagements of the new war have begun. I get up.

Pale light in the window. A cock is crowing furiously in the next-door yard. And the strange boy is already up and about, poking in the junk and dragging discarded packing cases hither and thither. Six o'clock in the morning. A new day, and I must put the kettle on for my shaving water and my early-morning coffee. For another half hour I can still keep the night-child alive, our son, the baby you bore me and hid from me. At half past six the newspaper arrived, and at a quarter past seven I heard on the news that the London *Times* has warned the Zionists against a reckless gamble that may prove fatal, and advised them to make a realistic revision of their aspirations and to understand once and for all that the idea of a Jewish state will lead to a blood bath. Another solution must be devised that may be acceptable to the Arabs, too, at least to their more moderate elements. However, the paper will in no way sanction handing over the achievements of the Zionist settlers to Moslem religious fanatics; the achievements themselves are admirable, but the inflated political aspirations of the leaders of the Jewish Agency verge on adventurism. After the news, while I made my bed and dusted the highboy and the bookshelves, David Zakkai gave a talk about the night sky in September. Then there was a program of morning music, while outside in the street the kerosene vendors and icemen rang the bells of their pushcarts. Over and over again I weighed the words in my heart: Recklessness. Gamble. Adventurism.

At eight o'clock, I decided to go to the Hadassah Hospital on Mount Scopus, to invade Professor Dushkin's office for a quarter of an hour and ask him again how my illness was developing and what he made of last week's tests. The piercing desert light had already engulfed Jerusalem. A dry wind was blowing among the hills. And in the dusty bus the students were joking, mimicking the German accents of their lecturers with a Polish twist of humor. Along the way, in the suburb of Sheikh Jarrah, there were wickerwork stools spilling over onto the sidewalk from a coffeehouse, and on one of them I saw a young, educated Arab in a pin-striped suit and horn-rimmed spectacles sitting in motionless contemplation, the tiny coffee cup seemingly frozen in his hand. He did not take the trouble to direct so much as a glance at the Jewish bus. In my mind I could not refrain from comparing his silence with the clamor of the students in the bus and the histrionic laughter of the girls. And I was filled with apprehension.

Professor Dushkin roared my name delightedly and immediately shooed out of his office a clucking, shriveled nurse who had been filling out index cards. He slammed the door after her, thumped me on the shoulder, and proclaimed in a Russian bellow:

"Out with it! Let's talk frankly, as usual."

I asked him four or five short questions concerning the results of last week's tests and received the expected replies.

"But look here, my dear Emanuel," he exclaimed rumbustiously, "you remember what happened in the summer of '44, with Rabbi Zweik, the mystic from Safed. Yes. We came to exactly the same conclusions with him, and yet his tumor dissolved and his condition was, how shall we say, arrested. And he's still alive and kicking. It's a fact."

I smiled. "So what are you suggesting, that I should settle down to study mysticism?"

Professor Dushkin poured out tea. He pressed me to accept a biscuit. Idiocy, he declared, was rampant on all sides. Even among his own faculty. Even in politics. The leaders of the Jewish Agency, he considered, were political infants, loudmouthed amateurs, small-town autodidacts, illiterates, ignoramuses, and these were the people who had to pit their wits now against the sophisticated experts of Whitehall. It was enough to drive you crazy. Another glass of tea? What's the matter with you, of course you will. I've poured it out already, what do you want, have you only come here to irritate me? Drink! In a word, Shertok and Berl Locker. What more need I say: political Svidrigaïlovs everywhere. In December we'll have you in for some more tests, and if there's been no change for the worse by then, we'll be entitled to take it as an encouraging sign. No, more than a sign, a turning point! That's right. Meanwhile, how shall I put it, keep your spirits up, my friend. One cannot help admiring your composure.

As he spoke, I suddenly noticed a film of tears in his eyes. He was a heavily built, muscular, compact-looking man. He invariably wept at the first onset of emotion; he was always flushing and boiling over. I had secretly nicknamed him "Samovar."

I rose to take my leave.

So, no new tests just yet. And no treatment. Just as I had expected.

"Thanks, Dushkin," I said. "Thank you very much."

"Thanks?" he cried out as if I had wounded him. "What's the matter? What's got into you? Are you crazy? What have you got to thank me for all of a sudden?"

"You've been frank with me. And you've hardly uttered a single superfluous word."

"You're exaggerating, Emanuel," he said with sadness and emotion in his voice. "For once you're exaggerating. But of course," he added in his former tones, "of course when idiocy is on the rampage, any meeting like ours today is almost an occasion. Svidrigaïlovs, I say: political Svidrigaïlovs, and medical Svidrigaïlovs as well. Even here in our department there are all sorts of Shertoks and Berl Lockers living it up. Well. The bus into town leaves in ten minutes. Number nine as usual. No—don't run! There's no hurry, it'll be late. I swear it'll be late. After all, it's Hammekasher, not the Royal Navy. If you notice any change, come and see me at once. At two o'clock in the morning, even. You can be sure of a hot glass of tea. How I love you, Emanuel, how my heart weeps for you. Na! Enough. Since we were talking about that grubby saint Rabbi Zweik, who broke all the rules in our book and literally rose from the dead, let me repeat a little saying of his. He used to tell us that the Almighty sometimes plays a trick on His worshipers and shows them that if He wills He can save a life even by means of doctors and medicine. Now, fare you well, my friend. Be brave."

His eyes glistened again. He opened the door for me furiously and suddenly roared out in a terrible voice:

"Svidrigaïlov! Shmendrik! Come here at once! Run and clear the X-ray room for me immediately! Use force if necessary!

Throw a bomb in, I don't care! But on the way show Dr. Nussbaum here to the elevator. No, to the bus stop. You're turning this Jerusalem of ours into a veritable Bedlam! As you see, gentlemen, at times I can be a terrible man. A cannibal. A Tartar. That's what I am. Na! Be seeing you, Emanuel. And don't worry about me. You know me. I'll get over it. And also . . . Forget it. Good-bye, good-bye, good-bye."

Despite all this, I missed the bus. But I bore no grudge against Samovar. I waited on the bench at the bus stop for close to an hour. The city and the mountains seemed amazingly quiet. Minarets and domes in the Old City, buildings overflowing down the slopes of gray hills in the new town, here and there tiled roofs, empty plots, olive trees, and apparently not a soul in Jerusalem. Only the dry wind in the woods behind me, and birds chattering calmly from the British military cemetery.

But on the other side lay the desert. It was literally at my feet. A neglected, rock-strewn terrain dotted with pieces of newspaper, thistles, and rusting iron, a wasteland of limestone or chalk. In other words, from the scenic point of view Mount Scopus is the threshold of the desert. I have a horror of this propinquity between myself and the desert. Over there are forsaken valleys, rocks baking in the sun, shrubs sculpted by the wind, and there are scorpions in the crevices of the rocks, strange stone huts, minarets on bald hilltops, the last villages. On the opposite slopes and in the Jordan valley are traces of ruined biblical towns, Sumieh, which my English pilgrim identifies with Beth-jesimoth, Abel-shittim, Beth-haran, Nimrin, which may be the ancient Beth-nimrah. And scattered among these ruins are camps of Bedouin tribes, goatskin tents, and dark shepherds armed with daggers. Justice through bloodshed. The simple law of the desert: love, honor, and death. And there is a venomous biblical snake called the asp. How I shudder, Mina, at this closeness to the desert.

Yes. Forgive me. You have already heard the gist of all this from me, in Haifa, at the Lev Ha-Carmel Café, over strawberry ice-cream sundaes. You remember. And you dismissed it all as "Viennese *angst.*" I won't deny it: it is indeed *angst.* And perhaps even Viennese *angst.*

Did I ever tell you this as well?

From my window as a child, I could see the canal. There were barges. Sometimes at night a noisy holiday cruiser went past, a riot of multicolored lights. The water was spanned by two bridges, one arched and the other modern. Perhaps in your student days you chanced to pass by these places. Perhaps we passed each other in the street unawares. Night after night I could see the consumptive sidewalk artist smoking and choking, smoking as though he reveled in the agony of coughing, vomiting in the gutter, and smoking again. I have not forgotten. The row of street lamps along the quay. The shivering reflections in the water. The smell of that gray water. The streetwalker on the corner of the old bridge. The boardinghouse whose ground floor was a tavern called the Weary Heart, where I could always see art students, all sorts of women; one of them stood there once and cried without a sound and stamped her foot. On warm evenings, gentlemen wandered around as if searching for inspiration, their faces either lost in thought or bereft of hope. The souvenir vendor wandered from shop to shop. "Like trying to sell ice to Eskimos," my father would jest. Every hour we could hear the bell of the local church, over whose door was inscribed the legend THERE IS A WAY BACK in four languages, Latin, German, Greek, and Hebrew (only the Hebrew was written in curious characters, and there was a slight spelling mistake). Next to the church was the antique shop run by two Jewish partners, the fakers Gips and Gutzi, whom I told you about when we went to Degania together on the valley train. Do you remember, Mina? You laughed. You accused me of "poetic license." And you forgave me.

But you were wrong. Gips existed, and so did Gutzi. I am putting this down in writing now because I have come to the point where I feel obliged to insist, even if it means contradicting you: the truth comes first. As I wrote the word "truth," I paused for a moment. Yes, a slight hesitation. For what is the truth, Mina? Perhaps this: I did not give up Vienna for Jerusalem; I was driven out, more or less, and even though at the time I thought of this expulsion almost as the destruction of the rest of my life, in fact it gained me eight or nine years of life, and it has enabled me to see Jerusalem and to meet you. All the way from there to Malachi Street. To Mount Scopus. Almost to the edge of the desert. If I were not afraid of making you lose your temper I would use the word "absurd." You and Jerusalem. Jerusalem and I. We and the heirs of prophets, kings, and heroes. We turn over a new leaf only to smudge it with ancient neuroses. My child, my neighbors' child, Uri, sometimes shows me his private poems. He trusts me, because I do not laugh at him, and because he thinks of me as a secret inventor who is lying low because of a conspiracy while perfecting wonderful secret weapons for the Hebrew state. He writes poems about the ten lost tribes, Hebrew cavalrymen, great conquests, and acts of vengeance. Doubtless some little teacher, some messianic madman, has captured the child's imagination with the usual Jerusalemite blend of apocalyptic visions and romantic fantasies of Polish or Cossack cavalrymen. Sometimes I try my hand at writing my own educational stories, about Albert Schweitzer in Africa, the life of Louis Pasteur, Edison, that wonderful man Janusz Korczak. All in vain.

In the laundry on the roof of his house, Uri has a rocket made from bits of an old icebox and parts from an abandoned bicycle. The rocket is aimed at the Houses of Parliament in London. And I alone am responsible for the delay, because it is up to me, Dr. Einstein, Dr. Faust, Dr. Gog-and-Magog, to develop in my laboratory the formula for the secret fuel and the Hebrew atomic bomb.

He spends hours on end immersed in my huge German atlas. He is quiet, polite, clean, and tidy. He listens respectfully to what I say but rebukes me for my slowness. He pins little flags in the atlas to trace the course of the advance (with my permission, naturally). He plans a mock landing of Hebrew paratroops on the Suez Canal and along the Red Sea coast. He captures the British fleet off Crete and Malta. Occasionally I am invited to join in this game that is more than a game, in the role of Perfidious Albion, hatching dark plots, conducting desperate rear-guard actions on land and sea, in the Dardanelles, Gibraltar, the Red Sea approaches. Eventually I am forced to capitulate graciously, to cede the whole of the East to the forces of the Hebrew Kingdom, to enter into negotiations, to pencil in lightly the limits of spheres of influence, and to admit sportingly that I have lost the diplomatic war of minds just as I have already been conclusively routed on the battlefield. Only then will the ground be prepared for a military alliance, and the two of us together, Kingdom of Israel and British Empire, will be able to operate against the desert tribesmen. We would advance eastward in a carefully coordinated pincer movement until we encountered a forward patrol of the forces of the ten lost tribes, right at the edge of the map. I have permitted Uri to sketch in in blue pencil a large but Godforsaken Israelite kingdom in Central Asia, somewhere among the Himalaya Mountains.

The game is not entirely to my taste, but I join in nonetheless, and at times I even experience a certain secret thrill: A child. A strange child. My child.

"Dr. Nussbaum," Uri says, "please, if you don't feel well again, I can give you your supper. And I can go to the greengrocer's for you and to Ziegel's and buy whatever you need. Just tell me what."

"Thank you, Uri. There's no need. On the contrary; there's some chocolate in the kitchen cupboard—help yourself, and you may find some almonds, too. And then you must go home, so they don't worry about you."

"They won't worry. I can even stay overnight and keep an eye on the laboratory so you can get some sleep. Mommy and Daddy have gone away to a sanatorium. There's no one at home except Auntie Natalia, and she won't make any trouble for us—

she's too busy with her own business. I can even stay out of doors all night if I want to. Or just stay quietly here with you."

"What about your homework?"

"It's done. Dr. Emanuel—"

"Yes, Uri."

"Nothing. Only you . . ."

"What did you want to ask me, Uri? Don't be shy. Ask."

"Nothing. Are you always . . . alone?"

"Recently, yes."

"Haven't you got any brothers or sisters? Haven't you thought about . . . getting married?"

"No. Why do you ask?"

"No reason. Only I haven't, either."

"Haven't what?"

"Nothing. I haven't got any brothers or sisters. And I . . . I don't need anybody."

"It's not the same, Uri."

"Yes, it is. And you don't call me a crazy child. Am I a crazy child?"

"No, Uri, you're not."

"Just the opposite. I'm your assistant. And that's a secret between you and me."

"Naturally," I say without a smile. "Now you must go. Tomorrow, if you like, we'll spend some time in the lab. I'll show you how to reduce certain substances to their elements. It will be a chemistry lesson, and you tell them that at home, please, if they ask you about your visits to me."

"Sure. You can count on me not to talk. I'll say it was chemistry lessons like you said. Don't worry, Dr. Emanuel. Bye."

"Wait a minute, Uri." I hesitate. "Just a minute."

"Yes?"

"Here, your sweater. Good night."

He leaves the house. Slips away down the back stairs. From my balcony I can watch his furtive passage among the shrubs. Suddenly I feel a surge of regret. What have I done. Have I gone mad. I mustn't. Then again: he's the neighbors' child, not mine. And naturally my illness is not catching. But all this will end badly. I'm sorry, Mina. You will certainly view this strange relationship in a totally negative light. And you will be right, as usual. I'm very sorry.

ꝏ

September 5
Evening again

Dear Mina,

I should have told Professor Dushkin there and then on Mount Scopus that I could on no account accept his harsh words about Moshe Shertok and Berl Locker. After all, these poor delegates of a tiny, isolated community are almost empty-handed. And I should have told the engineer from the Jewish Agency that it would be better for them to give up their useless fantasies about mysterious weapons and start making clear-sighted preparations for the departure of the British army and the impending war. And I should have tried to put up a fight—forgive me for using such a hyperbolic expression—to put up a fight for the soul of my child, my neighbors' child, to put a firm stop to his games of conquest, to get him out of my laboratory, to produce sensible arguments to counteract the romantic dreams with which his Cossack Bible teacher has apparently filled the boy's head.

But I cannot deny that these romantic dreams sometimes take hold of me, too, at night, in between the attacks of pain. Last night I helped Dr. Weizmann, disguised as a Catholic priest, to make his way secretly in the dark to one of the bridges over the Danube and empty phials of plague bacillus into the water. After all, we are already infected, Dr. Weizmann said; there's no hope for either of us, he said; if only we live long enough to see that our death does not go unavenged. I tried to remonstrate, I reminded him that we had both always despised such language, but he turned a tortured, eyeless face toward me and called me "Svidrigaïlov."

Early in the morning, I went out onto the balcony again. I found the light on in my neighbors' window across the yard. Zevulun Grill, who is a driver in the Hammekasher bus co-operative and a member of our local civil-defense committee, was standing in his kitchen slicing a sausage. He was probably making his sandwiches. I, too, put the kettle on for my shaving water and my morning coffee, and a strange, irrelevant phrase kept grating in my mind like a trashy popular tune that refuses to go away: a thorn in the flesh. I am a thorn in her flesh. We are a thorn in their flesh.

Dear Mina, I must record that yet another bad sign has joined all the others: for the first time I fell asleep fully dressed on the sofa. I woke up rumpled and disheveled at two o'clock and dragged myself to bed. So I shall have to hurry up.

"I went to the Tel Arza woods by myself after school," Uri said. "I've brought you a canful of that honey stuff that drips from pine trees when you break off a branch; hello, Dr. Nussbaum, I forgot to say it when I came in, and nobody followed me here because I was careful and made several detours on the way. This stuff smells a bit like turpentine, only different. My suggestion, which I thought of on the way back, is that we could try mixing it with a bit of gasoline and some acetone, then lighting it and seeing what the blast's like."

"Today, Uri, I suggest that we do something completely different. For a change. Let's close the windows, make ourselves comfortable, and listen to some classical music on the phonograph. Afterward, if you want to ask any questions, I may be able to explain some of the musical terms."

"Music," Uri said. "We get enough of that at home all day from my mother and her piano. Today you're not feeling well again, Dr. Emanuel, I can see, so maybe it's better if I come back tomorrow afternoon or Saturday morning to work by myself all alone on the experiments that are written in your notebook on the desk in the lab, with the sodium nitrate like you said, or the other thing, what's its name, nitric acid and nitrobenzene, does it say? Sorry to hurry you, only you're always saying that we must hurry up."

"I said that, Uri, I don't deny that I said it. But that was just in the game."

"You only call it a game because of the secrecy. Don't try to say you didn't really mean it 'cause I could see that you did. But never mind. I'll come back some other time."

"But Uri . . ."

"If it's one of your attacks, God forbid, then I'll run and call Dr. Kipnis, and if not, I'm ready to wash all the test tubes from the experiments in ten minutes and especially to fill the spirit lamp. Or if you like I'll go home now, and I'll report for duty the minute I see a slanting chink in your bathroom blinds like we arranged. Meanwhile, bye-bye, Dr. Emanuel, and be well, 'cause what'll I do if anything happens to you suddenly."

Do I have the strength, do I have the right, to try to influence his mind?

The education of children is totally outside my province.

Outside, in the yard, the Grill children ambush him and make fun of him. I can't hear the words, and even if I could I don't suppose I could understand them. I can hear their evil laughter. And Uri's heroic silence.

What can I do.

I sit at the table on the balcony, writing you an account that is incapable of yielding results or conclusions. Forgive me.

Meanwhile, it is almost dark outside. I have stretched the desk lamp out here again from my study so that I can write to you under this evening sky. Soon the first stars will appear. It is almost as if I could still expect some illumination. As if here in Jerusalem even a man like me could momentarily be chosen for the role of messenger.

Moths around the lamp. I have stopped writing for a moment to make myself some coffee by the most primitive method: boiling water poured on the black powder. No milk, no sugar. I had a biscuit, too. Then I had an attack of weakness and nausea; a sour taste rose in my throat. I took a pill and gave myself an injection. Forgive me, Mina, these physical complaints bore me and have nothing to do with the matter at hand.

But what *does* have to do with the matter at hand? What *is* the matter at hand?

That is the question.

Maybe this: that my neighbors' children have reduced Uri to despair outside, and he has climbed up the mulberry tree like a hounded cat. I ought to intervene to protect him, or call his parents. His parents are away. His aunt, then, that Natalia who has come from some kibbutz. Not now: late at night, when he is asleep, I should go and talk to her. Explain, warn, apologize.

How absurd. What can I say? And how can I, a total stranger, call on her late at night?

And I know nothing at all about the education of children.

I shall go on watching. Now the boys who chased Uri have begun a sort of commando raid across the broken-down railings. Is it a hunt, from yard to yard, in the cellars, in the peeling entrance halls, and among the dusty shrubs that are dying here in the drought? They have Hebrew names that savor of the desert: Boaz, Joab, Gideon, Ehud, Jephthah. And because the darkness is still not complete, still touched by the last vestiges of light, I can manage from my balcony to make out the rules of the game: it is an air raid. They spread their arms wide, group themselves in spearhead formation, bend the top halves of their bodies forward, and stamp along pretending to be warplanes. Spread-eagle. Uttering sounds of explosions, drone of engines, and tattoo of machine guns. One of them happens to look up at my balcony, catches sight of me calmly writing by the light of the desk lamp, aims an invisible gun at me, and annihilates me with a single salvo. I accept it.

That is, I raise my hands in a gesture of surrender, and even spread a smile on my face, no doubt a Dutch uncle's smile, so as to reward him with a victorious thrill. But the dedicated warrior refuses to accept my surrender. He rejects it outright. He disregards my smile and my raised arms. The logic of war is pursued without favor or exception. I have been annihilated, and now I no longer exist. He goes on his way, surging forward to wipe out the last traces of the Jew-haters.

Friday night, and Jews in cheap suits are carrying prayer books under their arms as they go past my balcony on their way to the Faithful Remnant Synagogue to welcome the Sabbath. Probably they are secretly delighted at the sight of these child airplanes, muttering contentedly to themselves, "little pagans."

All through the summer the children have exposed their skin to the blazing rays of the sun. Needless to say, I have done my duty. I have warned my neighbors, their parents, time and again that excessive exposure is bad for the skin and can even harm their general development. In vain. The settlers here, Orthodox shopkeepers, municipal and Jewish Agency officials, refugees, thinkers and stamp collectors, former pioneers, teachers, and clerks—they all agree in elevating sunbathing almost to the level of a religion. Perhaps they imagine that Jewish children who take on a bronze color cease to be Jewish children and become Hebrews. A new, tough race, no longer timid and persecuted, no longer sparkling with gold and silver teeth, no longer with sweaty palms and eyes blinking through thick lenses. Total liberation from the fear of persecution by means of this colorful camouflage. But I must put in a word of reservation here: I am not at all well read in either zoology or anthropology, and hence the comparison between what is happening here and the mechanism of protective coloration that is found in a certain type of lizard whose name escapes me cannot be regarded as substantiated.

However, I shall record my own private observations.

Jerusalem, Kerem Avraham, mid-1940s: Bunem begat Zischa, and Zischa begat Myetek, and Myetek begat Giora. A new leaf.

Nevertheless, needless to say, I can see no benefit in this effort. At the close of a summer's day, Kerem Avraham exudes a smell of Eastern European immigrants. It is a sour smell. If I try to isolate its ingredients: Their sweat. Their fish. The cheap oil they use for frying. Nervous indigestion. Petty intrigues among neighbors motivated by repressed greed. Hopes and fears. Here and there a partially blocked drain. Their underwear, drying everywhere on clotheslines, especially the women's underwear, has a sanctimonious air. I am tempted to use the word "puritanical." And on every windowsill here, cucumbers are pickling in old jam jars, cucumbers floating in liquid with garlic, dill, parsley, bay leaves. Is this also a place that in years to come someone will remember with longing? Can it be that when the time comes, someone will dream nostalgically of the rusting washtubs, the broken-down railings, the rough, cracked concrete, the peeling plaster, the coils of barbed wire, the thistles, the immigrant smells? Indeed, will we survive the war that is coming? What will happen, Mina—perhaps you have some suggestion, some consolation, to offer? No? This morning, on the shortwave broadcast of the Underground radio, they played a stirring song: "We shall climb together to the mountains,/ Climb toward the light of breaking day:/We have left our yesterdays behind us,/But tomorrow is a long, long way away." Here are the mountains, Mina, and here we are among them. Jewish immigrants. Our last reserves of strength. The tomorrow in the song is not for me, I know that. But my love and fears are directed desperately—forgive me—toward the darling child you bore me and hid away in a kibbutz in the Jezreel Valley. What lies in store for him? I imagine him lean and bronzed, barefoot, even his dreams filled with taps, screws, and cogwheels.

Or Uri.

Look, just like Dushkin, I have a tear in my eye. Suddenly I, too, am a Samovar. It is not sadness at my death, you know that, it's sadness for the people and their children and for the mountains all around. What will happen? What have we done, and what shall we do now? Yes. *Angst.* Don't smile like that.

Friday night. In every kitchen now they are cooking chicken necks stuffed with groats, stuffed intestines, stuffed peppers. The poor people have cheap sausage with mustard. For me, of course, only raw vegetables and fresh fruit. Even the quarrels, the insults hurled every now and again from balcony to balcony, are in Yiddish: *Bist du a wilde chayye, Mister Menachem, du herst mich, bist du a meshuggener?*

That is how it is in Jerusalem.

They say that in Galilee, in the valley, in Sharon, and in the remote parts of the Negev a kind of mutation is taking place: A new race of peasants is emerging. Laconic. Sarcastic. Single-minded. Dedicated.

I don't know.

You're the one who knows.

For two and a half years now, you have been wandering among the kibbutzim, dashing from place to place in their dusty trucks, making notes, interviewing, drawing comparisons, in khaki trousers and a man's shirt with large breast pockets, compiling statistics, sleeping in pioneer huts, sharing their frugal fare. Perhaps you can even speak to them in their own language. Perhaps you even love them.

A tough, spartan woman, uncompromising, strolling around those camps without the least embarrassment, collecting material for an original piece of social-psychological research. Stubbing out your cigarette as if you were pressing a pushpin into the table. Lighting up again at once, not blowing the match out but waving it almost violently to and fro. Entering the details of the dreams of the first native-born generation on little cards. "Patterns of Behavior and Normative Ideas Among the Products of a Collective Education." Mina, I am prepared to give my wholehearted admiration to those children, and to their pioneering parents, the enthusiasm, the silent heroism, the iron will, and the graceful manners.

And to you.

Mina, I take my hat off to you.

That is to say—forget it. A Viennese gesture. There, I've already regretted it.

As for me—what am I?

A weak Jew. Consumed by hesitations. Dedicated but apprehensive. And now, in addition to everything else, seriously ill.

My modest contribution: here, in Jerusalem, in a neighborhood of lower-middle-class immigrants from Russia and Poland, I have put up a fight, as long as my strength lasted, without counting the hours, even working at night sometimes, against the dangers of diphtheria and dysentery.

Moreover, there are my chemical interests. Homemade explosives. It is possible that Uri can already see what I refuse to see. Perhaps a formula is really taking shape in my mind for the large-scale production of homemade explosives. Or at least I may be able to suggest a starting point to the Hagganah. In this area, at any rate. In the early hours of this morning, I devoted some thought to the salts we possess in relative abundance, such as potassium chlorate and barium nitrate. Any porous substance, such as chalk or charcoal, can be saturated with liquid oxygen. I must stop recording details like these. My heart is heavy because I do not want to devise formulas for explosives or to contribute to wars, but Uri is right, and so I am obliged to do so. But the sadness, Mina, how great it is. And the humiliation.

I have tried to resist this obligation. I have even taken certain steps. I refer to the poignant conversations I had at the beginning of the summer with an Arab friend, a colleague, a doctor from Katamon, Dr. Mahdi. Need I go into details? The abyss that divides two doctors of moderate views, who both abhor bloodshed. My pleas. His pleas. The historical argument. On the one hand and on the other. The moral argument. On the one hand and on the other. The practical argument. On the one hand and on the other. His certainty. My hesitations. I must try again. I must appeal to him at this late hour and ask him to arrange for me to meet the members of the Jerusalem Arab Committee and make them think again. I still have an argument or two left.

Only the heart says: It's all in vain. You must hurry up. Uri is right, and so is the Underground broadcast on the shortwaves: "To die—or to conquer the mountain."

I will not deny it, Mina: as usual I am very frightened.

And I am also ashamed of my fear. Let us not be halted by the corpses of the weak, as Bialik says, they died in servitude, may their dream be sweet to them, onions and garlic in plenty, bountiful fleshpots. I am quoting from memory. My copy of Bialik's poems is in the bookcase some five or six paces away, but I don't have the strength to get up. And anyway, I strenuously reject the line about the dream of onions and garlic. Insofar as it concerns me, you know full well what is in my dreams. Wild, even rough women—yes. Murderers and shepherdesses from the Bedouin—also. And my father's face with his lawyer, and sometimes longing for river and forest. But no onions and no garlic. There our national poet was mistaken, or perhaps he merely exaggerated so as to rouse the people's spirit. Forgive me. Once more I have trespassed on a domain in which I am no expert.

And you are in my dreams, too. You in New York, in a youthful dress, in some paved square that reminds me of Moshavot Square in Tel Aviv. There is a jetty there, and you are at the wheel of a dusty jeep, smoking, supervising Arab porters who are carrying cases of arms for the beleaguered Hebrew community. You are on duty. You are on a secret mission. You are throbbing with efficiency or moral indignation. "Shame on you," you reproach me. "How could you, and at a time like this? Disgusting." I admit it, fall silent, recoil, and retreat to the far end of the jetty. Reflected like a corpse in the water, I hear distant shots and suddenly agree with you in my heart. Yes, you are right. How could I. I must go at once, just as I am, without a suitcase, without an overcoat, this very minute.

The shame is more than I can bear. I wake up in pain and take three pills. I lie down again, wide awake and alarmed, and hear outside, just beyond the shutters, on a branch, at a distance of perhaps two feet from me, a night bird. It is uttering a bitter, piercing shriek, in a kind of frenzy of wounded self-righteousness, repeating its protest over and over again: Ahoo. Ahoohoo. Ahoo. Ahoooo.

ꝏ

Jerusalem
Saturday evening
September 6, 1947

Dear Mina,

It will not be easy for me to wean myself from this child.

He spent the whole morning here, painstakingly copying facts out of the gazetteer and sketching a military plan for the capture of the mountain ranges that command Jerusalem from the north. Then he marked on his map the crossroads and the strategic points. On a separate sheet of paper, he allocated storm troops to each of the key buildings in Jerusalem, such as the central post office, the David Building, the radio station, the Russian Compound, the Schneller Barracks, the YMCA tower, and the railway station. And all the while he did not disturb me as I lay resting on the sofa. He is a thin, fair-haired child; his movements are abrupt, embarrassment and aspirations shine in his green eyes, but his manners are impeccable. Twice he interrupted his game and made me some coffee. He straightened my blanket and replaced the sweat-drenched pillow under my head with a fresh one. It was almost noon before he apologetically asked me my opinion of his work. Despite all my principles I praised it.

Uri said:

"I've got to go home soon and have my lunch. Please rest so you'll be strong enough to do the experiment tonight. I'm leaving a Matosian cigarette pack here, Dr. Emanuel; inside there are four live bullets we can take the gunpowder out of. And in my sock I've got the pin from a hand grenade. It's a bit rusty, but it's all there. I found it, and I've brought it for you. From our roof I counted nine British tanks in a shed in Schneller. Cromwells. Is it true, Dr. Emanuel, that a tank is finished if you put some sugar in the engine?"

Again the excited glint flickers in his eyes and dies down. He still trusts me, but his patience is beginning to wear thin: "How much more time will you need for the experiments? A fortnight?

More? By about December the Irgun and the Stern Group will have started to blow up enemy districts in the city, because the English are already moving troops to Haifa."

I smile:

"There may still be an agreement, Uri. I read in the paper that America may yet agree to govern the country until the storm dies down and the Arabs start getting used to the idea of a Hebrew state. There is still some such possibility. Why must you be so enthusiastic for wars? I have already explained to you more than once that a war is a terrible thing, even if you win it. Perhaps we shall still manage to prevent it."

"You don't really mean that. It's just because I'm still a child and you think you've got to improve me, like my daddy. But nothing comes from words. I'm very sorry. Everything is war."

"And how, if you don't mind my asking, did you arrive at that rather sweeping conclusion?"

Now he stares at me in utter disbelief. He stands up. His hands are thrust deep into the pockets of his shorts. He comes over to the sofa, and as he leans over me his voice is trembling:

"I'm not an informer. You can speak frankly to me. Surely everything is war. That's how it is in history, in the Bible, in nature, and in real life, too. And love is all war. Friendship, too, even."

"Are you acquainted with love already, Uri?"

Silence.

And then:

"Dr. Emanuel, tell me, is it true that there's a Jewish professor in America who has invented a huge atomic bomb made from a drop of water?"

"You are referring apparently to the hydrogen bomb. That lies outside the range of my knowledge."

"All right. Don't tell me anything. There are military secrets that I'm not allowed to know. The main thing is that you do know all about it, and no one will ever get a word out of me."

"Uri. Listen. You are quite mistaken about that. Let me explain something to you. Listen carefully."

Silence.

I don't know what to explain to him, or in what words.

It's not true:

The truth is that I am afraid of losing him. In his short trousers, with the buckle shining on his army belt, with his gentle hand once or twice on my forehead, am I still perspiring, have I got a slight temperature.

And so once again I give in. I start explaining to him what a chain reaction is and, in schematic terms, about the relationship between matter and energy. For a long while he listens to me in silent concentration, his eyes fixed on my mouth, his nostrils flaring as if they have caught a distant whiff of the fire storm in Hiroshima, which I am telling him about. Now he really worships me, he loves me with all his heart.

And now I feel better, too, as a result of his enthusiasm. Suddenly I feel strong enough to get up, to invite Uri into my little laboratory, I am suddenly animated by a kind of pedagogic enthusiasm, I light the spirit lamp and demonstrate a simple exercise to him: water, steam, energy, motor power.

"And that's the whole principle." I chuckle happily.

"My lips are sealed, Dr. Emanuel. I won't talk, even if the British arrest me and torture me, they won't get a word out of me, because I've got a way of keeping quiet that I learned from Ephraim Nehamkin. They won't get anything out of me about what you've told me, you can trust me a hundred percent."

Once more the beautiful rage flashes in his green eyes and dies away. My child.

Eventually he takes his leave and promises to come back tomorrow afternoon. And even in the middle of the night, if he sees a slanting crack of light at my bathroom window. In which case, he'll slip out and come to me at once. He'll be at my command, he says. Bye.

When he had gone, I suddenly began to argue with you in my mind. To apologize for it all. To justify myself about our first meeting. To re-examine how I went, two years ago, in the summer of '45, for a rest to the sanatorium at Arza. How I decided then, mistakenly, that my morning attacks of sickness were the result of general fatigue. How I made up my mind to relax completely, and how you came bursting into my solitary life, you and my illness. And as I reflected, I put the blame, if one can so express it, on you.

Dear Mina, if you mind my writing all this, then skip the next few lines.

Please. Try to see it like this: a bachelor, a doctor, with reasonable financial security, in receipt of an occasional mail remittance from his father, who is a confectioner in Ramat Gan. His expenditures are few: a moderate rent, simple clothing, and food in keeping with the times and his surroundings, the occasional expenses of his scientific hobby. He has a little put away.

Moreover, for some time now he has experienced a certain tiredness, and slight attacks of nausea early in the morning, before the first cup of coffee. A medical colleague diagnoses the first signs of ulcers and orders complete rest. Besides, certain European habits of his youth persist: summertime is holiday time.

And so, Arza, in the hills behind Jerusalem. A relaxed Dr. Nussbaum, dressed in a light summer suit and an open-necked blue shirt, sits in a deck chair under the whispering pines, half reading a novel by Jacob Wassermann. The paths are covered with fine white gravel. Every footstep produces a crisp crunching sound, which charms him and reminds him of other times. In the background, inside the building, the phonograph is playing work songs. Nearby, in a hammock, a prominent figure in the community and the Labor Movement is dozing, the gentle breeze ruffling the pages of the newspaper spread open on his stomach. Dr. Nussbaum does not admit even to himself that he is waiting for this public figure to wake up so that he can engage him in conversation and make an impression on him.

A Health Service nurse named Jasmine circulates among the reclining figures, distributing to each a glass of fresh orange juice and biscuits, a kind of midmorning snack. This Jasmine is a robust, buxom girl. The fine black down that covers her arms and legs stirs a sudden lust in Dr. Nussbaum. The capricious physical attraction he feels for simple Oriental women. He politely declines the orange juice and tries to engage Jasmine in a lighthearted conversation, but the words come with difficulty, and his voice, as always happens to him in such situations, sounds false. Jasmine lingers to bend over him and smooth his shirt collar over the lapels of his jacket. A momentary glimpse of her breasts arouses a certain boldness in him: as in his student days in Vienna, when he would drain a glass of brandy at a single gulp and find the courage to utter a mild obscenity. So he gives voice to a false explanation of his refusal of the orange juice, a sort of ambiguous hint about forbidden as against permitted pleasures. She does not understand. However, it seems that she is in no hurry to move on: she must find him not unattractive, this gentleman in his light suit and his graying hair. She probably thinks him highly intelligent and respected, but modest. It is possible that she can detect his welling lust. She laughs and asks what she can offer him instead of the juice. He can have whatever he wants, says Jasmine. No, he replies, with a polite smile in his eyes, what he wants she may not be able to give him out here, surrounded by all these other convalescents. Jasmine shows her teeth. She blushes, and her dark skin takes on a darker hue. Even her shoulders participate in her laughter. "If that's the way you are, then have a glass of my juice anyway." And he, now caught up in sweet game-fever, suggests she try another temptation. Again she does not understand. She is slightly taken aback. "Coffee, for instance," he hastens to add, in case he has gone too far. Jasmine reflects for a moment; perhaps she is still not quite sure—does he really want a cup of coffee, or is the game still on? On the clear summer air there comes the buzzing of a bee, the caw of a crow, and a British airplane droning far to the south over the Bethlehem hills. "I'll see to some coffee for you," Jasmine says, "as a special favor. Just for you."

It was at that point that you came into the picture. Actually, you were there already: an intense woman on a nearby rocking chair, in a simple, severe summer dress. Sitting and judging.

"If I might be permitted to intrude in this exchange," you say.

And I, in a trice, return from the harems of Baghdad to my Viennese manners:

"By all means, dear lady. Need you ask? We were merely indulging in idle banter. Please."

And so you advise me to choose fresh orange juice, rather than coffee, after all. From bitter experience that morning, you have discovered that the coffee here is ersatz, a kind of greasy black mud. Incidentally, I am not a total stranger to you: you once heard me lecture at a one-day conference at the Hadassah Hospital on Mount Scopus. I spoke about hygiene and the drinking water in Palestine, and impressed you with my sense of humor. Dr. Nussbaum, if you are not mistaken. No, you are surely not mistaken.

I hasten to reassure you, and you continue:

"Very pleased to meet you. Hermine Oswald. Mina for short. A pupil of pupils of Dr. Adler. Apparently we both share the same Viennese background. That is why I permitted myself to intervene and rescue you from the Health Service coffee. I have a bad habit of interfering without being asked. Yes. Nurse, please leave two glasses of grapefruit juice on the table here. Thank you. You may go now. What were we talking about? Ah, yes. Your lecture on the drinking water was entertaining, but quite out of place in that one-day conference."

You imagine I will agree with you on this point.

Dr. Nussbaum, naturally, hastens to agree wholeheartedly.

Meanwhile, Jasmine is receiving a noisy dressing down: the Trade Union official is grumbling, half an hour ago or more he asked her—or one of the other nurses, what's the difference—to put through an urgent telephone call for him to the office of Comrade Sprinzak. Has she forgotten? Is it possible?

You indicate him with your chin, smile, and explain to me *sotto voce:*

"Beginnings of egomania and overbearing behavior typical of short men. By the time he's seventy, he will be a positive monster."

We drift into lighthearted conversation. Jasmine, rebuked, has moved out of sight. You call her an "*enfant sauvage.*" I ask myself whether you have overheard my foolish exchange with her, and find myself devoutly hoping that you have not.

"I react in exactly the same way as you," you are saying, "only in reverse. An Oriental taxi driver, or even a Yemenite newsboy, can throw me quite off balance. From a purely physical point of view, of course. These '*enfants sauvages*' still retain—or so it would appear—some sort of sensual animal language that we have long forgotten."

Dr. Nussbaum, as you will surely recall, does not blush to hear all this. No. He blanches. He clears his throat. Hurriedly he produces a freshly laundered handkerchief from his pocket and wipes his lips. He begins to mumble something about the flies, which he has just noticed are all around. And so, without further delay, he changes the subject. He has an anecdote to relate about Professor Dushkin, who, you will recall, was in the chair at that medical conference at the Hadassah. Dushkin called everyone—the doctors, the High Commissioner, the leaders of the Jewish Agency, Stalin, everyone—Svidrigaïlovs.

"How unoriginal of him," you remark icily. "But Dr. Nussbaum, you may invoke whomsoever you will, Dushkin, Stalin, Svidrigaïlov, to change the direction of our conversation. It is not you but I who should apologize for the embarrassment I have caused."

"Perish the thought, Dr. Oswald, perish the thought," Dr. Nussbaum mutters like an idiot.

"Mina," you insist.

"Yes, with great pleasure. Emanuel," Dr. Nussbaum replies.

"You are uneasy in my company," you say with a smile.

"Heaven forbid."

"In that case, shall we take a little stroll together?"

You get up from your rocking chair. You never wait for an answer. I get up and follow you. You take me for a leisurely amble along the gravel path and beyond, down the wooded slope, to the shade of the cypress trees, toward the smell of resin and decay, until we come to the famous tree that was planted by Dr. Herzl and was later felled by some Arabs. And there we discovered, in the dry summer grass, a rusty earring with a Cyrillic inscription.

"It's mine!" you suddenly exclaim possessively, like a high-spirited schoolgirl. "I saw it first!"

A tearful grimace played around your mouth for a moment, as if I were really about to prize the earring from your fist by brute force.

"It's yours," I said, laughing, "even though I believe I saw it first. But have it anyway. As a gift."

Suddenly I added:

"Mina."

You looked at me. You did not speak. Perhaps for a full minute you looked at me and did not speak. Then you hurled the earring into the thistles and took hold of my arm.

"We are out for a stroll," you said.

"Yes, out for a stroll," I agreed happily.

What happened to us. What did you see in me.

No, I do not expect an answer. You are in New York. Up to your eyeballs in work, I expect. As usual. Who can rival your power of periodically turning over a new leaf.

If I were to try to examine myself through your eyes that day in Arza, I should not be much the wiser. You saw before you a withdrawn man with a pensive expression and a cautious way of moving. Rather a lonely man, to judge by outward appearances. Not lacking in sensuality, though, as you must have learned when you overheard him flirting with the girl Jasmine. Not bad looking, either, as I have already stated. A tall, thin man, inclined to turn pale in moments of emotion or embarrassment, his features angular and decidedly intellectual. Hair going slightly gray, but still falling luxuriantly over his forehead, enough perhaps to attract attention. He may have struck you as a rootless artist, he may have looked to you like an unconventional musician from the conservatoire of some German-speaking land, who had turned up here in Western Asia and now bore his degradation with silent, tight-lipped resignation: there is no way back. A melancholy man, yet capable nonetheless, in unusual circumstances, of wholehearted enthusiasm.

In brief, an orphan and a dominating aunt, according to your definition. A definition, however, that you only voiced some time later.

By lunchtime, we were already sharing a table. Chatting about the poet Gottfried Benn. And putting our heads together like a couple of conspirators, trying to work out the order in which the various tables were served. It was Jasmine who served us. As she poured the mineral water I was splashed slightly, because she was not paying attention. I did not complain; on the contrary, as she leaned over me her firm breasts almost brushed my shoulder. At their base, glimpsed through the opening of her white overall, there showed a network of blue veins, such as one sometimes finds in marble from Galilee.

My lust did not escape your notice. You were amused and began to tease me. You started asking me certain questions about my bachelor life. All without batting an eyelid, as if you were inquiring where I bought my shirts. Apparently your practical experience as a psychologist (before you devoted yourself to research) enabled you to ask me questions of a sort not normally exchanged by new acquaintances.

As for me, I blanched as usual. But I made up my mind this time not to evade your questions. Only I found the choice of words very difficult.

"This time you have not changed the subject to Svidrigaïlov," you observed ruthlessly.

Again we went for a walk together, this time beyond the perimeter, toward the buildings of the small farming settlement of Motza. My loneliness, and perhaps my extreme caution in the choice of my words, aroused your sympathy. You liked me, and you said so in a matter-of-fact tone of voice. Afternoon light on the hills. The gentle cypresses. A blaze of geraniums among the houses of the settlement, red-tiled roofs, a poinciana flaming red like a greeting from Tel Aviv. A light, dry breeze. Our conversation now is impersonal, Viennese as it were, a sort of exchange of views on the question of sexual pleasures and their relation to the emotions. You are remarkably free in the way you speak about anatomical and physiological details. You find my hesitancy appealing perhaps, but definitely surprising nonetheless: After all, Emanuel, we are both doctors, we are both perfectly familiar with these mechanisms, so why are you so embarrassed, secretly praying for me finally to change the subject?

I apologize; my embarrassment springs from the fact that in Hebrew the intimate particulars of the anatomy—very well, the sexual organs—have newly invented names, which seem rather sterile and lifeless, and that is why, paradoxically, I find it hard to utter them. You describe this explanation as "pilpulistic." You do not believe me. When all is said and done, what is to prevent my switching to German, or making use of the Latin terms? No, you do not believe me. Unhesitatingly you identify psychological inhibitions. Latent puritanism.

"Mina," I protest, "forgive me, please, but I'm not one of your patients yet."

"No. But we are making each other's acquaintance. We are taking a walk together. Why don't you ask me questions about myself?"

"I haven't got any questions. Only one, perhaps: you have been humiliated by someone, a man, perhaps a cruel man, a long time ago perhaps, viciously humiliated."

"Is that a question?"

"I was . . . voicing an impression."

Suddenly, forcefully, you take my head between your hands.

"Bend down."

I obey. Your lips. And a small discovery: tiny holes in the lobes of your ears. Is it possible that you once wore earrings? I do not ask.

Then you remark that I seem to you like a watch that has lost its glass. So vulnerable. So helpless. And so touching.

You touch my hair. I touch your shoulder. We walk on in silence. Darkness is falling. Overhead a bird of prey in the last rays of twilight. A vulture? A falcon? I do not know. And there is a hint of danger: outside the grounds of the sanatorium, Arab shepherds roam. Not far away is a notorious brigand village called Koloniyeh. We must be getting back. All around us the sadness of darkening rocks. Night is falling on an arid boulder-land. Far on the northern horizon, in the direction of Shu'afat and Beit Ikhsa, a star shell splits the sky, fades, shatters to shivers of light, and dies in the darkness.

After supper, a vulgar entertainer from the Broom Theater appeared in the dining room. He told jokes and made fun, in a heavy Russian accent, of the hypocrisy of the British government and the savagery of the Arab gangs. Finally, he even made faces at the audience. The Trade Union bigwig flushed, rose from his seat, and condemned such frivolity as being out of place in such critical times. The entertainer retired to a corner of the room and sat down, abashed, on the verge of tears. The audience was totally silent. When the speaker used the word "self-restraint," you suddenly burst into loud, resounding laughter, youthful laughter, which instantly provoked a reaction of astonished rage all around. At once people were laughing with you, or perhaps at you. We left the dining room. Darkness in the corridors and on the stairs. Almost immediately we were in each other's arms. Whispering, this time in German. You liked me, you said, you had a small volume of Rilke in your room, you said, and after all we were both adults and free agents.

In your room, almost without an exchange of words, rules were established at once. Orphan and dominating aunt. I must play the part of an ignorant, awkward, shy, but obedient pupil.

But grateful. And very diligent. Yours to command in a whisper, and mine to obey in silence. You had all the details drawn up ready in your mind, as if you were carrying out an exotic program taken from an erotic handbook: Here. Now here. Slowly. Harder. More. Wait. Wait. Now. That's right.

Dear Mina, we both intended that night to be the first and the last. Adults, you said, free agents, you said, but, after all, who is an adult or a free agent, both of us were captured by a force that carried us away like twigs in a river. Perhaps because I was subjugated. Perhaps you had decided from the outset to subjugate me that night, and so I found myself a slave. But you, too, became a slaveowner, Mina, through my very subjugation. And again the following afternoon. And the next night. And again. And after the holidays you began sending postcards to me in Jerusalem with curt commands: Come to Haifa the day after tomorrow. Expect me on Saturday night. Come to Kate Graubert's pension in Talpiyot. I'll come to you for the festival. Tell Fritz that his fast is almost over. Hug Gips and Gutzi for me.

Until you finally taught me to call you Jasmine, to unleash the panting satyr, to conjure up a Baghdad harem in low-ceilinged boardinghouses. To torment and be tormented. To scream aloud. Again and again to grovel at your feet when it was all over, while you lit a cigarette, shook out the match, and studied our lovemaking in precise terms, like a general returning to a battlefield to analyze the fighting and learn lessons for the future.

No, Mina, there is no bitterness, no regret. On the contrary. Unbearable longing. Longing for your rare words of praise. And longing for your rebukes. For your mockery, too. And for your fingers. My own Jasmine, I am a sick man now, I don't have much time left. One might say I fell into your clutches. Or one might say I loved you out of humiliation.

New paragraph.

Let me return to my record of the place and the time. As I have already said, here I am, on the lookout.

Jerusalem, evening, summer's ending, signs of autumn, a man of thirty-nine, already retired for reasons of serious ill health, sitting on his balcony writing to a girl friend, or a former girl friend. He is telling her what he can see, and also what he is thinking. What the purpose is, what can be called the "subject," I have already said I do not know.

The daylight has been fading for an hour and a quarter now, and it is still not quite dark. I am at rest. On the face of it, this is a peaceful hour. Every Saturday evening there is a miracle of sound in Jerusalem: even the noises of the children playing, the cars, and the dogs, and in the distance a woman singing on the radio—all these sounds are assimilated into the silence. Even the shouting down the road. Even a stray burst of machine-gun fire from the direction of Sanhedriya. The silence cloaks it all. In other words, on Saturday evening total silence reigns in Jerusalem.

Now the church and convent bells have started to ring out from nearby and far away, and they, too, are inside the silence. Tomorrow is Sunday. The color of the sky is dark gray with a segment of orange between the clouds. They are fast-moving autumn clouds. And there is a flock of birds flying past. Larks, perhaps. Various people pass below my balcony in Malachi Street. A woman from next door with a basket. A student with an armload of books. And now a boy and a girl walking past rapidly, separated from each other by a good yard or so, not exchanging a word, yet there is no doubt that they are together and that their hearts are at rest.

Opposite, on the corner of Zechariah Street, an old Arab woman is sitting on the sidewalk. A peasant woman. Cross-legged and almost motionless. In front of her there is a large brass tray full of figs for sale. At the edge of the tray, a little pile of coins, no doubt milliemes and half-piasters, her day's takings. She comes here all the way from Sheikh Badr, or perhaps even from Lifta or Malha. How calm she is, and what a long journey she still has to make this evening. Meanwhile she is waiting. Chewing something. Mint leaves? I do not know. Soon she will get up, I almost said arise, balance the tray on her head, and pick her way in the dark among the thistles and boulders. Like a fine network of nerves, the footpaths stretch across the fields, joining the suburbs to the villages all around Jerusalem. A slow, sturdy old woman, at peace with her body and the desolate mountains; my heart yearns for that peace. As she goes on her way, the yellow lights of the street lamps will come on all over the neighborhood. Then the ringing of the bells will cease, and only the sadness of the evening will remain. Iron shutters will be closed. All the doors will be locked. Jerusalem will be in darkness, and I shall be alone in its midst. Suppose I have an attack in the night. Will the child really watch out for the slanting crack of light at my bathroom window, will he really slip out and come to me, be at my command?

Panic seizes me at the very possibility of such a thought's occurring to me. No. Tonight, as usual, I shall be alone. Good night.

Sunday
September 7, 1947

Dear Mina,

I do not know what words one can use to describe to you a blue autumn morning such as we had here today, before the westerly wind blew up, bringing with it a cold, cloudy evening. The whole morning was flooded a deep sky-blue. Much more than a tone or a color: it was such a pure, concentrated blue that it felt like a potion. The buildings and plants responded with a general awakening, as though redoubling their hold on their own colors, or giving concrete expression to a national slogan that is current at the moment in the Hebrew newspapers and Underground broadcasts: To any provocation we shall react twofold; we are determined to stand by what is ours to the last.

That is to say, the blazing geraniums, for instance, in gardens, in backyards, in olive cans on verandas, in window boxes. Or the Jerusalem stone: this morning it is truly "shouting from the walls," in a powerful, concentrated gray. An unalloyed gray, like the color of your eyes. Or the flowering creeper climbing up the olive tree next to the grocer's, dotted all over with points of dark blue brilliance. It all looked like a painting by an over-enthusiastic amateur who has not learned, and has no wish to learn, the secret of understatement. I am almost tempted to use biblical Hebrew words, like sardius, beryl, carbuncle—even though the precise meaning of these words is unknown to me.

Should this miracle be attributed to the clarity of the desert air? To the breath of autumn? To my illness, perhaps? Or to some change that is impending? I have no answer to all these questions. I must try to define my feelings in words, and so I go back to writing: Today I feel painful longings for sights that are present, as though they were recollected images. As though they had already passed, perhaps as though they had passed beyond recall forever. Longings so powerful that I feel an urgent need to do something at once, something unusual, perhaps to put on a light jacket and go out for a walk. To the Tel Arza woods. Among the knitting mothers and their infants sprawled on rugs. To recall the Sunday outings of my childhood to the Vienna woods, and suddenly to sense a smell of other autumns, elsewhere, a smell of lakes, mushrooms, droplets of dew on the branches of fir trees, the smell of lederhosen, the smoke of holiday-makers' campfires, the aroma of freshly ground coffee. How strange I must have seemed this morning to the neighbors' wives in the Tel Arza woods: Look, there is Dr. Nussbaum out for a walk, tall and elegantly dressed, his hands clasped behind his back, smiling to himself as he treads the pine needles underfoot, as though he has just discovered an amusing solution.

"Good morning, Dr. Nussbaum, how are you this morning, and what are they saying at the Jewish Agency?"

"Good morning, a beautiful morning, Mrs. Litvak, I'm fairly well, thank you, and how your lovely little boy is growing. Little girl, I'm sorry. But still lovely."

"As you know, sir, happy are we who have been permitted to behold the light of Jerusalem with the eyes of the flesh and not merely with the eyes of the spirit, and surely what our eyes behold today is as nothing compared to the light that tomorrow will bring. Happy is he who waits."

"Yes indeed, Mr. Nehamkin, yes indeed. It's a wonderful day today, and I am very glad to see you so hale and hearty."

"Since you are also out for a stroll, sir, permit me to accompany you. Together we shall walk, and together our eyes shall behold, for, as it is written, the testimony of two witnesses is valid."

Only in this case the two witnesses were none too healthy. We were soon tired. My neighbor the poet Nehamkin apologized and turned for home, but not before assuring me that a momentous change would soon take place in Jerusalem.

And I, as usual, turned into the Kapitanski brothers' milk bar for a vegetarian lunch: tomato soup, two fried eggs, eggplant salad, buttermilk, and a glass of tea. Then I came home, and, without any pill or injection, I fell into a deep afternoon sleep: as if I had been drinking wine.

At half past four there was another meeting of the local committee in my apartment. As I must have written to you already, even Kerem Avraham is setting up its own civil-defense council.

Four or five representatives of the neighbors came, including Mrs. Litvak, who qualified as a nurse before she married. She brought some homemade biscuits with her, and refused to allow me to help her serve the coffee; all I had to do was to tell her where I kept the sugar and the tray—no, no need, she'd already found them. She had found the lemon, too. And how wonderfully tidy my kitchen was! She would bring her husband, Litvak, here one day to let him see with his own eyes and learn a thing or two. The head of a school for workers' children, and he couldn't even wash a glass properly. Still, it was her fate. She mustn't complain.

And so the meeting began, while we were still being served coffee and shortcake, and I was being treated like a guest in my own home.

"Well," said Mrs. Litvak, "let's get down to business. Dr. Nussbaum, would you like to begin."

"Perhaps we might take up where we left off last week," I suggested. "There's no need to start from scratch every time."

"We were talking about the possibility of an apartment we could use as an HQ," Comrade Lustig said, "somewhere where the committee could organize itself, which could be manned day and night in an emergency. Or at least a room, or a basement."

He spoke standing up, and when he had finished he sat down. Lustig is a little man, with puffy bags under his brown eyes, and a perpetual look of silent amazement on his face, as though he has just been called some terrible name in the street for no reason. Zevulun Grill, a flaming redhead, whose two missing front teeth give him the look of a dangerous brawler, added:

"We were also talking about a radio transmitter. And, as usual, we did nothing about it."

Ephraim Nehamkin, the curly-haired radio technician, nodded his head twice, as if Grill's words corresponded precisely to what one might expect from him, and anyone who harbored any illusions about him had better wake up before it was too late.

"Ephraim," I said, "it might be better if we conducted our discussion by means of words, rather than dumb show. Perhaps you'd like to tell us all what has made you so angry?"

"We've got one," Ephraim growled. "It's always the same old story with us: we talk about the past instead of the present."

"What have we got?"

"A radio. Didn't I say last week that I was putting a battery transmitter together for you. Anyway," he suddenly exploded, "what the hell do we need a transmitter for? To beg the English to do us a favor and stay here to save us from the Arabs? To prick the conscience of the world with biblical quotations? To explain nicely to the Arabs that they mustn't kill us, otherwise there'll be no one to cure their ringworm and their trachoma? What's the point of this whole committee, with two doctors and a bus driver? What the hell do you think you're doing?"

"Don't get so steamed up," Nachtshe said, smiling. "Simmer down. Everything'll be all right."

Nachtshe is a slim, strongly built young man who is a sort of occasional leader in one of the Socialist youth movements. His short trousers displayed his muscular, hairy legs. His hair was tousled. You must have heard of his father, Professor Guttmacher, the expert on Oriental mysticism, a world-famous scholar who is semiparalyzed. Sometimes, in the evenings, Nachtshe and his young charges light campfires in the woods, carry out night exercises with quarterstaves, or make the neighborhood re-echo to songs of rage and longing sung to Russian tunes.

"Instead of poking fun, why don't you tell us what you suggest," Grill demanded of Ephraim Nehamkin.

"An attack," Ephraim erupted in a deep growl, as if his heart were hoarse with emotion. "Organize a raid. That's what I suggest. Take the initiative. Go out to the villages. Shu'afat. Sheikh Jarrah. Issawiya. Burn down the mufti's house in the middle of the night. Or blow up the Najjara HQ. Hoist the blue-and-white flag on the minaret of Nabi Samwil, or even on the Temple Mount. Why not. Let's make them tremble, at long last. Let *them* start sending *us* deputations. Let *them* plead. What's the matter with us all."

At this point, Dr. Kipnis, the vet from Tel Arza, intervened. He was standing with his back to the window, wearing a gray battle-dress blouse and neatly pressed long khaki trousers. As he spoke, he kneaded his brown cap between his fingers, and he looked not at Ephraim but at Mrs. Litvak, as though she—or her black coif—were giving him hints on some vital principle.

"It seems to me, ladies and gentlemen," he began cautiously, "that we are venturing along the wrong road. I may claim to have some acquaintance with the neighboring villages."

"Of course you have," Ephraim whispered venomously. "Only they know you, too, and other Jews like you, and that's what's whetted their appetite."

"Excuse me," said Dr. Kipnis, "I didn't mean to get into an argument with you about your principles. At any rate, not at this moment. All I wanted to do was to try to evaluate the present situation, to discover what the possible lines of development are, and to make one or two suggestions."

"Let's get organized!" Comrade Lustig suddenly exclaimed, and he even thumped on the table. "Quit chattering! Let's get organized!"

As for me, the chairman, it was only with some difficulty that I resisted the temptation to return Nachtshe's fleeting smile, which was apparently directed at me alone.

"Dr. Kipnis," I said, "please continue. And it would be better if we did not keep interrupting one another."

"Very well. We have three possibilities open to us," said Dr. Kipnis, raising three piteously thin fingers and folding one of them back with each possibility he enumerated. "Firstly, the committee hands the whole country over to the Arabs, and we have to choose between a new Masada and a new Yavneh. Second, it recommends partition, and the Arabs either accept the verdict or have it imposed on them with the help of foreign powers. Not the British, naturally. In this eventuality, one of our tasks will be to be prepared for possible riots and—at the same time—to attempt to restore good relations with the Arab districts that surround us. To bury the hatchet, as they say."

"They must be driven out," Ephraim said wearily, "expelled, kicked out, what's the matter with you, let them go back to the desert where they belong. This is Jerusalem, Mr. Kipnis, the Land of Israel—maybe you've forgotten that, with your appeasement."

"Thirdly," the vet continued, apparently determined not to be deflected from his purpose by provocations, "total war. And in that case our local committee will not, of course, function independently, but will await orders from the national institutions."

"That's what I said," Lustig exclaimed delightedly, "we must get organized, organized, and again organized!"

"Dr. Kipnis," I insisted, "what exactly are you suggesting?"

"Yes, well. First of all, a delegation representing us, the Jewish districts of northwest Jerusalem, approaches the Jewish Agency, to explain the special difficulties arising from our geographical situation and to request instructions. I propose Dr. Nussbaum, Mrs. Litvak, and, naturally, Comrade Nachtshe. Second, a meeting with our neighbors. I mean the sheikhs and mukhtars. I am willing to volunteer myself for this assignment. We inform them that we, the inhabitants of the Jewish districts of northwest Jerusalem, will not take any hostile initiative, but will continue, no matter what happens, to maintain neighborly relations. So that if they nevertheless choose the course of bloodshed, all the responsibility will fall on them, and they must accept the consequences and cannot complain that they have not been warned. And now I suggest that Comrade Nachtshe talk to us about the defense of our districts. He should at least outline the plans, on the assumption that we may have to withstand a local assault on our own for a while. That is all I have to say."

"Then I suggest that we start erecting barricades," said Lustig, and suddenly he burst out laughing. "Imagine—our Kerem Avraham as the Zionist Stalingrad."

"Let's be practical, please," I urged. "We still have to settle the allocation of tasks and so on."

"There's no risk," Ephraim remarked sadly, "of anyone here being practical. Forget it. Not here. Not in this *Judenrat.*"

"I must insist," I said, with unnecessary sharpness.

Meanwhile, Nachtshe had returned from the kitchen. He had clearly made himself at home. He was chewing vigorously on a thick sandwich. From his bloodstained chin I detected that, besides cheese and onion, he had put some slices of tomato in it.

"Sorry," he said with a grin. "I was famished, so I raided your icebox. I didn't want to ask permission, in case I interrupted your symposium." As he spoke, he dropped crumbs shamelessly on the armchair and the rug. More crumbs clung to his mustache.

"Feel free," I said.

"Good," said Nachtshe. "Have we got over the ideological stage yet? Right. Well, then."

Nobody spoke. Even Comrade Lustig was silent for once.

"The English are going to pull out soon. That much is certain. And we're going to have problems. But I don't want to talk about the problems now. I'm here to talk about solutions. Well, then. We've got arms in the neighborhood. Only light arms at the moment. And thank God we've got a few boys who know what to do with them. We needn't go into details now. Sonya. Mrs. Litvak, I mean. You get all the old dears together in your apartment tomorrow—as you were today—to sew bags. Never mind what from. That's instead of knitting balaclava helmets for the troops. Balaclava helmets you can knit us another time. I need a thousand, twelve hundred bags. The youngsters can fill them with sand and gravel. They'll be used firstly for armed positions, then for windows in general. Protection against bullets and shells. Next. As of tomorrow morning, we keep a permanent watch on Schneller from the Kolodnys' balcony. That's another job for the youngsters. And another lookout post on Kapitanski's roof, toward Sheikh Jarrah and the police training school. I want Litvak to release twenty or thirty boys from the school for this, so that we know precisely what Tommy and Ahmed are both up to. Next. In the event that the English do pull out, or if we see that they're going to hand over the keys to King Abdullah's Bedouins, my boys will chip in and take over Schneller. That's got nothing to do with your committee, of course, but I wanted you to know, so that you can sleep soundly at night. Next. Communications. Ephraim. Tonight we'll come and look over what you've been putting together there, and if it's really what you say it is, then we'll tune you into Hagganah HQ. You and Lustig will take turns listening in, twenty-four hours a day. You'll sit quietly with the earphones on, and you won't argue with each other; you won't get up unless you need to take a piss or you have something to report to me. Now you, Grill. Listen carefully. There are two things. First, start collecting gardening tools from all over the district in your shed. Never mind whether people like it or not—requisition them. Whatever you can find, except watering cans. Spades, forks, hoes, everything. At a signal from me—as you were; at a signal from an authorized person—you and a few other neighbors grab the tools and get cracking, dig up the road at the bottom of Zephaniah Street, at the corner of Amos and Geulah, and the Tel Arza road. Dig in zigzags. Yes. Trenches. So they don't hit us with armor. And another thing, Grill. The HQ will be in your bedroom. That's because your house has three exits. You've got two days to get your wife out before we move in. Now, Kipnis. You, Kipnis, are not going to talk to the sheikhs and mukhtars. We don't want to risk any of the boys to go and rescue your mutilated corpse. Let's face it, doctor, after the war—by all means, why not, you're welcome to go and smoke the pipe of peace with them, and I'll even come with you for a good shish kebab. But in the meantime, if you're so set on your idea, why not send every sheikh a special-delivery registered letter proposing good neighborly relations. Go ahead. If it works, I shall personally beat my sword into a dagger. But till then, you just stay here and take charge of the grocer, the greengrocer, and the kerosene man for me. Make sure they bring in whatever they can get hold of. Only no black market and no panic. That's right, Sonya: hoarding. You heard. I want all the women to lay in supplies of canned food, biscuits, kerosene, sugar, as much as they can. Now let's talk about water. I want all the members of this committee—yes, all of you—to go from house to house and help move the water cisterns down from the roofs into the cellars. And then make sure they're full. And I want Almaliah to start making us tanks in his workshop. Water tanks, Ephraim, that's what I'm talking about, so don't jump off your chair. To begin with, anyway. Now our host. Nussbaum. You go to old Mrs. Vishniak's pharmacy tomorrow morning and check exactly what she's got and what she needs. Whatever she's short of, order it, at the committee's expense. And plenty of it. Your apartment here will be the first-aid station, with morphine and dressings and whatever else you need. Another thing: you, Grill, gradually start getting in supplies of gasoline for us. From your bus company or out of the rocks, I don't care where it comes from. Fifty gallons or so. The children are to collect several hundred bottles, and we—that's Ephraim and I—we'll start mixing cocktails. Nussbaum, you said you had something to suggest on this subject? Very good. But not now. It doesn't interest everyone. Now, is there anything else?"

"Yes," said Lustig, "we need to have some cyanide or something. If the Arabs do manage to get through despite everything, they'll butcher the children and violate the women. We need to be organized against even the worst eventualities."

"We're not in Warsaw now," said Nachtshe. "And if you come out with things like that outside this room, you'll be in trouble. And that's that."

"All right," muttered Comrade Lustig. "I've got the message."

"Any more questions?"

"Excuse me," I said. "What happens if the English don't pull out? Or if they hand over the whole of Jerusalem en bloc to King Abdullah?"

"If they don't go, they don't go. Don't ask me questions like that, ask Ben-Gurion. Who do you think I am? Right, then. Sonya, give these good people another cup of coffee. They're looking a bit pale all of a sudden. Dr. Nussbaum, thank you for your hospitality. I must be off now. As of lunchtime the day after tomorrow, anyone who wants me can find me or Akiva or Yigal in the Grills' bedroom. By the way, if the English come along to search or ask questions, don't forget that this district has a committee. Nobody knows me. I don't exist. Let the doctors talk to them. Nussbaum or Kipnis. That's all. Only don't worry, anybody: we haven't lost our hope, as the song says. Just one thing more: Ephraim, I want to say I'm sorry. If I've upset you at all, I didn't mean to. And now, good-bye."

He brushed the crumbs from his mustache, wiped the tomato juice off his chin, bared his perfect teeth in a broad grin, and left.

Hans Kipnis remarked softly:

"What can one say?"

Ephraim said:

"Don't you start all over again. You heard what you were told: you can write letters to all the sheikhs in the neighborhood."

Sonya Litvak said:

"Pray God he takes care of himself. What boys!"

Comrade Lustig:

"Like Cossacks. Always talking instead of getting organized. They'll end up by killing us, heaven forbid!"

And Dr. Nussbaum, dear Mina, your Dr. Nussbaum, said in an indulgent, ironic tone:

"With your permission, it seems to me that the meeting is over."

In my mind's eye I followed this angry, lissome youth as he disappeared from my apartment into the evening shadows. Nachtshe, short for Menahem or Nahum, Guttmacher, in his shorts, with his tousled hair, his eyes the color of late-summer dust, his loneliness. No doubt he went back to his comrades, in the woods or the wadi. Dropping with fatigue, perhaps. Probably he hasn't eaten a proper meal in days. And I asked myself: Has he known a woman, and if so, was it the same way as he tore into the sandwich, or was he perhaps trembling, confused?

And what could I do, Mina? What would you have done in my place? Trusted him and said nothing? Rebuked him and made fun of his bravado? Tried to analyze his dreams? Or perhaps fallen in love and conquered him for yourself?

I feel at a loss. Perhaps I should have silenced him, squashed his arrogance, called him to order? But could I have done it? In my heart of hearts, as you must surely have guessed, I had made him into the secret child you bore me and hid from me in a kibbutz somewhere in Galilee, or in the valleys; he had grown up surrounded by horses and agricultural machinery, and now he had come up to Jerusalem to rescue us all. I must stop and conclude this letter at once.

Only this: when my visitors had left, while I was still washing the coffee cups and picking the crumbs off my rug, the sky suddenly altered. A damp, icy rage began to blow up from the northwest. Gone was the savage blue. Jerusalem darkened. Subsided. Then the first drops, and it was wintry night outside. I shall also start collecting empty bottles. At any rate, Nachtshe will have to come to me to learn what to put into a Molotov cocktail if he wants it to blow up an armored car. I shall stop now. I'll take a pill. I won't go to bed, I'll spend this rainy night in my laboratory. Time is short. Henry Gurney, the British administration secretary, is on the radio urging the members of all communities in Palestine to calm down and maintain law and order until the situation improves. The "Voice of Jerusalem" announcer translates into official Hebrew: It is strictly forbidden to congregate in the streets, it is forbidden to interfere with the normal course of life.

September 8, 1947

Dear Mina,

The rain was light. Not the autumn rains yet, but a slow night drizzle. This morning the city brightened again, and a damp, fresh smell rose from the gardens. Even the falling leaves today were washed clean of dust. I could not get to sleep until just before the dawn. I did not even want to. An idea for a formula kept running through my head after yesterday's meeting, a simple, fascinating chemical possibility, and I could not relax. From time to time the pain became so intense that the desk, the ceiling, and the walls went misty. I deliberately did without an injection, because it seemed to me that it was precisely in this mist that my hope of clarifying my idea lay. You are smiling. The notion of illumination or inspiration coming out of a fog of pain may strike you as immature romanticism. So be it. I even jotted down in the night various symbols and figures on a scrap of paper. Suddenly, long after midnight, as the Schneller clock struck three or two, with my tongue and palate parched from thirst and pain, in a mood of ecstatic longing, I had the feeling that I had discovered the way to produce a chain reaction by an amazingly simple means, with no need for fantastic temperatures. A way of releasing energy from the cheapest and commonest substances. It may be precisely thus that the elemental life force may erupt with holy dreadfulness in the mind of, say, a composer who hears in the night the strains of his final symphony, which is not yet his, and who knows that there is no way of capturing it in notes. Ecstasy and despair. I can decipher the meaning of all this: it's the rumor of approaching death. The bit of paper I scrawled on in the night is in front of me now, and it is all nonsense. Scientific ravings in the style of Jules Verne or H. G. Wells. It is worthless. What is more, at the time I was so feverish that I could see the Dead Sea blazing in the eastward-facing window, illuminating the night with a kind of mineral glare as of hellfire, and I did not doubt for a moment that my nocturnal discovery was already operating in the outside world. In a twilight. You and Uri were concocting something in the laboratory. You and Jasmine and Nachtshe on the rug, making love and calling me to join you. And outside a mushroom of fire bursting into the heart of the night sky, while I, with the help of a simple mirror, followed it from here, from my room, over the mountains and across the valleys. I fell asleep fully dressed again, toward dawn, on the floor of my laboratory, and in my sleep I knew that the time had come to send for Dushkin, and with him came Rabbi Zweik, the sick mystic from Safed, and together they tried to talk you into agreeing that the only way to arrest the tumor in my glands was to operate and remove my head, while you maintained strenuously that a heavy concentration of X-rays directed at a mixture of sodium and phosphorus would unleash a chain reaction that would save my life and also radically alter the overall military situation.

In the morning, after my coffee and a shave, I found I had a slight temperature and also some blurring of vision. I could read the newspaper, and I can still write. But when I reached out to pick up a piece of buttered toast from the kitchen table, I missed and upset a pot of yogurt. I may add, with no reference at all to this development, that a British reconnaissance plane has been circling low over Jerusalem since the early hours of this morning, perhaps because it was announced semiofficially in this morning's paper that the commission of inquiry will indeed recommend the partition of the country, and that Jerusalem and Bethlehem will be under international control, and will not be handed over either to the Jews or to the Arabs. It was Uri who told me, on his way home from school, that without Jerusalem there would be no Hebrew state, or else a terrible war would break out between the Hagganah and the Palmach, on the one hand, and the Irgun and the Stern Group on the other, and that that was precisely what the British were planning.

Incidentally, he is now in command of my laboratory. He does whatever he likes. He made me comfortable on the sofa, covered me with a woolen blanket, made me some lemon tea, and even selected a record and put it on the phonograph to please me. He also put a hot-water bottle on my feet. And while I was lying there, too weak to object, the boy began unloading a crate of empty bottles. Then he went to the laboratory to brew some concoction, chop off match heads, mix solutions. I am gradually being driven out of my own home: Nachtshe and Sonya Litvak in my kitchen, Uri in my laboratory, you in my dreams. Soon I shall leave.

"Be careful there, Uri."

"I'm only doing what you showed me, Dr. Emanuel, don't worry, I'm doing exactly what it says in your notes on the desk here, and when you're better we'll work together again."

I am at peace. Mozart on the phonograph, and from the laboratory sounds of test tubes, the spirit lamp, simmering.

Outside, at the window, another early-autumn evening.

The simple, searing, trivial things, what urgent information are they straining to convey to me. The fading light, Mina, the cawing of crows, a yelping dog, a ringing bell, these things have been since time immemorial and will go on being forever. I can even hear a train hooting in the distance, toward Emek Refaim. And a baby crying. And the woman next door singing a Polish song. The simple, familiar, trivial things—why do they seem to be taking their leave of me tonight. And what am I to do except turn to the wall and die at once. At once, too, like an electric shock, this limpid certainty strikes me: there is a meaning. There is a reason. Perhaps there is a way. And there is still some time left for me to try to discover the meaning, the purpose. Only a sadness continues to gnaw: I have lived some forty years. I was banished, more or less, from one country to another. Here I have even achieved something, to the best of my modest ability. Here, too, I loved you. And now you are gone and I am still here. But not for long. I am being rudely banished from this place, too. And the conclusion, Mina, the moral, the reason? What, as they say here, is the matter at hand?

Maybe this: Autumn outside, and everything is closing in. Something needs to be done. It needs to be done immediately, hopeless though it may be. What it is, I wish I knew. The present moment—is irrevocable. It has been, and it is no more.

I remember: A summer's day in Vienna. Early afternoon. A nip in the air. Wispy clouds suspended in a pale, almost gray sky. In the street there is a subtle blend of smells, fried meat, garbage, and flowering gardens. Perhaps also the perfume of passing women. The cafés are crowded. Through their windows can be seen gentlemen in light suits, smoking, arguing, or doing business. Others are leafing through magazines or doing the crossword puzzle. Some are playing chess. I am on my habitual way home from the faculty library. My heart is empty. There is a slight temptation, not a real desire, to go and spend the evening with Charlotte or Margot on the first floor of the Weary Heart. As I pass the bridge, I pause for a moment. There, just by the bridge, stand a pair of Negro beggars. One is beating a drum while the other is wailing a kind of tune. There is a hat on the sidewalk with a few pennies in it. Neither of them is young. Neither of them is old, either. It is as if they are outside the European age scale, subject to another biological clock.

I stop and linger, watching them from a short distance away. Not long ago I took a course in anthropology, yet I believe these are the first Negroes I have ever seen. Outside the circus, of course. Yes, they are woolly-haired. Coffee-skinned, not cocoa-colored. A slight shudder ripples through me. I brush aside a fleeting mental image of the shape of their sexual organs. The taller of the two, the one who is wailing or singing, has a pierced nose but no nose ring. The other one's nose is so amazingly long and flat that it revives the suppressed image of their sexual organs. I can neither leave nor take my eyes off them. I am chained to the spot, as it were, by fear, fascination, and disgust. They are standing with their backs to the bridge and the water. One is wearing sandals held together with bits of string, the other a pair of large, worn-out shoes and no socks. I am suddenly overcome with shame, like the time when, as a child, I was caught gaping at the low neckline of my Aunt Grete's dress. Hurriedly I toss a coin into the hat.

Something is urging me, after all, to head for the Weary Heart, to spend the evening with Charlotte or Margot, or even both together for a change. But my feet are rooted to the ground. I look at my watch, pretending to be waiting for someone. And I wait. In any case, without prior arrangement by telephone there can be no Margot or Charlotte.

Just then a group of youngsters in the uniform of a national youth movement draws to a halt beside the black beggars. I am fixed to the spot. They are quiet-looking boys, handsome, thirsty for knowledge, all with close-cropped hair, and from their bronzed skin one senses that their prolonged hikes in the mountains and forests have instilled in them an element of military toughness, although without undermining their fundamental good manners. Then their leader steps forward. He is a short, taut, athletic man of middle years, with ruthlessly cropped gray hair and thin, molded lips. There is something about his gait or the set of his shoulders that suggests that he would be equally at home on a river, alone in the mountains, or in a spacious mansion. The sort of man that my father longs for his only son to resemble, at least in outward appearance. The leader is wearing the same clean, neatly pressed uniform, distinguished only by his lanyard and by the colors of his badges and epaulets. He starts to explain something to the youths. His voice is clipped. Each short sentence ends in a bark. As he speaks, he waves a finger in the air; he has no compunction about pointing it an inch or two from the head of the nearer of the two Negroes. He indicates the outline of the skull. He emphasizes and demonstrates. I edge closer, to catch what he is saying. He is expatiating in a Bavarian accent on the subject of racial difference. His short lecture, as far as I can follow it, is a blend of anthropology, history, and ideology. The rhythm: staccato.

Some of his charges produce identical notebooks and pencils from the pockets of their brown shirts and take eager notes. The two Negroes, meanwhile, grin relaxedly from ear to ear. They roll their eyes ingratiatingly. They are brimming with good will, perhaps stupidity, innocent gaiety, respect, and gratitude. I must admit that at this moment they look to me like a pair of stray dogs about to be taken in by a new master. And all the while the leader is employing such words as evolution, selection, degeneration. From time to time he snaps his fingers loudly, and the two Negroes respond as one man with high-pitched laughs and flashing, milk-white teeth.

The leader holds out his thumb and forefinger, measures their foreheads without touching them, then measures his own and says, "*Also.*"

The short lecture concludes with the word "*Zivilisation.*"

The boys put their pencils and notebooks back in their pockets. The spell is broken. Silently they go on their way. To me they look very worried as they march briskly away downstream, toward the city center and the museums. For an instant they resemble a military patrol, a forward-reconnaissance party that has stumbled on an outlying detachment of enemy troops, disengaged and retreated to seek reinforcements.

The spell was broken. I, too, resumed my homeward journey. On the way, ruminating, I was almost inclined to agree: Europe is indeed in danger. The jungle races are indeed on the threshold. Our music, our laws, our sophisticated system of commerce, our subtle irony, our sensitivity to double meanings and ambiguities—all are in mortal peril. The jungle races are on the threshold. And surely history teaches us that the Mongol hordes have already swept once out of the depths of Asia and reached the very banks of the Danube and the gates of Vienna.

At home, Lisel was silently serving dinner. Father was also silent. His face was overcast. Business was going from bad to worse. There was an ugly atmosphere in the city. Things would never be the same again. On the radio, a minister was vowing to crush Communism, cosmopolitanism, and other destructive elements. The government had displayed great forbearance toward the parasites, the minister declared, and had been repaid only with ingratitude. Father turned it off. Still he said nothing. Perhaps he privately blamed the Eastern Jews who were pouring in in droves, bringing us nothing but trouble. I, too, ate my dinner in silence, and retired to my room. Margot, her shoulders, her neck, was still at the edge of my thoughts. And what could I tell Father? He was always convinced that his only son was up to his neck in student flirtations and had no idea what was going on in the city and the world.

At midnight, I went downstairs to the kitchen for a glass of water and found him sitting there alone, in his dressing gown, silently smoking, with his eyes closed.

"Are you in pain again, Father?"

He opened an eye.

"What are you blathering about, Emanuel?"

And after a short silence:

"I got some Zionist prospectuses in the mail today. Brochures from Palestine. With pictures."

I shrugged, excused myself, said good night, and returned to my room.

Precisely a week later, the letter arrived.

It was anonymous. On the envelope Father's name was typed, in correct style, with the address of his factory. He opened it in the presence of his secretary, Inge, and suddenly his world went dark. Inside the envelope there was a small sheet of good-quality notepaper, with a watermark and gold-embossed edges, but with no heading, date, or signature. There was just a single word, inscribed in the very middle of the page, in a fine, rounded hand: *Jude*. And an exclamation point.

What do you think of that, Inge, Father asked as soon as he had recovered his voice. It's a fact, Inge replied politely, and she added: There's nothing to get upset about, Herr Doktor. It's just a plain fact.

Father muttered, with bloodless lips: Have I ever denied it, Inge, I have never attempted to deny it.

In less than a month, an eager buyer was found for the house with its beautiful garden. A partnership in Linz purchased the factory. Inge was frostily dismissed, while Lisel was packed off to her village in the mountains with an old suitcase full of Mother's clothes.

Father and I had no difficulty in getting immigration certificates for Palestine from the British consul himself: the privilege of wealth.

Father had already managed to collect information and draw up detailed plans for the establishment of a small factory in a new town not far from Tel Aviv. He had already learned something about conditions there and had even made certain calculations. But from time to time, he would talk about his longing to be speedily reunited with Mother in a world where there was no evil. Old family friends still tried to reason with him, arguing, pleading with him to reconsider. They were of the opinion that shock and humiliation had provoked a self-destructive impulse in him. The Viennese Jews firmly believed at that time that everything could be explained by psychology, and that the situation would soon improve because whole nations do not suddenly take leave of their senses.

Father was like a rock: gray and unshakable.

Nevertheless, he adamantly refused to admit that Dr. Herzl had foreseen all this. On the contrary, he argued, it was Dr. Herzl and his friends who had plunged us all into this mess.

But a year later, in Ramat Gan, he changed his mind completely. He even joined the General Zionist party.

I received my medical diploma four days before our departure, on the morning we got our visas. I was summoned to the rector's office. They explained politely that they did not think I would feel comfortable at the official graduation ceremony, they were bound to take into account the general mood of the students, and so they had decided to hand me my diploma informally, in a plain buff envelope. Wide vistas, they said, opened up for a young doctor in western Asia. The ignorance, dirt, and disease there were unbelievable. They even mentioned Albert Schweitzer, who was healing lepers in the middle of the jungle in Africa. They mistakenly stressed that Schweitzer, too, was of Jewish extraction. Then they turned to the bitter feelings I must be harboring in my heart, and begged me to remember, even when I was far away, how much Vienna had given me, and not only that she had humiliated me. They wished me bon voyage and, after a slight hesitation, shook hands.

I do indeed remember. And what I feel in my heart is neither bitterness nor humiliation but—how can I write it when I can see before me the expression of cold irony on your mouth and the cigarette smoke pouring contemptuously from your nostrils—Jewish sorrow and rage. No, not in my heart, in the marrow of my bones. I won't make homemade explosives for the Hagganah. I'll make them the ultimate explosive. I shall surprise Uri, Nachtshe, Ben-Gurion himself. If only my strength holds out. I myself shall be the jungle races on the threshold. I am the Mongol hordes.

I'm joking again, as usual, at the wrong time, as usual, joking without being funny, in my usual ludicrous way.

We reached Palestine by way of the Tirol, Trieste, Piraeus, and a French steamship. Father did indeed set up a candy factory in Ramat Gan that became well known. He even married again, a husky, bejeweled refugee from southern Poland. Perhaps it was his wife's influence that made him become an active member of the General Zionist Council and of several committees.

He occasionally sends me money. Unnecessarily. I have enough of my own.

Twice a year, at Passover and the New Year, I used to visit them and spend a few days among the vases, tea sets, and chandeliers. In the evenings there was a stream of visitors: middle-aged men of affairs, party workers and businessmen, middlemen who enjoyed *choolant* and snuff and cracked bawdy jokes in three languages with chesty, man-of-the-world laughter. "Felix," they would say as they winked at Father, "Reb Pinhasel, when are you going to marry off the boy? When are you going to initiate him into the mysteries of business? What are they saying about him, a Socialist you've got in your family?" While Father's wife, with a gold watch held between the jaws and tail of a gold snake wrapped around her freckled wrist, would leap to my defense: "What do you mean, business? Business nothing. Our Emanuel will soon be a professor at the Hadassah, and we'll all have to line up for three months before he'll so much as look at us, and even then only as a special favor."

I did indeed work at Hadassah for a while and put up uncomplainingly with Alexander Dushkin's rumbustious despotism. One evening he summoned me to his home in Kiryat Shemuel, and at the end of the tea, the jokes, and the gossip, I was informed: "Next week you're being handed over lock, stock, and barrel to the government of Palestine. To the bacteriological department. They've issued me an ultimatum to hand over to them some first-rate Svidrigaïlov who'll keep an eye on the whole water supply of Jerusalem and the surrounding area. So I sold you to them right away. Free, gratis, and for nothing. I didn't even claim my thirty pieces of silver. The pay's not bad, and you'll be able to travel around at His Majesty's expense, from Hebron to Jericho and from Ramallah to Rosh Ha'ayin. You'll have your own private empire. You'll like O'Leary. He's an educated, cultivated sort of chap. Not like me, a Tartar cannibal. You and I, Nussbaum, let's speak frankly, well, you're more the phlegmatic type, while I'm a madman—anyway, we're horses of a different color. I just want to say, Emanuel," Dushkin suddenly roared, as his eyes filled with tears, "that you'll always find my door and my heart open to you. Day or night. I really love you. Only don't let me down. Now what's the matter with your tea? Drink it up!"

So I took my leave of Samovar and joined Edward O'Leary and my dear friend Dr. Antoine al-Mahdi. And I started my tours of the springs and wells.

Two or three times a week, we went out into the country. We passed beautiful gardens, olive groves and vineyards, and tiny vegetable-patches. We saw minarets reaching upward from the hilltops. The three of us together forced our way through thorn hedges and tramped for hours on end to inspect some far-flung spring or Godforsaken well. The smell of dung and ashes brought me a sensation of peace and calm. Occasionally Antoine would say apologetically: "The cattle are cattle and so are the fellahin. You can't tell the difference." If O'Leary jokingly asked him, "Do you enjoy the thought that one day every villager will wear a tweed jacket and tie like you?" he would reply, "That would be against nature." Edward would chuckle: "And what about the Jews? In the kibbutzim you can find lawyers milking cows and mucking out." Antoine would flash me an affectionate smile: "The Jews are a remarkable people. They always go against nature."

We used to go to King Solomon's Pools. To Nahal Arugot in the Judean Desert. To the Elah Valley. We collected specimens in glass phials and took them back to the laboratory in Julian's Way to examine them under the microscope. O'Leary would lend us books by English travelers from the last century who described the desolate state of the country in all its details.

"How does she do it?" O'Leary would ask in tones of amusement. "How does this worn-out, barren old girl make them all fall madly in love with her? I was once in southern Persia: exactly the same miserable hills, dotted with gray rocks, with a few olive trees and pieces of old pottery. Nobody crossed half the world to conquer *them*."

"Woman comes from the earth," Dr. Mahdi said in a velvety whisper, in careful English. "Man comes from the rain. And desire comes from the Devil. Look at the Jordan. For thousands of years it has flowed into the Dead Sea, where there is neither fish nor tree, and it never comes out again. There's nothing like that in Persia, Edward, and the moral of the story is: if it's hard to get in, then it's hard to get out."

I would contribute an occasional remark, such as:

"The Land of Israel is full of simple symbols. Not only the Jordan and the Dead Sea—even the malaria and bilharzia here take on a symbolic significance."

"You two use similar words to express totally different sentiments. We all three do, actually."

"Is that really so?" O'Leary would murmur politely. He would refrain from offering an explanation and would deftly change the subject.

Antoine ran a private practice in the afternoons and evenings in Katamon, and I had my home clinic in Kerem Avraham. I learned to cultivate polite relations with my neighbors and to be a good listener in hard times. I lost track of the hours I spent battling against diphtheria and dysentery. If I was called out at night or over the weekend, when I was busy in my amateur laboratory or listening to music, I never complained. If the children made fun of me in the street for my German ways, I never lost my temper. I fulfilled my obligations, more or less.

Until you and I met in Arza, that is. And until my illness appeared.

So there you have a résumé of the story of my life. Some of it you knew already, and the rest you could probably have deduced, in your usual way, from an analysis of my behavior.

Now I shall return to my observations.

Uri has gone off, probably on instructions from one of Nachtshe's mysterious assistants, to stand on the Kapitanski brothers' roof and keep watch on the Sheikh Jarrah district and the traffic on the Ramallah road. And I, too, am on the lookout, sitting here on my balcony. The details I am amassing will be of no military use: A Jerusalem street vendor, what he sells, how he sells, who buys. My lower-middle-class Eastern European neighbors, and why they quarrel so much among themselves. And what, exactly, their communal ideal is. Their children, what is new about them and what is ancient. And the youths, boys like Nachtshe, Yigal, and Akiva, how, and with what measure of success, they all attempt to dress, talk, and joke on the basis of some abstract archetype from Galilee, from the Palmach, a venerated image of the pioneering hero.

And I myself: apart from my impending death and the code of pains and symptoms, why do I sometimes abhor these brave boys, and secretly call them "Asiatics," and sometimes feel a powerful love for them as though I have an unidentified son among them, a dark-skinned, barefoot, physically tough young man, an expert with machines and weapons, contemptuous of words, contemptuous of me and my worries? I don't know.

More rhetorical questions of an observer: What is regarded as funny here. What is considered embarrassing. What do they talk about and what do they pass over in silence. Who has come to Jerusalem, and where from, what did each of them hope to find here, and what has he actually found. Helena Grill compared to Sonya Litvak. The poet Nehamkin from the electrical and radio repair shop as contrasted with Comrade Lustig. What did they hope to find here and what have they actually found. And I don't exclude myself from the question.

Other questions: What is transitory in Jerusalem, and what is permanent. Why are the colors different here, the autumn colors and the evening colors. And on another level: What are the intentions of the British. Is there going to be a political vacuum. What are the real limits of our power, and how much is simply delusion and arrogance. Is Dr. Mahdi the real, deadly enemy. Is it weakness of will in me that I cannot desire his death, and that I keep trying to think up arguments that might convince him. Everything leads me on to the final point, to the single question: What is going to happen. What lies in store for us.

Because apart from this, what else have I got to think about? The sunsets, perhaps. The embers of my love for you. Doubts and hesitations. Pathetic preparations. Worries.

Mina. Where are you now, tonight. Come back.

These last words may seem to you like a cry for help. That was not what I meant. Forgive me. I'm sorry.

Tuesday, September 9

Dear Mina,

This morning I went to the Jewish Agency to hand in my report on readily available chemicals that may have military uses. On a separate sheet I offered some suggestions, even though it seemed to me that there was nothing new in them, and that any chemist in the university on Mount Scopus would have indicated precisely the same possibilities. My appointment was for nine o'clock, and I was a few minutes early. On the way, a fine drizzle lashed my cheeks. Later, the rain began to beat heavily on the windows of the office. They relieved me of the cardboard folder, thanked me, and then, to my great surprise, led me to Ben-Gurion's office. Somebody, apparently, had exaggerated and told him that there was a sick doctor here in Jerusalem who also happened to be an original chemist with daring ideas on the subject of explosives. In brief, he had asked to see me without further delay. Somebody had spun a meaningless myth about me.

Ben-Gurion began with an inquisition. I was asked about my origins, my family, was I related in any way to Nussbaum the well-known educationalist, were my views not close to those of the pacifist Brith Shalom movement. A volcanic man, with gestures reminiscent of Dushkin's, running backward and forward between the window and the bookcase, refusing to waste time on qualifications or reservations. He kept interrupting me almost before I had begun speaking, and goaded me on: The danger was imminent. A critical moment had been reached and we were almost without resources. What we lacked in materials we would make up in spirit and inventiveness. The Jewish genius, he said, would not let us down. We were up to our necks in it. Mr. Ben-Gurion, I tried to say, if you will permit me . . . But he did not permit me. On the contrary, on the contrary, he said, you will receive everything you need, and you will start work this very night. Make a note of that, Motke. Right. And now, out with it, doctor: tell us what you need.

And I stood there in confusion, with my arms held stiffly at my sides, and explained awkwardly that there appeared to be some misunderstanding. I was not a new Albert Einstein. I was simply a doctor with a modest competence in chemistry, who had volunteered a memorandum and some minor suggestions. The Jewish genius, by all means, but not me. A misunderstanding.

And so I came home, covered with shame and confusion. If only I could live up to their great expectations. Comrade Rubashov writes in the *Davar* newspaper that we will withstand the coming tests. My heart shuddered at these words. Tests. A real war is coming, we are without resources, and enthusiastic amateurs persist in using words like "tests." No doubt you will be smiling at this point, not at Comrade Rubashov's words but at mine: I wrote "a real war." I can imagine from far away the exhalation of smoke from your nostrils, the twist of your lips.

Last night I heard the drone of engines from the direction of Chancellor Street. Another British convoy on its way northward toward the port of Haifa, perhaps with blacked-out headlights.

Is this the beginning of the evacuation? Are we being left to shift for ourselves? What if there is no truth in the image of the fearless fighter from the hills of Galilee? What if regular armies cross the Jordan and the deserts and we fail the test?

This morning from my balcony I watched Sarah Zeldin the kindergarten teacher, a little old Russian woman with a blue apron and a wrinkled face. It was immediately after I got back from the Agency. She was teaching the little children to sing:

My pretty little village
Set on the mountainside,
With gardens, fields, and orchards
Extending far and wide,

and I could see at that moment an image of the little village, the mountainside, the broad expanse. I was seized with terror. But the children, Samson and Arnon and Eitan and Mrs. Litvak's Meirab, made fun of their teacher and piped, "My silly little village."

What's going to happen, Mina.

"The Irgun and the Stern Group will blow up all the bridges and capture the mountain passes as soon as the English start pulling out," Uri said, "because the Hagganah can't make up their minds if they really want us to have a Hebrew state or if they want us to go on begging on our knees. Look I've got a khaki battle dress, Dr. Emanuel, it's a present from Auntie Natalia because Mommy and Daddy are coming home today."

"Have you done your homework?"

"Yes, I did it at school during break. A drunk Australian soldier went into Kapitanski's to look for girls, and he left his jeep outside on the sidewalk. He took his pistol in with him, but he'll never see his magazines again. Look, I've brought them for you. Three full up and one only half. From a Tommy gun. Also, I found a small crack in the wall of Schneller, perhaps I can squeeze through it at nighttime, as soon as I get the order and some leaflets and dynamite. But don't breathe a word to Nachtshe because he always does whatever they tell him from the Hagganah, and nobody knows where Ephraim's disappeared to. So you decide."

"All right," I said. "No secret visits to Schneller. That's an order. And no more stealing from Australian soldiers. Otherwise I shall be very angry."

Uri gave me a look of amazement, nodded twice, came to a decision in his mind, and at the end of the silence requested permission to ask me a personal question.

"Go ahead," I said. And I added secretly: Little fool. Dear little idiot. If only I were your father. Only if I were your father I don't know what I would say or do to make you understand at last. Understand what. I don't know.

"Well," I said, "what's your question?"

"Never mind. You said no, so that's that."

"What I meant was, not without an order. Not before the time is right."

"Dr. Emanuel, is it the illness?"

"Is what the illness?"

"Is it the illness that makes your hands shake like that, and . . . one of your eyes is a bit closed, and it keeps blinking."

"I wasn't aware of that."

"Your illness . . . is it something very dangerous?"

"Why do you ask that, Uri?"

"Nothing. Only that if it is you ought to teach me about everything in the lab, so that if anything . . ."

"Anything what?"

"Nothing. Don't worry, Dr. Emanuel. Give me a list and a shopping basket and I'll go to the greengrocer and to Ziegel's and get you anything you need."

"Why are you so concerned about me, child? Is it just because of the bomb I've still got to make?"

"No special reason. I don't know. That too, maybe."

"What too?"

"You're like an uncle to me. No, not an uncle, I mean someone serious."

"What about your parents? And your Auntie Natalia?"

"They just laugh at me. They say my head's stuffed full of nonsense. You don't laugh."

"No. Why should I laugh?"

"You don't think my head's stuffed full of nonsense?"

"No, Uri, not nonsense. Or else we've both got the same sort of nonsense in our heads."

Silence.

And then:

"Dr. Emanuel, are you ever going to get better?"

"I don't think so, Uri."

"But I don't want you to die."

"Why me specially?"

"Because to you I'm not a crazy child, and because you never tell me lies."

"You must go now, child."

"But I don't want to."

"You must."

"All right. Whatever you say. But I'll come back again."

And from the doorway, from outside, a fraction of an instant before he closed the door behind him:

"Don't die."

His departure left behind a total silence. Inside the silence, the throbbing of the blood in my temples. What is there left for me to do now, Mina. Sit down, perhaps, and copy out for you a few items from this morning's paper, because in New York you probably lack details of what's going on here in Palestine. I shall skip the headlines. To judge from them, the British government is fed up with our bombs, our slogans, our delegations, our regular disgusted memorandums. One of these nights they will order a curfew, impose a deathly silence on Jerusalem, and in the morning we'll wake up to find that they have upped and gone.

And what then, Mina?

Hebrew traffic police have started to operate in Tel Aviv with the consent of the British governor. They have eight policemen working in two shifts. A thirteen-year-old Arab girl is to stand trial before a military court, accused of possessing a rifle in the village of Hawara, Nablus district. Some illegal immigrants from the *Exodus* are being deported to Hamburg, and they say they will fight to the last to resist disembarkation. Fourteen Gestapo men have been sentenced to death in Lübeck. Mr. Solomon Chmelnik of Rehovot has been kidnapped and badly beaten up by an extremist organization but has been returned safe and sound. The "Voice of Jerusalem" orchestra is going to be conducted by Hanan Schlesinger. Mahatma Gandhi's fast is in its second day. The singer Edith de Philippe will be unable to perform this week in Jerusalem, and the Chamber Theater has been obliged to postpone its performance of *You Can't Take It with You*. On the other hand, two days ago the new Colonnade Building on the Jaffa road was opened, containing, among others, the shops of Mikolinski and Freiman & Bein, and Dr. Scholl's chiropody. According to the Arab leader Musa Alami, the Arabs will never accept the partition of the country; after all, King Solomon ruled that the mother who was opposed to partition was the true mother, and the Jews ought to recognize the significance of this parable. And then again, Comrade Golda Myerson of the Jewish Agency Executive has proclaimed that the Jews will struggle for the inclusion of Jerusalem in the Hebrew state, because the Land of Israel and Jerusalem are synonymous in our hearts.

Late last night, an Arab set upon two Jewish girls in the vicinity of the Bernardiya Café, between Beit ha-Kerem and Bayit va-Gan. One of the girls escaped, and the other screamed for help until some of the local residents heard and succeeded in preventing the suspect's escape. In the course of investigations by Constable O'Connor, it emerged that the man is an employee of the Broadcasting Service and is distantly related to the influential Nashashibi family. Despite this, bail was denied, on account of the gravity of the alleged offense. In his defense, the prisoner declared that he had come out of the café drunk and had been under the impression that the two girls were prancing around naked in the dark.

One further item of news: Lieutenant Colonel Adderley, the presiding officer of the military court, hearing the case of Shlomo Mansoor Shalom, has found him guilty of distributing subversive pamphlets but found that he was of unsound mind. Mr. Gardewicz the probation officer requested that he not be sent to the lunatic asylum for fear of a deterioration in his condition, and pleaded with the judge that he be isolated in a private institution instead, so that his weak intellect might not be exploited by fanatics for their own criminal ends. Lieutenant Colonel Adderley regretted that he was unable to accede to Mr. Gardewicz's request since it was beyond his powers; he was obliged to commit the unfortunate man to custody pending a ruling by the High Commissioner, representing the Crown, on the possible exercise of lenience or clemency. I am copying out these tidbits of news to give you a clear idea of how things are here. No, that's not true: I am doing it to avoid sinking into all sorts of thoughts and emotions. On the radio, Cilla Leibowitz is giving a piano recital, and after the news we are promised a commentary by Gordus, and then some songs sung by Bracha Tsefira. I expect some of my neighbors will join me to listen to the news. Grill or Lustig, perhaps Litvak. Ephraim has not been seen around lately. Nachtshe has also disappeared. Only the poet Nehamkin strolls up and down Malachi Street, testing the substance of the stones of Jerusalem with the tip of his walking stick. Or perhaps he is tapping to discover a hollow spot, an ancient crevice in the rock on which we live, as is promised in his sacred scriptures. Happy is he who believes. My distant Jasmine, just as I was writing of a crevice in the rock a new pain came, unknown to me before, but resembling a certain piercing pleasure that you revealed to me not long before you left me. It appears that later in the autumn Dr. Nussbaum will begin to lose control of his bowel movements. He will have to be transferred to the Hadassah Hospital. From his window he may be able to watch the delusive desert light at dawn, and the shimmering skyline of the Mountains of Moab. Professor Dushkin will not stint on the morphine, nor will he try to spin out the death agonies unnecessarily; we have an unspoken agreement. Then there will be interference with breathing and vision. The heart will weaken. The consciousness will fade. From then on, the patient will only occasionally utter connected speech. He may ramble in German. He may whisper your name. How I hope he will not scream. His father and stepmother will come to take their leave of him, and he and his father will make a supreme effort and try to exchange an anecdote or two in German, even if it means speaking through clenched teeth. Afterward everything will go black, and he will struggle on for a few hours, a day or two at the most. It will be the rainy season. It is very likely that the January rain will already be falling on his grave on Sanhedriya or on the Mount of Olives. What is going to happen in Jerusalem he does not know. Nobody knows. It seems that Musa Alami and Golda Myerson will not budge from their positions. But in the end these hard times, too, will come to an end, and you will forget him and his troubles. Perhaps you have already forgotten. The one person who may remember as time goes by, with mixed feelings and perhaps even with longing, is Uri, the son of the printer Kolodny. I beg you, Mina, if Jerusalem survives and if these letters reach you and if you wish to dispose of them, please, in years to come, make an effort to find this Uri and to let him have them. I expect you are sick and tired of me now. Enough.

They are sitting on their balcony as I write, Kolodny the printer, his wife, his sister, Natalia, and our mutual neighbor the poet Nehamkin from the radio repair shop. They are surrounded by geraniums in cans and cacti growing in boxes of earth. Where is the child? I implore you to watch out for the child, in case he takes it into his head to sneak into the Schneller Barracks and launch a single-handed raid on the British army. I cannot see Uri. And they seem so unperturbed, sitting there chatting, talking about politics, I expect, apparently calm. I consider their calmness nothing short of outrageous. Above their heads there is a yellow light bulb around which the insects are swarming dementedly. Kolodny the printer is a pale-faced, equable man, yet even he for some reason chooses to dress in what is almost a military uniform: wide khaki shorts, a brass-buckled belt, long khaki socks held up just below the knees by garters. The poet Nehamkin, on the other hand, is wearing his habitual Polish suit and silk tie: ready at a moment's notice. It seems to me that with the exception of us two, everyone in the neighborhood is more or less a pioneering type. They are all positive, constructive characters, apparently incapable of panic. And death is not a possibility. They are chatting. Laughing, Mrs. Kolodny passes around a bowl of oranges, but nobody takes one, and she smiles distractedly. What is transitory in Jerusalem and what is permanent. What will Uri look back to nostalgically in times to come. Corrugated-iron sheds. Plywood partitions. Empty yogurt pots. European manners blended with a certain crude gaiety. A city of immigrants on the edge of the desert whose flat rooftops are all festooned with drying sheets. The inhabitants are always scurrying from place to place with sunglasses pushed up on their foreheads. A general expression of "I'm very busy but I'll stop a moment just for you." An expression of "Business calls." An expression of "Sorry, we'll have a nice long chat some other time, but right now I must dash, we all have to do our duty."

I am not complaining, Mina. These are crucial times, and soon there will be a war. Everybody, even a man like me, must do his best to make his modest contribution to the general effort. Perhaps it is true that this is the last generation to live in chains. But is it really the last generation. Is it true that different times will come that I shall not know.

Only the women, it seems to me, are not strong enough: lining up for rice, lining up for ice, waiting beside the kerosene cart, they seem to be on the point of fainting. And at times on summer afternoons, when Jerusalem is ablaze, swept by the desert light, I can hear Mrs. Kolodny playing her piano behind her shuttered windows, and it sounds like a desperate moan.

So the British will leave. The King David Hotel in Julian's Way will be emptied of its officers with their greased, neatly parted hair, emptied of its weary Englishwomen who sit on the hotel terrace looking out over the walls of the Old City as if fishing on the banks of the biblical past. No more morning sessions under the picture of the King in Edward O'Leary's office, where Dr. Mahdi from the Arab Council and Dr. Nussbaum from the Hadassah Hospital discuss ways of protecting the city's water supply from bacteria or destroying the breeding grounds of the mosquitoes in the Kedron Valley. Different times will come. "Excellent people like yourselves," says Dr. Mahdi, "such an intelligent, enlightened community, how have you all come to be captivated by such a terrible idea as Zionism?" I try my best: "For heaven's sake, Antoine, make an effort, just for once, try to see things from our point of view." And Edward, as always, firmly: "Gentlemen, perhaps we had better. Let's get back to the business at hand, if you don't mind."

What is the business at hand, Mina, my dear?

Perhaps you know?

Pitch-black outside. Crickets. Stars. Wind. I shall stop now.

Early hours of Wednesday morning
September 10

Dear Mina,

I shall not use the word "blame." You are not to blame for what you do to me in my dreams. But perhaps you are responsible, up to a point.

With a hint of a gray mustache, a smell of cigarette smoke emanating even from your hair, wearing army trousers and a large man's shirt with several pockets, you stand beside my bed.

Antoine is feeling my Adam's apple; he is clasping my chin in both hands, to keep me from wriggling during the operation. His polite face is so close to mine that I can see a yellow boil with a pink rim on his nose. A slight asymmetry between the two wings of his mustache. He is chubby and well mannered, and he smells of eau de cologne as he smiles at me. "There, there," he says in English; "let's both try together," he says. Two strong young men are holding my legs above the knees, but apparently their minds are not on the operation, because they are whispering to each other and chuckling. You are holding out a scalpel, or perhaps it is not a scalpel but a kitchen knife, a bread knife. Samovar thanks you in his usual way, with a slight bow, and takes it from you. "Slowly," you tell him. "With him there's no need for you to hurry." "There." "Now there." "And here." He does exactly what you say. He is wearing rubber gloves. He is a bright crimson. And he cuts amazingly gently. I must try to say something, at once, before my head is severed from my neck. Perhaps I shall remind Antoine how he came to see me late one night last winter, and begged me to cure him of a dose of gonorrhea that he had apparently contracted on his last trip to Beirut. And how I put him up here in my apartment for four days and gave him injections. But I promised Antoine to carry his secret with me to the grave. I shall remain silent. How strange is the deepening cut in my throat: no blood, no pain. On the contrary, Relief. "That is all, Dr. Oswald," says Ben-Gurion, as if he cannot believe his eyes. "It is a very simple operation, after all." And I indicate with a movement of the lips that the meeting is now over.

I am awakened by heavy rain. The light refuses to come on: it would seem that there is a power failure in Jerusalem. I strike a match. Look at my watch. One o'clock. I must get up. Wind and rain at the window. This time it is the autumn rain at last. The insects that have been dancing around the balcony light in the evenings have been swept away. The pine trees and the stone are what has endured, washed clean of dust, purified by wind and water.

I must get dressed. I must go at once. Go where, Mina. The dead praise not the Lord. In New York, you have said, a neo-Viennese school is reassembling. You must be there to report on the collective recovery that is taking place in the hills of Galilee and the Jezreel Valley. On the beginning of the eclipse of centuries-old ethnic neuroses. There is a way, ladies and gentlemen, you will proclaim to those scholarly refugees, there is a way, and it lies open.

Will you tell them about me, too? Will you be able to use me at least as an example, a curiosity, a detail that sheds a certain light or casts a shadow on the new pioneering reality among those ancient hills?

I must go. Tonight. At once. Perhaps to Katamon, to knock on Antoine's door and implore him by everything that's holy. To plead with him. To plead for the lives of our children, his and mine. Or perhaps not to Katamon but to Haifa and the kibbutzim in the valley. Is it already too late? Are the wind and rain meant for me this time? The Schneller bell rings once, twice, and is silent. I am sitting writing to you by the light of a kerosene lamp, in my gray flannel dressing gown. I ought to get dressed and go. There is a way and it lies open. Happy is he who waits, says Mr. Nehamkin; he will surely reach his goal. He who waits will never reach his goal, my dear fellow: only those who travel ever reach their goal. What is that goal. There is a way and I must get up and go. Which is the way, Mina, that is what I do not know, but we have a son and he will be able to travel it. The man who is writing to you is tired and ill. He must give himself an injection, take his pills, and go quietly back to bed. Enough. The inscription on the parish church was in four languages in the Vienna of my childhood; in four languages it promised every man and woman that there is a way back. It is a lie, I tell you, a bald-faced lie.

I must go. Not tonight, tomorrow morning. I must go to Mount Scopus and tell Dushkin, as I promised I would, that my condition has taken a turn for the worse. It is not for me to work a minor miracle in Jerusalem, to win over Dr. Mahdi or to make a discovery that may turn the military situation on its head. "Dew underfoot and the stars up above, / The Valley of Jezreel sparkles with love." So runs the song they are playing this early morning on the Hagganah shortwave broadcast. But here on Malachi Street, the trees are showing pale in the half-light of a murky dawn, and the rain has not stopped. As I wrote earlier, there is not much time left. You found me, used me, and set me aside. One of these days, you will come back to Jerusalem, a famous woman, a professor, the pioneer of a new discipline. You will bring fresh methods to the young Hebrew state. My death may even contribute to your fame. In the course of time they may mistakenly number me among the victims, and behind your back they will say that Professor Oswald lost her young fiancé in the war, an original scholar from Vienna. Jerusalem will overflow its boundaries and become a big city. Old men and old women shall dwell in her streets and rejoice therein, and no foe shall menace her gates. Just as my neighbor the poet promises us. There will be wide boulevards. There will be streetcars to link the various neighborhoods. Castles and towers will spring up. Perhaps they will make a river here and span it with bridges. It will be a beautiful, tranquil city. I shall close now, yours affectionately, and go back to bed. I have finished with recording time and place. This witness may stand down. He hopes that in due course, time, place, and witness will all be granted a kind of pardon. In Uri's longing, perhaps. Good night. Everything will be all right. ~

Interpretive Questions for Discussion

Why does the gentle Dr. Nussbaum, a man beset by doubts, spend his last days writing to Mina, his efficient, unsentimental lover who has left for America?

1. Why does Dr. Nussbaum want to record "the place and the time" of his home in Jerusalem, the "simple, familiar, trivial things"? (326, 327, 359–361, 375) Why does Dr. Nussbaum long for "sights that are present, as though they were recollected images"? (362)

2. Why does Mina, in contrast to Dr. Nussbaum, "not look back, remember, feel longing, regret"? (320)

3. Why is Dr. Nussbaum disparaging of Mina's resolve to "turn over a new leaf from time to time"? (320)

4. Even though he is dying and Mina is launching her career, why does Dr. Nussbaum say that Mina, like himself, is "a barren desert" within? (321)

5. Why does Dr. Nussbaum describe America as a place where "all eyes are constantly on the future, where even longing is directed to the future, and everybody agrees that the past is condemned to silence"? (326) Does Dr. Nussbaum disapprove of Mina's decision to make her career in America after completing her research on the dreams of the first native-born children of the kibbutzim? (345)

6. What does Dr. Nussbaum mean when he writes to Mina that the "truth" is that he and the other Jews who escaped the Holocaust—"the heirs of prophets, kings, and heroes"—"turn over a new leaf only to smudge it with ancient neuroses"? (335–336)

7. Why are we told that it is Dr. Nussbaum's sense of humor that first draws Mina to him? (353) Why does Mina suggest to Dr. Nussbaum that the reason they are physically attracted to "Orientals" is that they have retained "some sort of sensual animal language" that European Jews like themselves have long forgotten? (354)

8. Why do Dr. Nussbaum and Mina relate to each other as "an orphan and a dominating aunt," as slave and slaveowner? (356, 359) Why does Dr. Nussbaum write to Mina that he loved her "out of humiliation"? (359)

9. Why doesn't Mina respond to Dr. Nussbaum's suggestion that in her past she had been viciously humiliated by a man? Why is her reply to "forcefully" caress Dr. Nussbaum and tell him he is "so vulnerable. So helpless. And so touching"? (357–358)

10. Why does Dr. Nussbaum imagine Mina reacting with cold irony and contempt when he admits that his banishment from Vienna left him feeling not bitter or humiliated, but full of "Jewish sorrow and rage"? (380)

11. Why does Dr. Nussbaum dream that Mina directs an operation in which his head is severed from his body, with Samovar, Dr. Antoine al-Mahdi, and Ben-Gurion all participating? (394–395; cf. 373)

12. In his last letter to Mina, why doesn't Dr. Nussbaum write that he loves her? Why does he write instead that she found him, used him, and set him aside? (397)

Suggested textual analyses

Pages 319–321: beginning, "There is not much time left," and ending, "the termination of the British Mandate."

Pages 394–395: beginning, "I shall not use the word 'blame,' " and ending, "the meeting is now over."

Why does Dr. Nussbaum dream that Mina bore him a son and then hid him?

1. Why does Dr. Nussbaum come to think of Uri as his son? (337, 344, 350) Why does he think that his "strange relationship" with Uri will end badly? (339)
2. Why does Dr. Nussbaum confess to Mina that he ought to fight for Uri's soul—put a firm stop to their war games—but then decline to do so? (339; cf. 388) Why does Dr. Nussbaum wonder whether he has the strength or the right to influence Uri's mind? (341)
3. Why does Dr. Nussbaum try and fail to write educational stories about heroes like Albert Schweitzer, Louis Pasteur, and Thomas Edison, to counteract stories of war and vengeance told to children by "messianic" Jewish teachers? (336)
4. When trying to figure out "what *is* the matter at hand," why does Dr. Nussbaum describe the "evil" Grill children tormenting the "heroic" Uri? Is Dr. Nussbaum suggesting that a war to annihilate "Jew-haters" will alter the Jewish character? (341–343)
5. Why does Dr. Nussbaum both abhor and love the new children of Israel, whom he secretly calls "Asiatics"? (384) Why does he remark that a "new race of peasants is emerging. Laconic. Sarcastic. Single-minded. Dedicated"? (345)

6. When Dr. Nussbaum tries to temper Uri's enthusiasm for war, why does the boy reply, in utter disbelief, that "everything is war," even love and friendship? (349)

7. Why is Dr. Nussbaum so afraid of "losing" Uri that he allows the boy to think that he is working on a top-secret military assignment? (350)

8. Why does Dr. Nussbaum imagine that Nachtshe is his child by Mina, come to Jerusalem "to rescue us all"? Why does Dr. Nussbaum wonder about Nachtshe's loneliness and his relationships with women? (371–372)

9. Why is Uri portrayed as being both nurturing toward Dr. Nussbaum and totally committed to war? Why does Dr. Nussbaum learn from Uri that without Jerusalem there will be no Hebrew state? (374)

10. Why does Dr. Nussbaum want Uri to have the letters he writes to Mina? (392)

11. Why does Dr. Nussbaum imagine Mina reporting that "there is a way" toward overcoming the "centuries-old ethnic neuroses," a way that he does not know, but that their son will be able to travel? (396; cf. 375)

12. Why does Dr. Nussbaum conclude that perhaps he, Jerusalem, and the turbulent times "will all be granted a kind of pardon" in Uri's longing? (397)

Suggested textual analyses
Pages 339–344: beginning, "I should have told Professor Dushkin," and ending, "Or Uri."

Pages 396–397: from "I must get dressed," to the end of the story.

Why does the author have a young, dying European Jew narrate the events leading up to the formation of an independent Israel?

1. Why does the author have Dr. Nussbaum's indifferent lover abandon Israel for America on the eve of his death and the birth of the nation?

2. Why does the peace-loving Dr. Nussbaum participate in the war effort as an explosives expert? Why does the author have everyone—from Uri to Ben-Gurion—think that Dr. Nussbaum will discover the miracle formula that will give Israel the advantage in the war?

3. Why does Dr. Nussbaum feel humiliated by the fact that he is contributing to the war effort? (346)

4. Why is Dr. Nussbaum filled with apprehension at the contrast between the silent, young, educated Arab in the coffeehouse and the noisy, disrespectful Jewish students on the bus? (331–332)

5. Why does Dr. Nussbaum succumb in his dreams to the romantic notion of wiping out the enemies of the Jews? (339) Why, in his pain and "ecstatic longing," does Dr. Nussbaum suffer the delusion that he has discovered a simple scientific formula that will make Israel a great military power? (373)

6. Why does Dr. Nussbaum describe the "sour smell" of the Eastern European Jews in his neighborhood in such a pejorative, unflattering manner, and then wonder, "Is this also a place that in years to come someone will remember with longing?" (343–344)

7. Why is it suggested that the meetings of Dr. Nussbaum's neighborhood civil defense council come off as farces in which nothing is usually accomplished? Are we meant to think that Nachtshe indeed provides "solutions," or that his arrogance and bravado ought to be squashed, as Dr. Nussbaum contemplates? (368–372)

8. When searching for "the moral, the reason," why does Dr. Nussbaum recall the events leading up to his flight from Vienna to Palestine with his father? (375–378)

9. Why is it suggested that the "humiliation" felt by the elder Dr. Nussbaum at the anti-Semitism he experienced in Vienna led to his salvation in Palestine? (379) Why are we told that the elder Dr. Nussbaum initially believed that the Eastern European and Zionist Jews were responsible for anti-Semitism, but then changed his mind completely after a year in Palestine? (378, 380)

10. After describing what he felt when he was "banished" from Vienna, why does Dr. Nussbaum joke, "I am the Mongol hordes" who will create the ultimate explosive for Israel? (380)

11. Why does the author show the scientists O'Leary, al-Mahdi, and Nussbaum as being able to transcend their political differences to become dear friends? (346, 382–383, 394, 395)

12. Why does Dr. Nussbaum conclude his narrative with the assurance that Jerusalem will become a beautiful, tranquil city, and that "everything will be all right"? (397)

Suggested textual analysis

Pages 372–381: beginning, "The rain was light," and ending, "in my usual ludicrous way."

For Further Reflection

1. Why has Israel not yet achieved the tranquil vision put forth by Dr. Nussbaum?

2. When should world powers like the United States intervene in areas of ethnic strife, such as that between Jews and Arabs in Palestine in 1947? Is there a way in which superpowers can keep the peace, or must "centuries-old ethnic neuroses" be played out through violence?

3. Has the Jewish character changed since the end of the Holocaust and the establishment of Israel?

4. Is "humiliation" the ultimate cause of war?

POETRY

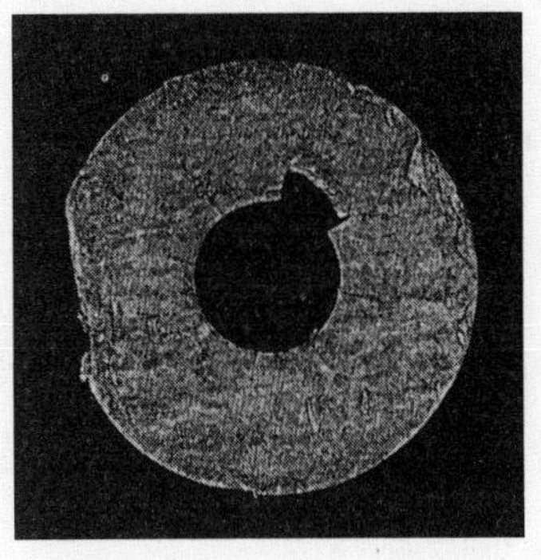

Lao-tzu

LAO-TZU (fl. sixth century B.C.) may have been an older contemporary of Confucius and an archivist in one of China's petty kingdoms. Nothing certain is known about his life; some scholars have even questioned whether a man named Lao-tzu—meaning "Old Person" or "Old Philosopher"—is historical. According to legend, Lao-tzu, upon leaving the court of the declining Chou Dynasty, passed on his teachings to a border guard who afterward compiled his words into the *Tao Te Ching,* which can be translated as *The Book of the Way and Its Power*—a guide to the art of living and government. Scholars, however, date the work in the fourth, third, and second centuries B.C., with some sections possibly as old as the sixth century B.C. The *Tao Te Ching* sets forth the philosophical and political doctrine of "not-doing"—effortless action and the renunciation of all striving—which is the foundation of Taoism, one of China's major religions.

Tao Te Ching

(selection)

1

The tao that can be told
is not the eternal Tao.
The name that can be named
is not the eternal Name.

The unnamable is the eternally real.
Naming is the origin
of all particular things.

Free from desire, you realize the mystery.
Caught in desire, you see only the manifestations.

Yet mystery and manifestations
arise from the same source.
This source is called darkness.

Darkness within darkness.
The gateway to all understanding.

2

When people see some things as beautiful,
other things become ugly.
When people see some things as good,
other things become bad.

Being and non-being create each other.
Difficult and easy support each other.
Long and short define each other.
High and low depend on each other.
Before and after follow each other.

Therefore the Master
acts without doing anything
and teaches without saying anything.
Things arise and she lets them come;
things disappear and she lets them go.
She has but doesn't possess,
acts but doesn't expect.
When her work is done, she forgets it.
That is why it lasts forever.

3

If you overesteem great men,
people become powerless.
If you overvalue possessions,
people begin to steal.

The Master leads
by emptying people's minds
and filling their cores,
by weakening their ambition
and toughening their resolve.
He helps people lose everything
they know, everything they desire,
and creates confusion
in those who think that they know.

Practice not-doing,
and everything will fall into place.

5

The Tao doesn't take sides;
it gives birth to both good and evil.
The Master doesn't take sides;
she welcomes both saints and sinners.

The Tao is like a bellows:
it is empty yet infinitely capable.
The more you use it, the more it produces;
the more you talk of it, the less you understand.

Hold on to the center.

7

The Tao is infinite, eternal.
Why is it eternal?
It was never born;
thus it can never die.
Why is it infinite?
It has no desires for itself;
thus it is present for all beings.

The Master stays behind;
that is why she is ahead.
She is detached from all things;
that is why she is one with them.
Because she has let go of herself,
she is perfectly fulfilled.

8

The supreme good is like water,
which nourishes all things without trying to.
It is content with the low places that people disdain.
Thus it is like the Tao.

In dwelling, live close to the ground.
In thinking, keep to the simple.
In conflict, be fair and generous.
In governing, don't try to control.
In work, do what you enjoy.
In family life, be completely present.

When you are content to be simply yourself
and don't compare or compete,
everybody will respect you.

9

Fill your bowl to the brim
and it will spill.
Keep sharpening your knife
and it will blunt.
Chase after money and security
and your heart will never unclench.
Care about people's approval
and you will be their prisoner.

Do your work, then step back.
The only path to serenity.

10

Can you coax your mind from its wandering
and keep to the original oneness?
Can you let your body become
supple as a newborn child's?
Can you cleanse your inner vision
until you see nothing but the light?
Can you love people and lead them
without imposing your will?
Can you deal with the most vital matters

by letting events take their course?
Can you step back from your own mind
and thus understand all things?

Giving birth and nourishing,
having without possessing,
acting with no expectations,
leading and not trying to control:
this is the supreme virtue.

11

We join spokes together in a wheel,
but it is the center hole
that makes the wagon move.

We shape clay into a pot,
but it is the emptiness inside
that holds whatever we want.

We hammer wood for a house,
but it is the inner space
that makes it livable.

We work with being,
but non-being is what we use.

13

Success is as dangerous as failure.
Hope is as hollow as fear.

What does it mean that success is as dangerous as failure?
Whether you go up the ladder or down it,
your position is shaky.
When you stand with your two feet on the ground,
you will always keep your balance.

What does it mean that hope is as hollow as fear?
Hope and fear are both phantoms
that arise from thinking of the self.
When we don't see the self as self,
what do we have to fear?

See the world as your self.
Have faith in the way things are.
Love the world as your self;
then you can care for all things.

15

The ancient Masters were profound and subtle.
Their wisdom was unfathomable.
There is no way to describe it;
all we can describe is their appearance.

They were careful
as someone crossing an iced-over stream.
Alert as a warrior in enemy territory.
Courteous as a guest.
Fluid as melting ice.
Shapable as a block of wood.
Receptive as a valley.
Clear as a glass of water.

Do you have the patience to wait
till your mud settles and the water is clear?
Can you remain unmoving
till the right action arises by itself?

The Master doesn't seek fulfillment.
Not seeking, not expecting,
she is present, and can welcome all things.

16

Empty your mind of all thoughts.
Let your heart be at peace.
Watch the turmoil of beings,
but contemplate their return.

Each separate being in the universe
returns to the common source.
Returning to the source is serenity.

If you don't realize the source,
you stumble in confusion and sorrow.
When you realize where you come from,
you naturally become tolerant,
disinterested, amused,
kindhearted as a grandmother,
dignified as a king.
Immersed in the wonder of the Tao,
you can deal with whatever life brings you,
and when death comes, you are ready.

17

When the Master governs, the people
are hardly aware that he exists.
Next best is a leader who is loved.
Next, one who is feared.
The worst is one who is despised.

If you don't trust the people,
you make them untrustworthy.

The Master doesn't talk, he acts.
When his work is done,
the people say, "Amazing:
we did it, all by ourselves!"

19

Throw away holiness and wisdom,
and people will be a hundred times happier.
Throw away morality and justice,
and people will do the right thing.
Throw away industry and profit,
and there won't be any thieves.

If these three aren't enough,
just stay at the center of the circle
and let all things take their course.

20

Stop thinking, and end your problems.
What difference between yes and no?
What difference between success and failure?
Must you value what others value,
avoid what others avoid?
How ridiculous!

Other people are excited,
as though they were at a parade.
I alone don't care,
I alone am expressionless,
like an infant before it can smile.

Other people have what they need;
I alone possess nothing.
I alone drift about,
like someone without a home.
I am like an idiot, my mind is so empty.

Other people are bright;
I alone am dark.
Other people are sharp;
I alone am dull.
Other people have a purpose;
I alone don't know.
I drift like a wave on the ocean,
I blow as aimless as the wind.

I am different from ordinary people.
I drink from the Great Mother's breasts.

22

If you want to become whole,
let yourself be partial.
If you want to become straight,
let yourself be crooked.
If you want to become full,
let yourself be empty.
If you want to be reborn,
let yourself die.
If you want to be given everything,
give everything up.

The Master, by residing in the Tao,
sets an example for all beings.
Because he doesn't display himself,
people can see his light.
Because he has nothing to prove,
people can trust his words.

Because he doesn't know who he is,
people recognize themselves in him.
Because he has no goal in mind,
everything he does succeeds.

When the ancient Masters said,
"If you want to be given everything,
give everything up,"
they weren't using empty phrases.
Only in being lived by the Tao
can you be truly yourself.

25

There was something formless and perfect
before the universe was born.
It is serene. Empty.
Solitary. Unchanging.
Infinite. Eternally present.
It is the mother of the universe.
For lack of a better name,
I call it the Tao.

It flows through all things,
inside and outside, and returns
to the origin of all things.

The Tao is great.
The universe is great.
Earth is great.
Man is great.
These are the four great powers.

Man follows the earth.
Earth follows the universe.
The universe follows the Tao.
The Tao follows only itself.

27

A good traveler has no fixed plans
and is not intent upon arriving.
A good artist lets his intuition
lead him wherever it wants.
A good scientist has freed himself of concepts
and keeps his mind open to what is.

Thus the Master is available to all people
and doesn't reject anyone.
He is ready to use all situations
and doesn't waste anything.
This is called embodying the light.

What is a good man but a bad man's teacher?
What is a bad man but a good man's job?
If you don't understand this, you will get lost,
however intelligent you are.
It is the great secret.

30

Whoever relies on the Tao in governing men
doesn't try to force issues
or defeat enemies by force of arms.
For every force there is a counterforce.
Violence, even well intentioned,
always rebounds upon oneself.

The Master does his job
and then stops.
He understands that the universe
is forever out of control,
and that trying to dominate events
goes against the current of the Tao.
Because he believes in himself,
he doesn't try to convince others.
Because he is content with himself,
he doesn't need others' approval.
Because he accepts himself,
the whole world accepts him.

48

In the pursuit of knowledge,
every day something is added.
In the practice of the Tao,
every day something is dropped.
Less and less do you need to force things,
until finally you arrive at non-action.
When nothing is done,
nothing is left undone.

True mastery can be gained
by letting things go their own way.
It can't be gained by interfering.

57

If you want to be a great leader,
you must learn to follow the Tao.
Stop trying to control.
Let go of fixed plans and concepts,
and the world will govern itself.

The more prohibitions you have,
the less virtuous people will be.
The more weapons you have,
the less secure people will be.
The more subsidies you have,
the less self-reliant people will be.

Therefore the Master says:
I let go of the law,
and people become honest.
I let go of economics,
and people become prosperous.
I let go of religion,
and people become serene.
I let go of all desire for the common good,
and the good becomes common as grass.

58

If a country is governed with tolerance,
the people are comfortable and honest.
If a country is governed with repression,
the people are depressed and crafty.

When the will to power is in charge,
the higher the ideals, the lower the results.
Try to make people happy,
and you lay the groundwork for misery.
Try to make people moral,
and you lay the groundwork for vice.

Thus the Master is content
to serve as an example
and not to impose her will.
She is pointed, but doesn't pierce.
Straightforward, but supple.
Radiant, but easy on the eyes.

59

For governing a country well
there is nothing better than moderation.

The mark of a moderate man
is freedom from his own ideas.
Tolerant like the sky,
all-pervading like sunlight,
firm like a mountain,
supple like a tree in the wind,
he has no destination in view
and makes use of anything
life happens to bring his way.

Nothing is impossible for him.
Because he has let go,
he can care for the people's welfare
as a mother cares for her child.

60

Governing a large country
is like frying a small fish.
You spoil it with too much poking.

Center your country in the Tao
and evil will have no power.
Not that it isn't there,
but you'll be able to step out of its way.

Give evil nothing to oppose
and it will disappear by itself.

65

The ancient Masters
didn't try to educate the people,
but kindly taught them to not-know.

When they think that they know the answers,
people are difficult to guide.
When they know that they don't know,
people can find their own way.

If you want to learn how to govern,
avoid being clever or rich.
The simplest pattern is the clearest.
Content with an ordinary life,
you can show all people the way
back to their own true nature.

66

All streams flow to the sea
because it is lower than they are.
Humility gives it its power.

If you want to govern the people,
you must place yourself below them.
If you want to lead the people,
you must learn how to follow them.

The Master is above the people,
and no one feels oppressed.
She goes ahead of the people,
and no one feels manipulated.
The whole world is grateful to her.
Because she competes with no one,
no one can compete with her.

67

Some say that my teaching is nonsense.
Others call it lofty but impractical.
But to those who have looked inside themselves,
this nonsense makes perfect sense.
And to those who put it into practice,
this loftiness has roots that go deep.

I have just three things to teach:
simplicity, patience, compassion.
These three are your greatest treasures.
Simple in actions and in thoughts,
you return to the source of being.
Patient with both friends and enemies,
you accord with the way things are.
Compassionate toward yourself,
you reconcile all beings in the world.

69

The generals have a saying:
"Rather than make the first move
it is better to wait and see.
Rather than advance an inch
it is better to retreat a yard."

This is called
going forward without advancing,
pushing back without using weapons.

There is no greater misfortune
than underestimating your enemy.
Underestimating your enemy
means thinking that he is evil.
Thus you destroy your three treasures
and become an enemy yourself.

When two great forces oppose each other,
the victory will go
to the one that knows how to yield.

70

My teachings are easy to understand
and easy to put into practice.
Yet your intellect will never grasp them,
and if you try to practice them, you'll fail.

My teachings are older than the world.
How can you grasp their meaning?

If you want to know me,
look inside your heart.

71

Not-knowing is true knowledge.
Presuming to know is a disease.
First realize that you are sick;
then you can move toward health.

The Master is her own physician.
She has healed herself of all knowing.
Thus she is truly whole.

78

Nothing in the world
is as soft and yielding as water.
Yet for dissolving the hard and inflexible,
nothing can surpass it.

The soft overcomes the hard;
the gentle overcomes the rigid.
Everyone knows this is true,
but few can put it into practice.

Therefore the Master remains
serene in the midst of sorrow.
Evil cannot enter his heart.
Because he has given up helping,
he is people's greatest help.

True words seem paradoxical.

79

Failure is an opportunity.
If you blame someone else,
there is no end to the blame.

Therefore the Master
fulfills her own obligations
and corrects her own mistakes.
She does what she needs to do
and demands nothing of others.

80

If a country is governed wisely,
its inhabitants will be content.
They enjoy the labor of their hands
and don't waste time inventing
labor-saving machines.
Since they dearly love their homes,
they aren't interested in travel.
There may be a few wagons and boats,
but these don't go anywhere.
There may be an arsenal of weapons,

but nobody ever uses them.
People enjoy their food,
take pleasure in being with their families,
spend weekends working in their gardens,
delight in the doings of the neighborhood.
And even though the next country is so close
that people can hear its roosters crowing and its dogs barking,
they are content to die of old age
without ever having gone to see it.

81

True words aren't eloquent;
eloquent words aren't true.
Wise men don't need to prove their point;
men who need to prove their point aren't wise.

The Master has no possessions.
The more he does for others,
the happier he is.
The more he gives to others,
the wealthier he is.

The Tao nourishes by not forcing.
By not dominating, the Master leads.

Lao-tzu

Interpretive Questions for Discussion

According to Lao-tzu, why is the best leader one who follows the Tao, practicing "not-doing" and letting the world govern itself?

1. Why does overesteeming great statesmen make a people powerless? (Chapter 3)
2. How does the Taoist leader govern without trying to control? (Chapters 8, 10, 48, 57) Why should a leader not impose his or her will upon the people? (Chapters 10, 58, 81)
3. Why is the subtle, behind-the-scenes leader more effective than the leader who is loved? (Chapter 17)
4. Why does Lao-tzu insist that the Taoist leader must never engage in a force of arms—that even well-intentioned violence will rebound upon the leader? (Chapter 30; cf. Chapter 69)
5. Why is the leader who practices "non-action" able to leave nothing undone? (Chapter 48) Why does the Master's work, when completed and forgotten, last forever? (Chapter 2)
6. Why does ceasing to strive for the common good lead to effecting the common good? (Chapter 57; cf. Chapter 78)
7. Why does Lao-tzu describe the Master as one who is "pointed, but doesn't pierce. / Straightforward, but supple. / Radiant, but easy on the eyes"? (Chapter 58)

8. Why does Lao-tzu counsel those who want to learn how to govern to "avoid being clever or rich"? Why does the good leader "show all people the way/back to their own true nature"? (Chapter 65)

9. Why does Lao-tzu recommend being patient with one's enemies? (Chapter 67)

Suggested textual analyses
Chapters 3, 17, and 20

Why does Lao-tzu say that people will act righteously and be happier if morality, justice, and wisdom are all thrown away?

1. Why is "the great secret" to following the Tao knowing that a good man is a bad man's teacher and a bad man is a good man's job? (Chapter 27)

2. Why is the pursuit of knowledge at odds with the practice of the Tao? (Chapter 48)

3. How does one lead "by emptying people's minds/and filling their cores"? (Chapter 3)

4. Why is it desirable for one to feel "I am like an idiot, my mind is so empty" and "I blow as aimless as the wind"? (Chapter 20; cf. Chapter 16)

5. Why must the Taoist Master teach through example, rather than through words? (Chapters 2, 22, 58, 65)

6. Why do "fixed plans and concepts" inhibit the prosperity of a people, make them less virtuous, and render them more vulnerable to attack? (Chapter 57)

7. Why does Lao-tzu teach simplicity, patience, and compassion—the "greatest treasures"—as opposed to morality, justice, and wisdom? (Chapter 67; cf. Chapter 19)

8. Why does underestimating one's enemy destroy one's "three treasures"? Why does underestimating an enemy lead to becoming one's own enemy? (Chapter 69)

Suggested textual analyses
Chapters 19, 48, 57, and 58

Why can't the Tao be understood by the intellect?

1. Why is "the tao that can be told" not the eternal Tao? (Chapter 1) Why does Lao-tzu call the origin of all things the Tao—that is, the way or path? (Chapter 25)
2. Why can those who are free of desire "realize the mystery" of life, while those who are enslaved by desire see only its "manifestations"? (Chapter 1)
3. Why is "darkness within darkness" the "gateway to all understanding"? (Chapter 1)
4. Why are "good" and "bad," "ugly" and "beautiful" not useful terms when one lives according to the Tao? (Chapters 2, 5)
5. Why does following the Tao lead to personal fulfillment? (Chapter 7; cf. Chapters 15, 22)
6. What is meant by the lines, "We work with being, / but non-being is what we use"? (Chapter 11)
7. Why does Lao-tzu insist that his teachings are easy to understand and put into practice if one does not try to grasp them intellectually? (Chapter 70)
8. Why must the Master heal herself of all knowing? (Chapter 71)

Suggested textual analyses
Chapters 1, 25, 70

For Further Reflection

1. Is the Tao a practical guide, or an exercise in idealism that ignores harsh realities?
2. Why would it be impossible for most Americans to practice the Tao? Until we do, will we lack a "center" as individuals and as a people?
3. Can the ordinary person practice the Tao, or does one have to be extraordinary—a Master?
4. Can a Taoist leader be effective if the people do not practice the Tao? Would you want to be governed by a leader who follows the Tao?
5. Are the greatest leaders those who teach their people through example?
6. Is "hold on to the center" in the Taoist sense good advice for all leaders?

Questions for

Age of Iron

J. M. Coetzee

J. M. COETZEE (1940–) was born in Cape Town, South Africa. Upon completing bachelor's degrees in mathematics and English, he moved to England to work as a computer programmer, writing poetry and studying literature in his spare time. Coetzee then traveled to the United States, where he received his Ph.D. in English and taught at several American universities. In the early 1970s, he returned to South Africa to teach literature at Cape Town University. Coetzee has won numerous awards for his fiction, including the James Tait Black Memorial Prize for *Waiting for the Barbarians,* and the Booker Prize for *The Life and Times of Michael K.* A noted essayist and scholar, he has also produced translations of works in Dutch, German, French, and Afrikaans.

NOTE: All page references are from the Vintage International edition of *Age of Iron* (first printing 1992).

Interpretive Questions for Discussion

In the last days of her life, why does Mrs. Curren grow close to Mr. Vercueil and more remote from her daughter in America?

1. Why does Mrs. Curren take in the derelict Mr. Vercueil although he is physically repulsive and his lassitude revolts and mystifies her? (8) Why does Mrs. Curren find comfort and companionship in a man who is "beyond caring and beyond care"? (22)

2. Why, during the last days of her life, does Mrs. Curren write to her daughter about Mr. Vercueil? Why does she say that her letter is not a baring of her heart, "it is a baring of something, but not of my heart"? (15)

3. Why does Mrs. Curren write that by speaking her heart to Mr. Vercueil, she is taking a "crooked path" to her daughter? (82; cf. 131) Why does Mrs. Curren say that "when I write about him I write about myself"? (9)

4. Why does Mrs. Curren ask the unreliable Mr. Vercueil to mail her letter to her daughter? Why does he agree to do it? (31–33)

5. Why does Mr. Vercueil advise Mrs. Curren to tell her daughter everything about her condition "right now" or not at all? Why is his rebuke of her keeping her daughter in ignorance like a slap in the face to Mrs. Curren? (74)

6. Why does Mrs. Curren feel something break inside her when Mr. Vercueil says that she, like her daughter, is "like iron"? (75)

7. What is the "sore spot" that Mrs. Curren touches in Mr. Vercueil when she offers to buy him a ticket to America so that he can deliver her letter in person? Why does she imagine her daughter saying, "*This is what I came here to get away from*"? (194)

8. Why does Mrs. Curren think of Mr. Vercueil as being as ignorant as a child about death and sex—a non-nourisher who needs a woman's help because he "does not know how to love"? (193, 196)

9. Why does Mrs. Curren become "Mrs. V."? (190)

10. When Mrs. Curren suggests that he could learn Latin, why does Mr. Vercueil find himself "at a threshold he could not cross"? Why does Mrs. Curren say, "I am like a woman with a husband who keeps a mistress on the sly, scolding him, coaxing him to come clean"? (193)

11. Why does Mrs. Curren come to understand that it was not Mr. Vercueil who fell under her care, nor she under his, but that they "fell under each other"? (196)

12. Why is Mrs. Curren's last thought that of Mr. Vercueil taking her in his arms and holding her "with mighty force," so that the breath goes out of her in a rush? Why does she say, "From that embrace there was no warmth to be had"? (198)

Suggested textual analysis
Pages 186–198: from "I have the story now," to the end of the novel.

Why does Mrs. Curren's fatal disease bring her into consciousness about the politics of South Africa?

1. Why does Mrs. Curren identify her cancer with "the accumulation of shame" she has endured in her life? (145)
2. Why does Mrs. Curren consider the story of her mother not knowing what was rolling over her—the wagon wheels or the stars—to be her own story? Why does she believe it is "there that I come from . . . there that I begin"? (120)
3. Why does Mrs. Curren toy with, but ultimately reject, the idea of incinerating herself in front of the "House of Lies"? Why does she conclude that "there was always something false about that impulse"? (141)
4. Why does Mrs. Curren think "Florence is the judge"—that in Florence's eyes a serious death would be one that "crowns a life of honorable labor" or comes "unannounced . . . like a bullet between the eyes"? (141–142)
5. Why does Mrs. Curren have a vision of Florence as a silent, unsmiling Aphrodite, striding down Government Avenue with her daughters, Hope and Beauty? (177–178)
6. Why is Mrs. Curren forced to witness the horrors in Guguletu without her caretaker, Mr. Vercueil? (88–108)
7. Why does Mr. Vercueil give Mrs. Curren a box of matches after she gives him a speech about trying to hold on to her resolve? Why does Mr. Vercueil encourage Mrs. Curren to take more pills, to drink, to "do it now" and kill herself—and offer to help by strangling her? (122, 184–185)

8. Why does Mr. Vercueil ask Mrs. Curren if she wants to go for a sightseeing drive when she is contemplating going down Signal Hill with a petrol bomb? (117–118) Why do Mr. Vercueil and Mrs. Curren have a drunken quarrel during which he throws away her car key and leaves her? (126)

9. Why does Mrs. Curren reproach her daughter by saying, "What I bear, in your absence, is pain. I produce pain. You are my pain"? (139)

10. Why is Mrs. Curren worried that Mr. Vercueil is trying to trivialize her by dancing to the anthem of the Republic? (180–181)

11. Why does Mrs. Curren conclude that "life is drowning"? Why does she risk offending her daughter by writing that her American grandchildren will die "as stupid as when they were born," and are "in any event already dead"? (195; cf. 122)

12. Why is Mrs. Curren portrayed as helpless to do anything to right the wrongs of apartheid, even though she is willing to try?

Suggested textual analyses

Pages 140–147: beginning, "In the middle of the night," and ending, " 'Poor child,' I whispered."

Pages 177–181: beginning, "I have had a dream of Florence," and ending, "to roll round for the next pill."

Why does Mrs. Curren conclude that to avoid dying in a state of ugliness the first step is to "love . . . the unlovable"?

1. Why does Mrs. Curren think that her love for her daughter is called into question by her inability to love Bheki's friend? Why does she think that the more she loves her daughter, the more she should love Johannes? (137)

2. What does Mrs. Curren mean when she says, "I trust Vercueil because I do not trust Vercueil. I love him because I do not love him"? Why does she believe that the alms she gives Vercueil are the "hardest of all"? (131)

3. Why does Mrs. Curren believe that hers "is the true voice of wisdom" even though she has not suffered under apartheid as much as others have? (164)

4. Why does Mrs. Curren conclude that what the times call for is not goodness, but heroism—that her mistake has been to think that goodness was enough? (165)

5. Why does Mrs. Curren argue with Mr. Thabane about politics? (97–103, 148–150) Why, despite her shame and feeling of uselessness, does she stand her ground? (163)

6. Why is no one—not Mrs. Curren, Florence, Mr. Thabane, nor Mr. Vercueil—able to save Bheki and Johannes?

7. When Bheki and Johannes beat up Mr. Vercueil, why does Mrs. Curren defend him and tell Florence, "There are no rubbish people. We are all people together"? (47) Why does Mrs. Curren's attitude seem more enlightened than Florence's on this point?

8. Why is Mr. Vercueil unable to help Mrs. Curren as she experiences the horror surrounding the deaths of Bheki and Johannes, but able to care for her afterward?

9. Why, despite her dislike of him, does Mrs. Curren say that Johannes is "with me more clearly, more piercingly than Bheki has ever been"? (175)

10. Why does Mrs. Curren tell her daughter to "spare a thought for this man left behind who cannot swim, does not yet know how to fly"? (197)

11. Does the derelict Mr. Vercueil represent for Mrs. Curren what she should aspire to be, or what she must avoid becoming?

12. In loving Mr. Vercueil, does Mrs. Curren succeed in loving the unlovable? Is she saved from her shame by loving Mr. Vercueil?

Suggested textual analyses
Pages 136–140: beginning, "So this house," and ending, "Daughter."

Pages 162–168: beginning, "Forgive me," and ending, "That is why I keep turning to you for guidance, for help."

For Further Reflection

1. What should the ordinary, non-heroic South African have done to fight the policy of apartheid?

2. In what sense must Americans "love the unlovable" in order to correct injustices in our society?

3. How does an evil system like apartheid take over a whole country? How much guilt must each individual bear when an unjust government is in power?

4. Do you agree that goodness is not enough to combat injustice? Is violent protest necessary to bring about needed change?

5. Were people like Mrs. Curren responsible for the demise of apartheid, or were they ultimately ineffectual?

6. Should the United States Constitution be the model of government for all nations?

Questions for

Paradise of the Blind

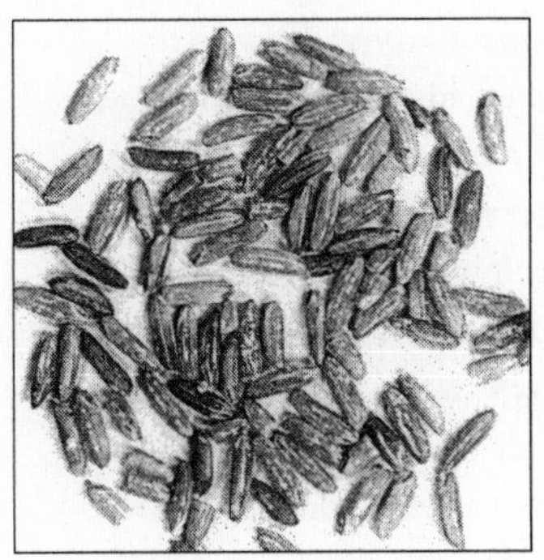

Duong Thu Huong

Duong Thu Huong (1947–) was born in Hanoi, Vietnam. When she was twenty years old, she led a Communist youth brigade sent to the heavily bombarded 17th parallel during the Vietnam War. When China attacked Vietnam twelve years later, Duong was among the first female combatants to volunteer for the front lines. Duong Thu Huong was expelled from the Vietnamese Communist party in 1989 as a result of her outspoken advocacy of democratic political reform and human rights. In 1991 she became a political prisoner and was held without trial for seven months. *Paradise of the Blind* was published in 1988, one year after the Communist party called for Vietnamese writers and journalists to abandon their stilted Marxist style and to reassert their traditional role as social critics. The novel was well received by the Vietnamese public before the Vietnamese government suddenly banned it, along with Duong's other novels.

NOTE: All page references are from the Penguin Books edition of *Paradise of the Blind* (first printing 1994).

Interpretive Questions for Discussion

Why doesn't Que ever understand the tragedy that Communism inflicted upon her?

1. Why does Que accept with submission Chinh's dissolution of her marriage to Ton, a man she loved passionately? When Que speaks of how Ton "couldn't bear the humiliation" of Communist persecution, why does her voice become "oddly vacant, bearing neither reproach nor admiration"? (29)

2. Why does Que tell Hang, "To live with dignity, the important thing is never to despair. . . . Unhappiness forges a woman, makes her selfless, compassionate"? (14) Does Que live with dignity?

3. Why does Que wait so long to tell Hang about her father, even though her silence makes Hang suffer? (46, 56, 59)

4. Why does Que let her self-serving, petty, and greedy brother ruin her life? Even though Chinh has a wife and two sons, why does Que say that she is "all he's got"? (178)

5. Why does Que submit to Chinh's every wish except his demand that she give up her street-vending business to work in a factory? (50–51, 93–96)

6. Why does Que stop doting on Hang once Tam comes into their life, even though she is jealous of Hang's love? (102, 112) Why does Que eventually become indifferent to Hang and transfer her affection to her two nephews? (137)

7. Why does Que refuse to sell the earrings from Tam when Hang asks to have a new roof for their home, but then sell the rings from Tam to help Chinh? (101–102, 180–188)

8. Why does Que only feel confident when she is raking in the money? (103) Why does Que assume the air of a woman "in perfect control of herself" once she takes on the role of providing for her brother and nephews? (137)

9. Why does Que implore Hang to never stop loving her just before she has Hang deliver food to her nephews—her "two little drops of Do blood"? (111–112)

10. Why does the author have Que lose everything she has at the height of her business season, in her effort to save a few coins? Why does Que call her misfortune "fate"? (116)

11. Why does Que banish Hang from her house after being dressed down by Tam? (188–190) Why does Neighbor Vi, but not Hang, understand why Que kicked Hang out? (196)

12. Why does Hang see her mother's life as "a whole life lived for nothing, for no one"? (17)

Suggested textual analyses

Pages 101–103 (from Chapter 6): beginning, "That same autumn," and ending, " 'And all without Aunt Tam's earrings,' she said."

Pages 111–115 (from Chapter 6): beginning, "I pulled the latch," and ending, "let alone a human being."

Pages 184–192 (from Chapter 10): beginning, "Aunt Tam stared at my mother," and ending, "I dreamed of a stick of barley sugar."

Why does Tam have "one obsession: to get rich" after the Communists take over?

1. Why can Tam, but not her brother Ton, humiliate herself before Chinh, saying, ". . . we accept our shame. Even without your orders, my family will never try to rise above this"? (29)

2. When meeting her aunt for the first time, why does Hang feel a wave of fear, as if she were "drinking to some solemn, merciless vow, some sacred, primitive rite"? (74)

3. Why is Tam described as both coarse and delicate, powerful and peasantlike, but also beautiful, graceful, and dainty? (72, 250)

4. Why does longing to see the undoing of the "reformers" Bich and Nan enable Tam to survive the humiliation of the land reform? (76) Why does Tam vow to make her ancestral home "even more opulent than before. . . . Even if I have to tear this body of mine apart"? (79)

5. Why does Tam succeed in becoming rich, whereas Que, who also works as a petty capitalist, never does?

6. Why is Tam, a traditional peasant, determined to have her niece become an educated professional woman? (87) Why does the vision of Hang's future liberate Tam from her suffering and humiliation? (99)

7. Why can't Tam and Que, who are bound together by love for Hang and Ton, bury their hatred? (81, 136–137, 188–189, 241)

8. Why is the hardworking Tam contemptuous of Que's dedication to her street vending, which doesn't allow Que to sacrifice a day of business? (134)

9. When on her deathbed, why does Tam say that she detests Hang's mother, but go on to say that she herself is the cause of Hang's unhappiness and suffering? Why does Tam seek Hang's forgiveness? (241–242)

10. Why does Hang think of her aunt's life as "a victory born of the renunciation of existence"? (248)

11. What does Hang mean when she says that Tam's passing seals her life's "most insistent mystery"? (251)

12. Why does Hang honor all the traditions of a Vietnamese funeral for Tam even though she thinks they are "phony" and "ephemeral," but vow to sell Tam's house against the dearest wishes of her aunt? (251, 258)

Suggested textual analyses
Pages 76–81 (from Chapter 5): beginning, "Remember now:" and ending, "crushing everything that blocked her way."

Pages 97–101 (from Chapter 6): beginning, "From then on, until Tet," and ending, "letter after letter."

Why, unlike everyone else in the novel, does Hang remained untouched by ambition or greed for material gain?

1. Why does Hang "show the same selflessness" as her mother by helping her uncle Chinh even though she despises his personal and political values? (14–16, 167)

2. Why does Hang stay silent when her roommate in Russia complains, "It's a bitch of a life. Better to get it over with once and for all"? Why, unlike her roommate, does Hang not despair while in exile but rather live with dignity, as her mother has taught her? (14)

3. Why does Hang think of "revolt" as a kind of love and "the most essential force in human existence"? (39)

4. On her journey to Moscow, why does Hang remember waiting to see her first snowfall and recall that "this beauty pierced my soul like sorrow. Extremes have always wounded me"? (82) Why is Hang haunted by the landscape of a pond filled with purple flowers, an image that "is at once both the purest balm and the most overpowering poison" of her existence? (130–131)

5. Why does the incident involving the roommate who thought her friends had stolen her sewing machine lead Hang to realize that "in every life, there must come a moment when what is most sacred, most noble, in us evaporates into thin air"? (85–86)

6. Why is Hang petrified by Tam's lavish gifts of jewelry, food, and money? (88, 98–101) Why does Hang resist Tam's desire to celebrate her acceptance to the university? (134–135)

7. Why does Hang see her future both in her mother's sad, feverish, sleeping figure and in watching Tam oversee the butchering of the pig in preparation for the banquet to celebrate Hang's acceptance to the university? (111, 143)

8. After her mother's injury, why does Hang choose to be an imported worker in Russia, an exile from her native land? Why does she see her separation from Vietnam as part of a vulgar and hideous spectacle, "a deviation from all rules of human nature"? (133–134)

9. Why does Hang refuse to see any men while she is at the university? (193)

10. Why does the ugly man who comes to purchase Tam's gold serve as Hang's "key" to understanding her despair? Why is Hang grateful to the man, a person who disgusts and frightens her? (257)

11. Why is Hang able to endure a life of "endless humiliation" while her father, who committed suicide out of shame, was not? (229, 80)

12. Why does Hang find through her uncle Chinh a hint of a better life with the Bohemian? (232) Why is Hang's final vision of better, "different worlds" that of a university auditorium and a distant port where a plane could land and take off? (258)

Suggested textual analyses

Pages 81–86 (from Chapter 5): beginning, "My neighbor yawned loudly," and ending, "no one is spared."

Pages 128–131 (Chapter 7)

Pages 141–143 (from Chapter 8): beginning, "The scene was lively but well ordered," and ending, "I saw a vision of my future."

Are we meant to see Communism as a mistake for Vietnam or as a necessary step in the advancement of its society?

1. Why does the author portray the Do and Tran women as more adaptable and effective than their male relations?
2. Are we meant to think that Que and Chinh represent two starkly different ideologies—the traditional and the Communist—or that they both suffer from the same cultural myopia?
3. Why are we told that, during the Rectification of Errors, the villagers tried to kill the innocent Que for the unfair cruelty imposed upon them by her brother? (33–34)
4. Why does the author have Hang's father saved by following proverbial wisdom—"water nourishes wood"—and starting a new life in a Muong village as a respected husband and father, teacher, and sage? (65–66)
5. Why are we told that Chinh elevated two village outcasts—the lazy, lascivious Bich and the glutton Nan—to the status of "pillars of the peasantry"? (28) Why do worthless people become powerful during the denunciation of the class of "exploiters"? (25)

6. Why is Chinh's devotion to Communism and the "people" stronger than his sense of familial duty to his wife and sons, sister, and deceased parents? (49, 107–108, 170, 222–223)

7. Why don't Tam's stories about Ministers Chinh and Tran Binh dissuade the village vice president from confiscating the poor peasant's land for his daughter's dowry? (154–162, 245–246)

8. Why does it turn out that Chinh's only proficiency is cooking authentic Vietnamese food? (206–207) Why is he portrayed wearing women's sandals and being ridiculed by his "comrades," who speak of him like housewives complain about their servants? (205, 212)

9. Why is the young Bohemian the only person able to rebuke Chinh and tell him that the old Party cadres "never deserved our respect, or our fear. They're just a bunch of illusionists"? (214–215)

10. Are we meant to conclude that Vietnam was always ruled by corrupt officials—that the Communist leaders are no worse than the old mandarins? (156–161, 213–216)

11. Why does Hang compare the prosperous and confident Japanese tourists to her own people, who are "taut, lean with fear," desperate, and humiliated? (229)

12. Why does Hang come to see her village, which she had remembered nostalgically when she was working in Russia, as a "cesspool of ambition"? (257)

Suggested textual analyses

Pages 153–162 (from Chapter 9): beginning, "Aunt Tam served the tea herself," and ending, "Good night, everyone."

Pages 227–230 (from Chapter 11): beginning, "I did some shopping," and ending, "under a real roof . . . "

Pages 255–258 (Chapter 12)

For Further Reflection

1. Are women better equipped than men to deal with social upheaval?
2. Did Tam, like Que, fail Hang?
3. Could legitimized persecution of a class of people, like that imposed by the Vietnamese Communists on the "middle peasantry" during the land reform, ever happen in the United States?
4. Why has Communism failed in the twentieth century, even though its promise of shared wealth and social equality is rational and desirable?

ACKNOWLEDGMENTS

All possible care has been taken to trace ownership and secure permission for each selection in this anthology. The Great Books Foundation wishes to thank the following authors, publishers, and representatives for permission to reprint copyrighted material.

Letter from Birmingham Jail, by Martin Luther King Jr. Copyright 1963 by Martin Luther King Jr.; renewed 1991 by Coretta Scott King. Reprinted by permission of The Heirs to the Estate of Martin Luther King Jr., c/o Writers House, Inc. as agent for the proprietor.

Sorrow-Acre, from WINTER'S TALES, by Isak Dinesen. Copyright 1942 by Random House, Inc.; renewed 1970 by Johan Philip Thomas Ingerslev, c/o The Rungstedlund Foundation. Reprinted by permission of Random House, Inc.

Kongi's Harvest, from COLLECTED PLAYS 2, by Wole Soyinka. Copyright 1967 by Wole Soyinka. Reprinted by permission of Oxford University Press.

The Melian Dialogue, from THE HISTORY OF THE PELOPONNESIAN WAR, by Thucydides. Edited in translation by Sir Richard Livingstone (1943). Reprinted by permission of Oxford University Press.

Longing, from THE HILL OF EVIL COUNSEL, by Amos Oz. Copyright 1976 by Amos Oz and Am Oved Publishers Ltd. English translation copyright 1978 by Amos Oz. Reprinted by permission of Harcourt Brace & Company.

Tao Te Ching, from TAO TE CHING: A NEW ENGLISH VERSION, by Stephen Mitchell. Translation copyright 1988 by Stephen Mitchell. Reprinted by permission of HarperCollins Publishers, Inc.

Cover photography: Hunter Freeman, San Francisco

Cover and book design: William Seabright and Associates